D0993290

VISUAL QUICKSTART GUIDE

VISUAL BASIC 6

Harold Davis

 Peachpit Press

Visual QuickStart Guide
Visual Basic 6
Harold Davis

Peachpit Press

1249 Eighth Street
Berkeley, CA 94710
(510) 524-2178
(510) 524-2221 (fax)

Find us on the World Wide Web at: http://www.peachpit.com

Peachpit Press is a division of Addison Wesley Longman

Editor: Clifford Colby
Production Coordinator: Kate Reber
Compositor: Owen Wolfson
Indexer: Cheryl Landes

Notice of rights

Notice of liability

Trademarks

ISBN: 0-201-35383-0

0 9 8 7 6 5 4 3 2

Printed and bound in the United States of America

 Printed on recycled paper

For the love of my life, Phyllis.

Acknowledgements

Without the wonderful crew at Peachpit Press, this book would not exist. Special thanks to: Marjorie Baer, Cliff Colby, Kate Reber, Nancy Ruenzel, Kathy Simpson, and Owen Wolfson.

I'd like to thank Phyllis and Julian for putting up with me—or rather, the lack of me—while I was writing this book. Also, I'm grateful to my consulting clients for patience while I was working on this project.

About the Author

Harold Davis is a software developer who specializes in the Web and e-commerce. He works as a consultant for clients ranging from Web startups to Fortune 500 corporations.

Harold's most recent book is *Red Hat Linux 6: Visual QuickPro Guide,* also published by Peachpit Press. He is the author of many books on programming and software development, including the best-selling *Visual Basic Secrets series, Web Developer's Secrets,* and *Delphi Power Toolkit.* He is also the author of a number of books about photography, art, and publishing.

Harold holds a B.A. degree in Computer Science and Mathematics from New York University and a J.D. degree from Rutgers Law School.

He lives in Berkeley, California, with his wife, Phyllis, and son, Julian. When not programming, writing, or performing technical architecture reviews, he enjoys spending time in the garden.

TABLE OF CONTENTS

TABLE OF CONTENTS

INTRODUCTION

I wrote this book to help people who want to learn to program. For my money, if you want to learn to program, learning Visual Basic is the best and easiest way to start.

The sequence of chapters in *Visual Basic 6: Visual QuickStart Guide* has someone in mind who has used Microsoft Windows but has never programmed. The approach is to provide a step-by-step, visual guide to performing Visual Basic tasks. The many visuals in my book work well with a development environment such as Visual Basic's—which is visual to the max.

Each chapter shows you how to accomplish specific tasks, many of which frequently come up in the real world. In this book, I'm not big on theoretical disquisition; you'll learn the hows and whys of programming in the course of creating actual projects. If you follow the chapters in order and create Visual Basic projects by following the directions in the text, I promise that by the end of this book, you *will* have learned to program.

This book is not intended for advanced readers. In addition to being for those who want to learn to program, it is intended to be a focused, task-based reference guide for beginning to intermediate readers. If you've written some Visual Basic programs or have worked in a Windows development environment, *Visual Basic 6: Visual QuickStart Guide* will help you quickly find out how to perform many necessary tasks.

As my grandmother might have asked, "So you vant to program?" Eeef so, start reading. You will learn how here.

How to Use This Book

Visual Basic 6: Visual QuickStart Guide presents easy, step-by step directions and illustrations to help you get started creating applications with Visual Basic.

If you are a first-time Visual Basic user and new to programming, I suggest reading the book in order. You will get the most out of the book if you work through the examples as you go.

More experienced users should regard *Visual Basic 6: Visual QuickStart Guide* as a reference guide that will help you achieve specific tasks.

What Is Visual Basic?

Visual Basic 6—VB or VB6 for short—is a development environment that runs under Microsoft Windows. It is used to write programs that also run under Microsoft Windows.

There are many ways to answer the question "What is Visual Basic?" For one thing, it is the development environment used by more programmers than any other in history (more than 3 million and counting). For another, it combines extraordinary ease of use with great power and flexibility. Visual Basic is used in many ways and at many levels, from programmers just taking those first baby programming steps to veritable Jedi knights of the art of programming.

Any development environment with such a range must be very feature-rich, and of course, Visual Basic is. It has many more features that could possibly be described in a book of this length.

Visual Basic is a development language with several faces. One face is visual. This face is made up of objects and tools that easily—almost magically—assemble themselves into a modern Windows interface.

Another face is the Visual Basic language, which is a descendant of the original BASIC (Beginner's All-Purpose Symbolic Instruction Code). BASIC was invented in the early 1960s by two Dartmouth College professors, John G. Kemeny and Thomas Kurtz. It was intended to be as easy to understand and as close to everyday language as possible.

Visual Basic has kept the BASIC tradition intact in this respect. It is one of the easiest computer languages to work with and understand.

Visual Basic Editions

Visual Basic 6 ships in four editions:

◆ **The Working Model,** which lacks important functionality and ships with some books on Visual Basic.

◆ **The Learning Edition,** formerly known as the Standard Edition. This edition is inexpensive and contains everything that you need for many purposes.

◆ **The Professional Edition,** a true high-end development environment that includes features not available in the Learning Edition, such as ActiveX controls and component development capability.

◆ **The Enterprise Edition,** which includes the features of the Professional Edition in the context of enterprise and remote development.

Visual Basic 6: Visual QuickStart Guide assumes that you are working with the Learning Edition. Everything in it is also valid for the Professional and Enterprise editions; the book just doesn't cover Professional or Enterprise features.

I made the decision to stick with this book's goal of helping people to learn to program. To learn to program, you shouldn't have to go out and buy an expensive program. It's true that a few Professional Edition features might have been nice to cover in this book. But a book explaining software cannot be all things to all people. If you need to learn the advanced features of Visual Basic, many good books are available, specifically intended for an advanced audience.

Visual Basic and Visual Studio

Microsoft's Visual Studio is an umbrella application that combines many of Microsoft's development tools. Visual Studio includes Visual C++, Visual J++, and Visual FoxPro. Significantly, from our viewpoint, it also includes Visual Basic.

Nominally, all the applications in Visual Studio have a common interface design (as well as libraries and some utilities).

As a practical matter, however, there is very little overlap between Visual Basic and the other applications in Visual Studio. (The only commonality you are likely to observe is the fact that Visual Basic shares some files with the other Visual Studio applications.)

You should know about Visual Studio, however, because it is a great suite of development tools. If you are serious about developing in the Microsoft Windows environment, it probably makes sense to buy a version of Visual Studio rather than just Visual Basic. The prices usually are such that it is cheaper to buy Visual Studio than only two of the applications that it includes.

Visual Basic and Microsoft Office

VBA—or Visual Basic for Applications—is the common macro language for Microsoft applications, including those in Microsoft Office. VBA is, in fact, a knocked-down version of the Visual Basic language and development environment.

If you open the VBA development environment from one of the Office components—such as Excel or Word—you'll see that it looks a lot like Visual Basic 6. It is not too strong to say that if you know Visual Basic, you also know VBA, which means that you'll find it easy to write small applications, or macros, that work in Office applications.

Design-Time vs. Run-Time Environments

You will be using Visual Basic in two modes as you work through this book. These modes are called *design time* and *run time*.

In the design-time environment, you create and modify objects and enter code. The run-time environment simulates running the program that you created in the design-time environment.

This run-time simulation has several advantages. For one, it makes the development process faster than it would be if you had to stop to compile a program, and then run the program, to determine the impact of each change you make in its source. For another, the VB run-time environment provides tools that help you understand exactly what is going on when your application is run.

Line Continuation Characters

The pages of this book are obviously narrower than a monitor screen. Because of that, in the code throughout this book, we often had to continue a long single line of code onto a second line. When this happened, we inserted an → at the beginning of the second line. For example,

```
This is the first part of the long line of code
  → and the line continues down here.
```

Errata, Source Code, and Contacting the Author

I have made every effort to be as accurate as possible. Inevitably, however, some errors may have crept in. I'd greatly appreciate any corrections. Drop me a line at harold@bearhome.com.

An errata page for the book will be available on the companion Web site for the book, http://www.peachpit.com/vqs/visualbasic.

I encourage you to follow the examples in the book by re-creating the objects in the projects and by using your keyboard to enter the source code. You will learn the most if you do this.

If typing is unbearably tedious for you, however, I have placed the source code for the projects in the book—organized by chapter in archives—on the companion Web site for you to download.

If Not Now, When?

This book is about learning to program. It doesn't assume any knowledge on your part about how to program.

If you already know a bit about programming, the goal of my book is to leverage the knowledge you already have so that you can quickly achieve tasks by following the illustrated steps in the book.

In either case—if you want to learn more about the wonderful world of software development, or if you have specific tasks to perform—why wait? With *Visual Basic 6: Visual QuickStart Guide,* you can get started now. As Hillel put it, "If not now, when?"

Projects, Forms, and Command Buttons

It is a very common practice to begin teaching—or learning—a programming language by creating a program that, when run, displays the phrase "Hello, World!" Although this is a cliché, it makes sense. In many programming languages it is hard enough to get anything to work, so it's a good idea to start with something simple. Additionally, in the real world, programs must often display text. It's particularly helpful to know how to do so when debugging a program. You can determine which parts of a program have been executed by noting which messages have been displayed. Although the messages are no substitute for the powerful debugging tools available in Visual Basic (see Chapter 4 for information on the Immediate Window), you may still find them useful at times.

This chapter goes far beyond the traditional "Hello, World!" approach. In it, you learn how to create a window, or form, that is displayed on the computer screen. (Objects called *forms* in Visual Basic become windows when a program is executed.)

Next, you learn how to position a button (actually, an ActiveX control called a Command Button) on the form.

In Visual Basic, you can associate program code with *events*. Events are *fired*—much as an alarm clock rings—in response to something a user does. Events can also be initiated by the computer system, or by other parts of a project.

In this chapter, you learn how to add code to the event that is fired when a user clicks the button that you added to the form.

Specifically, the code that you add to the button's click event displays a simple *message box*, which is a formatted text dialog or message box. (In Chapter 2, you learn about the different kinds of message boxes and how to invoke them.)

Finally, you learn how to let a user dynamically change the caption of a window when a program is running.

This chapter is like a dive right into the Visual Basic Integrated Development Environment (IDE) and into programming. Sometimes when you dive into deep water, you need to relax and take a deep breath.

You should be able to understand and follow all the steps in this chapter if you have Visual Basic installed on your computer. At times, however, you might want a little more background on the tools available in the VB IDE or more information on how programming works. That's OK! You'll find a great deal of information on these topics in the rest of *Visual Basic 6: Visual QuickStart Guide*.

Figure 1.1 When you start Visual Basic, the initial New Project dialog is displayed.

Starting a New Project

Visual Basic programs are organized in *projects*. That is to say, the objects and code contained in a VB project become a program when the project is *compiled*. The forms contained in a project become windows, for example.

You can have only one project open at a time in Visual Basic. It is possible, however, to have several *instances* (meaning, copies) of Visual Basic—each with a different project—open at the same time. (Project *groups* are a Professional and Enterprise feature usually involving a project that creates an ActiveX control and a project that uses the control.)

Usually, you'll want to see what a program does before you compile it. You can do this by *running* a project—that is, using Visual Basic to simulate the effect of executed the compiled program that your project could be used to create from within the Visual Basic environment.

You can start a new project by using the project dialog that Visual Basic displays the first time you start it. Alternatively, you can set VB to start without this initial dialog and begin a new project yourself. It's a matter of individual preference: It doesn't matter which way you do it. I'll show you both ways.

To start a new project:

1. Start Visual Basic.

   The Initial New Project dialog is displayed (**Figure 1.1**).

2. Make sure that Standard EXE is selected as the project type.

continues on next page

3. Click Open.

A new Visual Basic project opens (**Figure 1.2**).

✔ Tips

■ If you select VB Application Wizard rather than Standard EXE in the initial New Project dialog, the Application Wizard helps you build many aspects of your project's user interface. For more information, see Chapter 6.

■ By default, Visual Basic projects include a form module. The form is initially named Form1.

To disable the initial New Project dialog:

1. With the Initial New Project dialog open, put a check mark in the Don't show this dialog in the future checkbox.

2. Click OK.

The next time you open Visual Basic, the dialog will not be there.

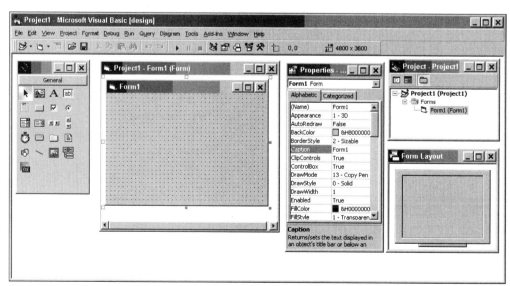

Figure 1.2 Voilà! Your new Visual Basic project is ready to roll!

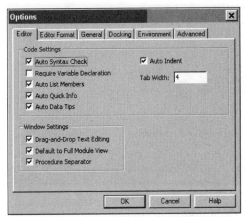

Figure 1.3 The Options dialog is used to configure Visual Basic.

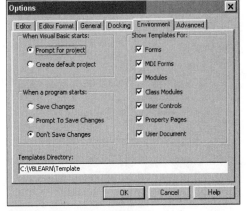

Figure 1.4 Choose Prompt for Project in the Environment tab of the Options dialog to display the initial New Project dialog the next time VB starts.

Figure 1.5 The New Project dialog is used to open a new project when VB is running.

✔ Tip

■ If the dialog has been disabled, Visual Basic automatically starts with a new project loaded.

To restore the initial New Project dialog:

1. From the Tools menu, choose Options. The Options dialog opens (**Figure 1.3**).

2. Choose the Environment tab (**Figure 1.4**).

3. In the When Visual Basic starts section, place a check mark in the Prompt for project checkbox.

4. Click OK. The next time you start Visual Basic, the initial New Project dialog is displayed.

To open a new project with VB running:

1. From the File menu, choose New Project. The New Project dialog opens (**Figure 1.5**).

2. Make sure that Standard EXE is selected.

3. Click OK. A new Visual Basic project opens.

Configuring Your Project

Visual Basic provides many options regarding the way in which it treats projects. In the interest of safe computing—to minimize the risk of losing any of your work in progress and to help enforce good programming practices—you should change some options right away.

To require explicit variable declarations:

1. From the Tools menu, choose Options. The Editor tab of the Options dialog opens (**Figure 1.6**).

2. In the Code Settings section, place a check mark in the Require Variable Declaration check box.

3. Click OK.

✔ Tip

■ Requiring variable declaration means that you must explicitly enumerate variables your code will use. This makes it harder to make careless mistakes.

By the way, if you have not run across variables before, you certainly will in this book. For now, think of a variable as a way that programs store values.

To save changes automatically when a program runs:

1. With the Options dialog open, choose the Environment tab (**Figure 1.7**).

2. In the When a Program Starts section, choose either Save Changes or Prompt to Save Changes.

3. Click OK.

Naming Your Project

You don't really have to name your project unless you want to do so. If you don't supply a name, Visual Basic will. Your project will be named *Project1*. Because this name doesn't tell you much about the project, you might prefer to give it a different name.

To name a project:

1. From the Project menu, choose Properties. The Project Properties dialog opens (**Figure 1.8**).

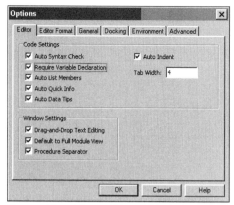

Figure 1.6 Requiring explicit variable declaration makes it harder to make careless mistakes.

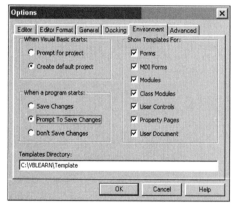

Figure 1.7 It's a good idea to have Visual Basic save the changes to your programs before running them.

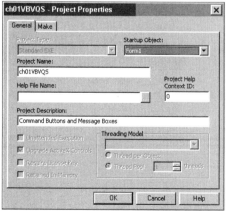

Figure 1.8 The Project Properties dialog is used to name a project.

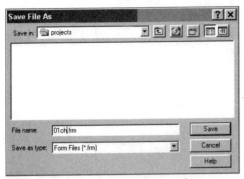

Figure 1.9 Each Visual Basic module—such as a form—is saved in a separate file.

2. Type a name for your project in the Project Name field.

3. (Optional) Type a description of the project in the Project Description field.

4. Click OK.

✔ Tips

- Project names—like other identifiers in Visual Basic—must start with a letter and can be a maximum 40 characters long. They can include letters, underscore characters, and numbers but not spaces.

- A project's name is internal to Visual Basic. You can use it within a Visual Basic project, but it is not necessarily the same as the name the project file is saved under or the name of the executable program created with the project.

Saving Your project

Even though you have set Visual Basic to save your projects automatically when you run them, you may want to save your projects manually. In fact, it's a good idea to do so from time to time so that you do not lose any work, just as you would in a word processing program.

To save a project:

1. From the File menu, choose Save Project or Save Project As.
   The Save File As dialog opens.

2. Each *module* in a project—such as a form—is saved in a separate file. Save each module with a file name and location (**Figure 1.9**).

continues on next page

3. When all the modules in your project have been saved, you are prompted to select a file name and a location for saving your project file (**Figure 1.10**).

4. Click Save to save the project file.

✔ Tip

■ As a matter of organizational clarity, it's a good idea to name the files in a project similarly so that you know that they go together. As your projects become more complex, you may also want to use a portion of each module file name to indicate the functionality of the module. For example, 01ch.frm is a file name for a form that clearly says that the form is used in Chapter 1. In any event, the files for a project should be saved in the same place on your hard disk so that you can find them easily.

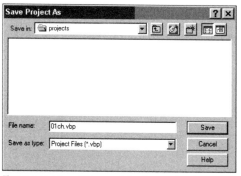

Figure 1.10 After all the modules in a project have been saved, you are asked to provide a file name and location for the project file.

Setting Form Properties

Now that you've learned how to open a new project and how to save it, it's time to get to work on your first form. As I've already mentioned, Visual Basic forms become windows when a program—or Visual Basic project—is run. This means that forms are the basis of the user interface in any program written in Visual Basic.

By default, a new Visual Basic project comes with a form already provided. Adding a form is easy enough, too, as I'll show you in a moment.

There are many ways to alter the appearance and behavior of Visual Basic forms. Typically, you achieve this by changing one of the form's *properties*. In this context, *property* is akin to *attribute*. BackColor, for example, is a form property. If you change a form's BackColor property to red, you've made the background color of the form red.

Some properties can be set dynamically when a program is running. When you click a form, for example, it turns blue. Under the hood, the form's BackColor property was set to blue in the relevant click event.

You can also set properties in Visual Basic's design-time environment before VB is run. You usually do this in VB's *Properties Window* or in *Property Pages*. A Property Page— explained in Chapter 8—is a mechanism for setting the custom properties of some controls (but not the intrinsic controls such as command buttons and text boxes that you will be working with in the first few chapters). The Property Page interface resembles the standard Windows Properties dialog.

This section shows you how to set some important form properties at design time.

To add a form to a project:

1. If the Project Explorer is not already open, open it by choosing Project Explorer from the View menu or by pressing Ctrl+R.

   The Project Explorer displays all the modules in a project (**Figure 1.11**).

2. Right-click anywhere within the Project Explorer.

3. Choose Add from the pop-up menu.

4. Choose Form.

   The Add Form dialog appears (**Figure 1.12**).

5. Choose the New tab, and then choose Form.

6. Click Open.

   A new form is added to your project.

✔ Tip

- You can choose among specialized form templates in the Add Form dialog to add a ready-made specialized form to your project.

Centering a Form

You'll often want a form to be in a specific position on the screen when a program is running. One of the most common requirements is to center a form on the screen.

To center a form:

1. Make sure that your form is displayed in the Visual Basic environment, if necessary, by double-clicking the form in the Project Explorer.

2. If the Form Layout window is not already open, open it by choosing Form Layout Window from the View menu.

   The Form Layout window displays the run-time position of forms on the screen (**Figure 1.13**).

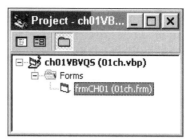

Figure 1.11 The Project Explorer displays all the modules in a chapter.

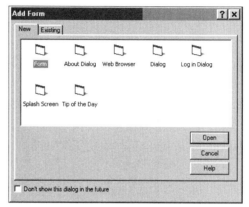

Figure 1.12 The Add Form dialog is used to add a form to a project.

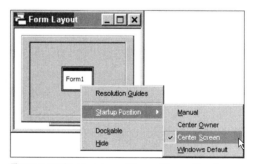

Figure 1.13 The Form Layout is used to position forms on the screen at run time.

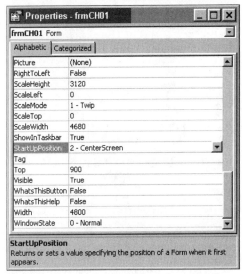

Figure 1.14 You can also center forms by setting the StartUpPosition property.

Figure 1.15 To change the background color of a form, set its BackColor property by using the Properties window.

3. Right-click the miniature representation of the form.

4. From the pop-up menu, choose Startup Position.

5. From the submenu, choose Center Screen.

The form is now initially positioned in the center of the screen when the project is run.

✔ Tip

■ You can achieve the same result—centering a form at run time—by using the Properties window to set the form's StartUpPosition property to 2 - Center-Screen (**Figure 1.14**).

Setting the Form BackColor Property

As you might expect, the BackColor property of a form sets the background color of a form. This color is displayed both at design time in the Visual Basic environment and when you run the project containing the form.

To set a form's BackColor property:

1. Make sure that your form is displayed in the Visual Basic environment, if necessary, by double-clicking the form in the Project Explorer.

2. If the Properties window is not open, open it by choosing Properties window from the View menu *or* by pressing F4.

3. Make sure that the form is selected in the top list box of the Properties window (**Figure 1.15**).

If the form is the only object in your project, this will happen automatically, but if there are other objects in the project—such as other forms and controls—you may have to scroll through the objects in the list to select it.

continues on next page

4. In the Alphabetic tab of the Properties window, select BackColor in the left column.

5. Click the down arrow in the right column.

The System tab of the color selector opens (**Figure 1.15**). Using the System tab, you can select a background color for the form based on the Windows color scheme in use on your computer by clicking the color.

6. To choose a color directly from a palette, select the Palette tab of the Color Selector (**Figure 1.16**).

7. Click the color you want to use.

Whether you selected a color from the System or Palette tab, a small square of that color appears in the right column of the BackColor property in the Properties window. You'll also see the hexadecimal representation of the RGB color that it represents. In addition, the form is displayed in the new color that you selected.

✔ Tips

■ You can enter a hexadecimal RGB color constant directly in the Properties window, rather than selecting a color from the System or Palette tab. For more information, look up the BackColor property in MSDN Help. (Using VB's MSDN Help is explained in Appendix A.)

■ You can change a form's BackColor property dynamically while a form is running by using code. You'll find an example of dynamically changing a form property later in this chapter.

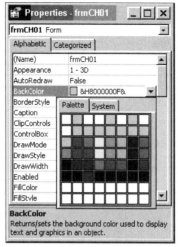

Figure 1.16 The Palette tab of the Color Selector is used to pick colors without regard to the Windows desktop scheme.

Setting the
Form Caption Property

A form's *caption* is what appears in the title bar of the form (**Figure 1.17**). The caption property is used to set the form's caption.

The text in the caption appears both at design time and when the form is running.

It is important to understand that a form's caption is different from the form's *name*—used to reference the form in code—and from the name of the file containing the form module.

Users of your programs will identify windows in the applications you create by their captions, not their names. So it is very important that you choose captions that adequately describe the windows.

SETTING FORM PROPERTIES

Object list

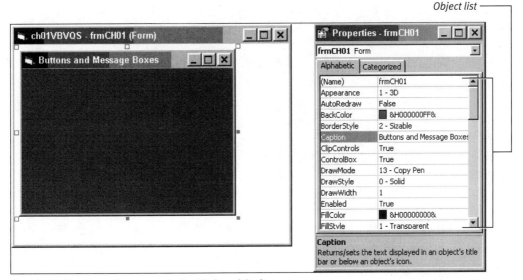

Figure 1.17 A form's caption appears in the title bar of the form.

To set a form's caption:

1. With the form open, open the Properties window.

2. Make sure that the form is selected in the Properties window, either by selecting the form or by selecting it in the top list of objects in the Properties window.

3. In the Alphabetic tab of the Properties window, choose Caption (**Figure 1.17**).

4. In the right column of the Properties window, enter the text for the caption.

The new text appears in the form's title bar.

✔ Tip

■ Like the BackColor property, a form's caption can by changed dynamically by user actions when the form is running. I'll show you how to do this later in this chapter.

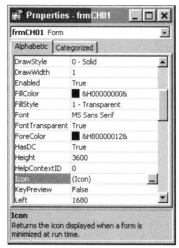

Figure 1.18 A form's Icon property is used to associate an icon with a form.

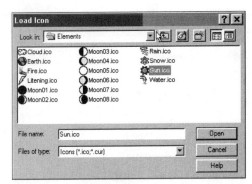

Figure 1.19 The Load Icon dialog is used to select an icon to associate with a form.

![Buttons and Message Boxes]

Figure 1.20 When an icon has been loaded, it is displayed in the title bar of the form.

Setting a Form's Icon

If you associate an icon with a form, the icon appears in the left end of the form's title bar. In addition, the icon can be displayed on the Windows Taskbar when the form is run and minimized.

You associate an icon with a form by using the form's Icon property.

To set a form's Icon property:

1. With the form selected in the Properties window, select Icon in the Alphabetic tab.

2. In the right column of the Properties window, click the button with three dots to the right of the word (Icon) (**Figure 1.18**). The Load Icon dialog opens (**Figure 1.19**).

3. Browse through the files in the Load Icon dialog until you find the icon you want to use; then select it.

4. Click Open.

   The icon you selected is now displayed in the title bar of your form (**Figure 1.20**).

✔ Tip

■ Visual Basic ships with numerous categorized icon files. (These icon files have the file suffix .ico.) No matter where you decided to install Visual Basic, these icon files are installed in a common location for Microsoft Visual Studio—usually, `C:\Program Files\Microsoft\Visual Studio\Common`.

   When you use the Load Icon dialog to browse for these files and are unable to find them, it may be because they were not installed. In this case, you need to rerun the Visual Basic installation program with Custom Installation selected. Make sure that you select the Icon Library option (which is available if the Graphics option is selected).

SETTING FORM PROPERTIES

Categorizing properties

It's very convenient to display form properties alphabetically. But if you are working with one kind of property—all properties related to the appearance of an object, for example—it would be useful to have the properties categorized.

To display properties in categories:

◆ In the Properties window, select the Categorized tab.

The properties appear in a categorized list (**Figure 1.21**).

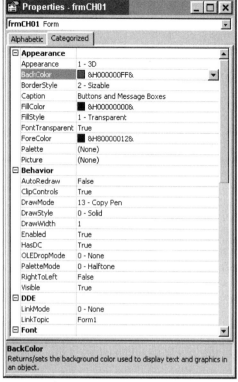

Figure 1.21 Properties are sorted by function in the Categorized tab of the Properties window.

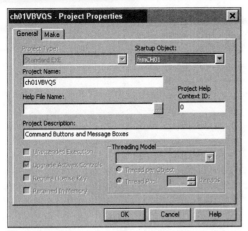

Figure 1.22 If your project contains multiple modules, a Startup Object should be selected in the Project Properties dialog.

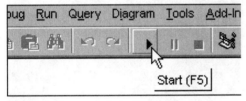

Figure 1.23 To run a project, click the right arrow on the Visual Basic toolbar.

Running a Project

So far, I've shown you how to set your form's properties in Visual Basic's *design-time* environment. Visual Basic also provides a *run-time* environment. VB's run-time environment gives you a chance to review the appearance and behavior of your program when it is running without having to first compile the Visual Basic project into an executable program. This greatly speeds the development process because you don't have to stop and go through the compilation process each time to see the impact of changes you've made. In addition, by running a project within the Visual Basic environment instead of first compiling it, you get the benefits of the debugging tools that Visual Basic provides (see Chapter 8).

You don't really know what impact the changes you make to a VB project have until you run the project. So let's go ahead and run the project containing our form!

To run a project:

1. Because your project contains only one module—the form—it is automatically set to be the project's Startup Object. If the project contained multiple modules, you would need to select a Startup Object in the General tab of the Project Properties dialog (**Figure 1.22**). You access the Project Properties dialog via the Project menu.

2. *Do one of the following:*
   - Click the right arrow in the Visual Basic toolbar (**Figure 1.23**).
   - Choose Run from the Run menu.
   - Press F5.

continues on next page

If you chose Prompt to Save Change in the Environment tab of the Options dialog box (see "Configuring Your Project" earlier in this chapter), you will be asked to save any changes made in your project since it was last saved (**Figure 1.24**).

3. Click Yes to save the changes.

The form is now displayed in running mode so that you can examine its appearance and behavior. You can move it to the Windows desktop by minimizing Visual Basic itself, if necessary—and its icon appears in the Windows Taskbar (**Figure 1.25**).

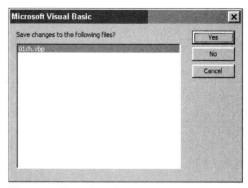

Figure 1.24 If you elected to prompt to save changes when a project is started, you are asked to save any changes before the project starts.

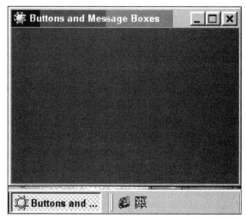

Figure 1.25 A running Visual Basic project behaves like any other Windows application; the form is shown with its Taskbar icon.

Adding a Button

Forms by themselves don't do very much! They are like the background scenery, waiting for the actors to come out on the stage. The actors in a form are usually *controls*. (You may be interested to know that the full technical name for a control is *ActiveX control*. There—now you know how to use the word *ActiveX* properly to impress your friends.)

The Visual Basic Toolbox displays the controls that are available for you to add to your forms.

Visual Basic controls are divided into *intrinsic* controls—which ship with the VB Learning edition—and *extrinsic* controls, which must be added to the Toolbox before they can be used. For now, we will be working with one of the most common and easy-to-use intrinsic controls: the Command Button. (For information on adding extrinsic controls to the Toolbox, see Chapter 5.)

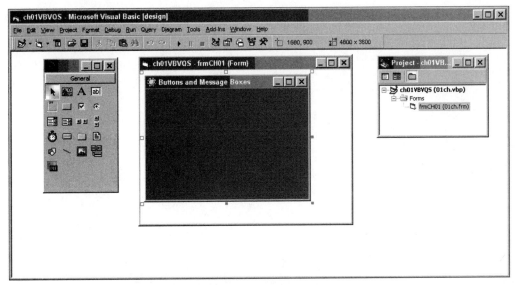

Figure 1.26 The Toolbox displays icons representing all available controls.

To add a button to a form:

1. Make sure that the form is open in Visual Basic, if necessary, by double-clicking it in the Project Explorer.

2. If it is not already open, open the Toolbox by choosing Toolbox from the View menu.

   The Toolbox displays icons representing any controls that are loaded (**Figure 1.26**).

3. In the Toolbox, locate the icon representing the Command Button (**Figure 1.27**).

4. Double-click the Command Button to move an instance of the control to the form; alternatively, you can drag the control into the form.

   In either case, the control now appear on the form (**Figure 1.28**).

Figure 1.27 When you've found the control you want to use, you can move an instance of it to a form by double-clicking it or using drag-and-drop.

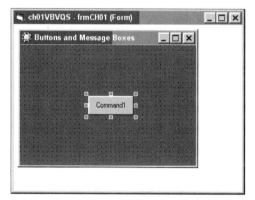

Figure 1.28 The control is displayed on the form.

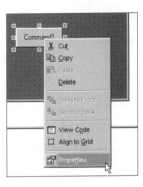

Figure 1.29 You can use a control's pop-up menu to open the Properties window.

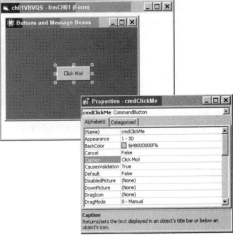

Figure 1.30 The Properties window is used to change control attributes.

Figure 1.31 To fully view the changes made in the Properties window, you should run the project.

To set button properties:

1. In the Properties window, select the Command Button.

   You can do this by right-clicking the Command Button and choosing Properties from the pop-up menu (**Figure 1.29**).

2. In the Properties window, change the name of the Command Button to cmdClickMe.

3. Change the value of the button's Caption property to Click Moi!

   As you enter this text in the Properties window, the caption appears on the Command Button (**Figure 1.30**).

4. Run the project by clicking the right arrow in the Visual Basic toolbar.

5. When prompted, save the changes to the project.

   Your form appears in run mode with its new button (**Figure 1.31**).

✔ Tip

■ You should name each kind of control using a prefix that says what the control is—cmd for command buttons, for example. This helps you know what an object is when you are reading program source code.

Adding Code to the Click Event

Visual Basic objects—such as forms and controls—have *events* that are associated with them.

One fundamental way that Visual Basic works involves events. When you create a project, you generally add code to specific events to make something happen when that event has been fired.

A very common event to use for this purpose is the Click event. A Command Button's Click event is fired when a user clicks the button with her mouse.

To add code to a click event:

1. Right-click the Command Button, and from the pop-up menu choose View Code.

   or

   From the View menu choose Code.

   The Code Editor opens (**Figure 1.32**).

2. From the Object drop-down menu, located in the top-left corner of the Code Editor, choose the Command Button.

   By default, the Command Button's Click event appears in the Procedure list in the top-right corner of the Code Editor (**Figure 1.33**). You should know that you can select another event by scrolling through the Procedure list, as shown in **Figure 1.33**.

3. In the Command Button's Click event in the Code Editor, between the Private and End statement, type:

   ```
   frmCH01.Caption = "I have a new
    caption!"
   ```

   When executed, this command changes the form's caption.

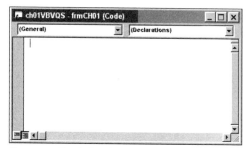

Figure 1.32 The Code Editor is used to add event procedures.

Figure 1.33 Code can be added to any of the events that appear in the Procedures list for an object.

Code Listing 1.1

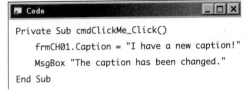

```
Private Sub cmdClickMe_Click()
    frmCH01.Caption = "I have a new caption!"
    MsgBox "The caption has been changed."
End Sub
```

Figure 1.34 Code statements are added between the beginning and end of the event procedure.

Figure 1.35 Event code is executed when the user fires the event by clicking the button.

4. In the Code Editor, in the next line, type:

MsgBox "The caption has been
→ changed."

This command displays a message to the viewer. The completed code, called an *event procedure,* is shown in **Figure 1.34** and **Listing 1.1**.

5. Run the program by clicking the right arrow in the VB toolbar.

6. When prompted, save the changes to the form file and project.

Now, when you click the button, the form's caption changes, and a message is displayed (**Figure 1.35**).

✔ Tip

■ For a complete explanation of the MsgBox statement, see Chapter 2.

ADDING CODE TO THE CLICK EVENT

Summary

In this chapter, you learned to:

- Start a Visual Basic project.
- Configure a project.
- Name a project
- Save a project.
- Add a form to a project.
- Set form properties.
- Center a form.
- Set a form's BackColor property.
- Set a form's caption.

- Assign an icon to a form.
- Run a Visual Basic project.
- Add a Command Button to a form.
- Set button properties.
- Add code to click events.
- Dynamically change a form caption in response to a user click.
- Display a message.

ADDING CODE TO THE CLICK EVENT

MESSAGE BOXES AND IF STATEMENTS

In Chapter 1, I showed you how to use the MsgBox statement to display a text message in a simple dialog. I'm sure you'll be pleased to learn that you can use MsgBox to create "instant" dialogs that are considerably fancier than that. Message boxes can even include buttons, which the user can click to indicate a desired course of action.

In this chapter, I'll show you the full gamut of MsgBox statements and functions. (A *function* is a programming statement that returns a value.)

The goal of this chapter is to create a form that can be used to display the most common variants of message boxes. To fulfill that goal, a form will require controls besides the Command Button (explained in Chapter 1). The additional controls, explained in this chapter, are Labels, TextBoxes, Frames, and OptionButtons.

Some simple programming is required to make these controls work together to display the different message boxes. This kind of programming can be thought of as wiring the controls together under the hood.

Primarily, this wiring involves the use of If statements. I'll explain how Visual Basic If statements—also called *conditional* statements—work and how to use them with the controls on the form.

Finally, some variants of the message box provide buttons for the user to click— buttons labeled Yes and No, for example. I'll show you how to evaluate user response to a message-box statement. (*Evaluate* is a fancy word meaning to determine what button the user clicked.)

So come on in! The water is fine! By the end of this chapter, you'll have built a real Visual Basic application.

Message Boxes

A message-box statement has five possible parts, called *parameters*. You can leave off all the parameters except the first one, which is required. This first parameter, the *prompt*, is the text that the message box displays. If you just include a prompt, Visual Basic fills in the rest of the parameter values as best it can (this is called "using default values").

In addition, as I've already mentioned, MsgBox can be used as either a statement, which does not return a *value*, or a function, which returns a value that allows you to determine a user action.

If this all sounds complex, don't worry: It's not. When you start using message boxes, you'll catch on quickly.

In this section, I'll explain the message-box parameters. I'll tell you how to work with buttons and icons. Next, I'll provide some examples of using MsgBox. Finally, I'll provide you more complete information about possible parameter values.

MsgBox syntax

A MsgBox statement has the following format:

```
MsgBox Prompt, Buttons, Title,
→ Helpfile, Context
```

If you're using MsgBox as a function, the parameters—also called *arguments*—must be enclosed in parentheses. For example:

```
Answer = MsgBox (Prompt, Buttons,
→ Title, Helpfile, Context)
```

Here's the meaning of the parameters, which must be entered in the order shown just above:

◆ *Prompt* contains the text that will be displayed in the message box.

◆ *Buttons*, which is optional, contains a code that indicates the buttons the message box will display.

◆ *Title*, which is optional, contains the text that will go in the message box title bar.

◆ *Helpfile*, which is optional, contains the name of the Help file to use with context-sensitive help in the message box. If a value for *Helpfile* is supplied, a value for *Context* must also be supplied. *Helpfile* will not be covered in detail. For more information on adding Help to your programs, see the "Adding Help to Your Visual Studio Applications" topic in the MSDN library that ships with Visual Basic or one of the many intermediate to advanced books that cover Help files.

◆ *Context*, which is optional unless *Helpfile* has been specified, contains a number referencing a help topic. *Context* will not be covered in detail.

One final wrinkle is the way middle parameters are omitted. Suppose that you want a message box to display a prompt and a title. The syntax to use is:

```
MsgBox Prompt, , Title
```

The missing Buttons parameter is indicated with the extra comma: , ,. In other words, you can't just leave out a parameter that is optional; you must replace it with an extra comma.

Buttons and Icons

The Buttons parameter is an integer value. Each possible button, set of buttons, or icon displayed by the MsgBox statement is represented by an integer. For example, 1 is the code representing OK and Cancel buttons, and 48 means an exclamation-point icon.

To display multiple buttons and icons, you can add their numbers. Thus, if 49 were used as the Buttons parameter of a MsgBox statement, an exclamation-point icon and OK and Cancel buttons would be displayed.

Although using a number for the Buttons parameter works just fine, it is better programming practice to use built-in Visual Basic constants instead. (A *constant* is a predefined value that does not change.) It is a better practice because it produces code statements that are easier to read.

Using these constants, to display the OK and Cancel buttons and the Exclamation icon, you'd replace the Buttons parameter with:

`vbOKCancel + vbExclamation`

At this point, you may be scratching your head and saying, "OK, but where do I find these constants?" Good question! You'll find some of them in **Tables 2.1** and **2.2**. (**Table 2.2** shows the return values from the MsgBox—in other words, what the user clicked—as explained later in this chapter.) In addition, when you are typing the MsgBox statement in the VB Code Editor, when you get to the Buttons parameter, a list of the available constants pops up (**Figure 2.1**).

Looking ahead a little, you may be interested to know that the collection of Button constants are the members of the vbMsgBoxStyle class. Using Visual Basic's Object Browser, you can find a list of these class members by searching for MsgBox (**Figure 2.2**). You'll find instructions on using the Object Browser and an explanation of Visual Basic classes in Chapter 10.

By the way, this is somewhat like the Chinese-restaurant menu system: You can have one choice from each group. In other words, if you select vbOKCancel for the buttons, you cannot also add vbAbortRetryIgnore (but you can have an icon with either choice).

Table 2.1

Common MsgBox Button Constants

CONSTANT	VALUE	DESCRIPTION
vbOKOnly	0	Display OK button only.
vbOKCancel	1	Display OK and Cancel buttons.
vbAbortRetryIgnore	2	Display Abort, Retry, and Ignore buttons.
vbYesNoCancel	3	Display Yes, No, and Cancel buttons.
vbYesNo	4	Display Yes and No buttons.
vbRetryCancel	5	Display Retry and Cancel buttons.
vbCritical	16	Display Critical Message icon.
vbQuestion	32	Display Warning Query icon.
vbExclamation	48	Display Warning Message icon.
vbInformation	64	Display Information Message icon.

Table 2.2

MsgBox Return Values

CONSTANT	VALUE	DESCRIPTION
vbOK	1	OK
vbCancel	2	Cancel
vbAbort	3	Abort
vbRetry	4	Retry
vbIgnore	5	Ignore
vbYes	6	Yes
vbNo	7	No

Figure 2.1 A list of available Button constants appears in the Code Editor when you enter a MsgBox statement.

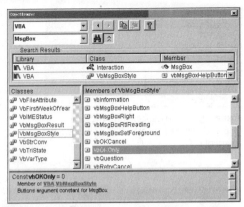

Figure 2.2 Using the Object Browser, you can list all members of the vbMsgBoxStyle class (constants that can be used in the Buttons parameter of the MsgBox statement).

Figure 2.3 You can use a message box to display prompts and titles without icons or buttons.

Figure 2.4 A message box can display an OK button and an icon along with the prompt and title.

MsgBox Examples

It's probably easier to get a feeling for the MsgBox statement in the context of actual examples. In this section, I'll show you a few message-box statements.

To display a prompt and a title:

Use code along these lines:

```
MsgBox "Your input has been received", ,
→ "Tell them about it!"
```

Your message box displays a prompt ("Your input has been received") and a title ("Tell them about it!") but no buttons or icons (**Figure 2.3**).

To display an OK button and icon:

This code displays a prompt, a title, an OK button, and the Information icon (**Figure 2.4**).

```
MsgBox "I'm Okay!", vbOKOnly +
→ vbInformation, "You're Okay!"
```

✔ Tip

■ Some wag has dubbed message boxes that display only an OK button a "not OK" dialog. This is because they sometimes say things along the lines of "Your data has been lost and your system is crashing. OK?" No, it's not really OK, but there is nothing the poor user can do other than click OK. Another problem with this style of message box is that it requires user intervention—clicking the OK button—without providing any other option (and thus is a waste of the user's input). As a matter of good interface design, avoid using the vbOKOnly style of message box when possible.

To display OK and Cancel buttons:

```
Dim Answer As Integer
Answer = MsgBox("Press OK to continue,
→ Cancel to cancel.", vbOKCancel +
→ vbQuestion, "Continue?")
```

This displays OK and Cancel buttons as well as a question-mark icon (**Figure 2.5**). I'll show you later in this chapter how to decode the user's answer to the question (meaning the button she clicked), which is stored in the variable *Answer*.

To display Yes, No, and Cancel buttons:

```
Dim Answer As Integer
Answer = MsgBox("Press Yes to accept
→ default values" +
→ ", Press No to enter new values," +
→ " and Cancel to exit.",
→ vbYesNoCancel + vbCritical,
→ "The Critical Question.")
```

This will generate a message box with Yes, No, and Cancel buttons (**Figure 2.6**). This time, the Critical icon is displayed.

As in the previous example, the user's choice is returned in the variable *Answer*.

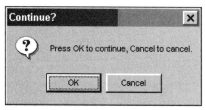

Figure 2.5 OK and Cancel buttons can be displayed, with the user's choice returned in a variable.

Figure 2.6 Yes, No, and Cancel buttons can be displayed, once again returning the user's response in a variable.

MESSAGE BOXES

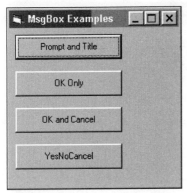

Figure 2.7 The Examples form is used to display the MsgBox examples.

Examples Form and Source Code

You can find this source code on the book's Web site in the 02ch.vbp project, in the form named Examples (**Figure 2.7**). **Listing 2.1** shows the complete code for the four MsgBox examples.

Listing 2.1 Sample MsgBox Code

```
Option Explicit

Private Sub cmdOKandCancel_Click()
    Dim Answer As Integer
    Answer = MsgBox("Press OK to continue, Cancel to cancel.", vbOKCancel + vbQuestion, "Continue?")
End Sub

Private Sub cmdOkOnly_Click()
    MsgBox "I'm Okay!", vbOKOnly + vbInformation, "You're Okay!"
End Sub

Private Sub cmdpromptandtitle_Click()
    MsgBox "Your input has been received", , "Tell them about it!"
End Sub

Private Sub cmdYesNoCancel_Click()
    Dim Answer As Integer
    Answer = MsgBox("Press Yes to accept default values" + ", Press No to enter new values," +
    → " and Cancel to exit.", vbYesNoCancel + vbCritical, "The Critical Question.")
End Sub
```

Frames

Frames are controls used to group related controls on a form. This is generally done to promote visual clarity, rather than because it is required.

The application that you will build in this chapter will employ three frames:

- ◆ A frame for the text and labels that will be used to display prompts and titles

- ◆ A frame for the option buttons used to select buttons

- ◆ A frame for the option buttons used to select icons

Before you can add a frame (or any other control) to a form, you must start a Visual Basic project and open a form. This procedure is explained in Chapter 1.

To add a frame to a form:

1. With a project and form open, display the Toolbox (if it is not already displayed) by choosing Toolbox from the View menu.

2. Locate the representation of the Frame control in the Toolbox (**Figure 2.8**).

3. Move the Frame control from the Toolbox to your form, either by double-clicking the Frame control icon or by dragging the control into the form.

4. With the Frame control on the form, use the handles on the form to size the frame control (**Figure 2.9**).

5. To set Frame properties, open the Properties window, by choosing Properties Window from the View menu or by right-clicking the frame and choosing Properties from the pop-up menu (**Figure 2.10**).

6. Make sure that the frame is selected in the Object list.

Figure 2.8 Move the Frame control from the Toolbox to your form, either by double-clicking the Frame control or by dragging the control into the form.

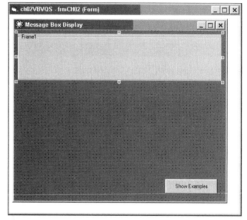

Figure 2.9 Position and size the Frame control when it is on the form.

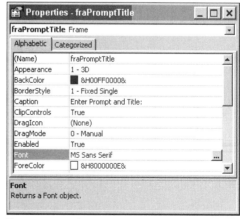

Figure 2.10 Use the Properties window to change the frame's name and caption.

FRAMES

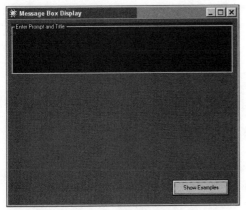

Figure 2.11 When the frame's Caption has been changed, the new caption is displayed on the form.

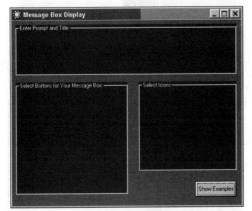

Figure 2.12 Frames can be sized and positioned on the form to make an attractive user interface.

7. Set the frame's name to `fraPromptTitle` and its caption to `Enter Prompt and Title:`; you can also set its BackColor property.

   The next time you run the form, the new caption appears in the frame (**Figure 2.11**).

✔ Tip

- The Show Examples button shown in the form in **Figures 2.9, 2.11,** and **2.12** is used to display the MsgBox examples explained earlier in this chapter.

To add button and icon frames:

1. With the form still open, use the Toolbox to add a second frame to the form.

2. Use the Properties window to name the frame `fraButtons`, and give it the caption `Select Buttons for Your Message Box`.

3. Position the fraButtons frame in the form.

4. Add another frame named `fraIcons` and captioned `Select Icons`.

5. Position the three frames in the form.

6. Run the project to save your work, and ensure that the frames are appropriately positioned and sized (**Figure 2.12**).

FRAMES

Labels and TextBoxes

Labels are controls used to display text on forms and other controls. *TextBox controls* are used to accept text input from the user. Generally, when you need to create a user interface that asks the user to enter text, you'll need a Label and TextBox pair. The Label is to tell the user what text to enter, and the TextBox is to retrieve the text actually entered.

To add a label to the frame:

1. Make sure that the project and form are open.

2. If the Toolbox is not already open, open it by choosing Toolbox from the View menu.

3. Locate the Label control (represented by a capital A) in the Toolbox (**Figure 2.13**).

4. Drag a Label control into the form, and drop it on the appropriate frame (fraPromptTitle).

   The label appears in the frame with the default caption Label1 (**Figure 2.14**).

5. Position and size the Label control, using its handles.

6. Open the Properties window, either by choosing Properties Window from the View menu, or by right-clicking the Label control and choosing Properties from the pop-up menu.

7. Make sure that the Label control is selected in the Objects list (**Figure 2.15**).

8. Change the label's Name property to lblPrompt.

   A label's Caption property contains the text that appears on the screen. In the next step, you change it.

9. Change lblPrompt's Caption property to Prompt: (**Figure 2.15**).

Figure 2.13 The icon for the Label control in the Toolbox is a capital A.

Figure 2.14 When you drag a Label control into the form, it appears with the default caption Label1.

Figure 2.15 The Properties window is used to set label caption, name, and appearance properties.

LABELS AND TEXTBOXES

Figure 2.16 To add a text box to the frame, first locate the TextBox control in the Toolbox.

Figure 2.17 When the TextBox control is positioned on the frame, it appears with the default text Text1.

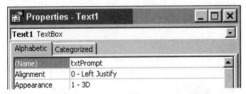

Figure 2.18 Text boxes should be named with the prefix txt.

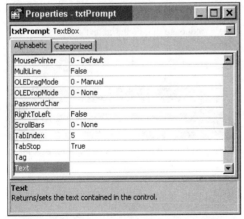

Figure 2.19 A text box's Text property is used to set and retrieve the text displayed in the control.

To add a TextBox to the frame:

1. With the form and Toolbox open, locate the TextBox control (**Figure 2.16**).

2. Drag the TextBox into the form, and drop it on the appropriate frame (fraPromptTitle).

3. Position and size the TextBox, using its handles (**Figure 2.17**).

4. In the Properties window, change the name of the text box to txtPrompt (**Figure 2.18**).

   A TextBox's Text property sets the text in the control (and is used to retrieve text from the control). In the following step, you change that property.

5. Using the Properties window, change txtPrompt's Text property so that it has no value (**Figure 2.19**).

   This causes txtPrompt to be displayed initially without text.

To add the next Label and TextBox:

1. Drag and drop another Label control onto the frame.

2. Position and size the label.

3. Use the Properties window to set the label's Name to `lblTitle` and the Caption to `Title:` (**Figure 2.20**).

4. Drag and drop a TextBox control onto the frame.

5. Position and size the text box.

6. Use the Properties window to set the text box's Name to `txtTitle` and its Text property to have no value (**Figure 2.21**).

7. Save and run the project.

   The fraPromptTitle frame appears with labels and input text boxes (**Figure 2.22**).

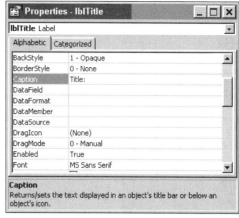

Figure 2.20 Use the Properties window to set the name and caption of the next Label control.

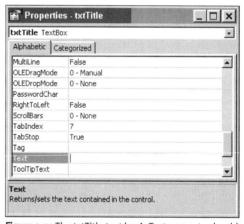

Figure 2.21 The txtTitle text box's Text property should have no value, so that no initial text appears on the screen.

Figure 2.22 The text boxes are now ready for user input.

LABELS AND TEXTBOXES

Figure 2.23 Option buttons are used to allow users to make a choice from a group of options.

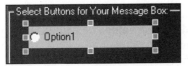

Figure 2.24 Option buttons can be positioned and sized like labels and text boxes after they have been added to a frame.

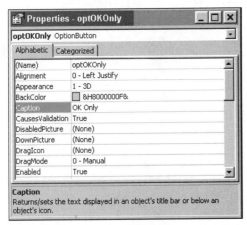

Figure 2.25 By convention, OptionButton names start with opt; the caption appears to the right of the control.

Option Buttons

Option buttons are controls that are typically used when you want to let the user make one—and only one—choice from a menu. It is important to understand that option buttons added to the same frame automatically behave this way. In other words, all the option buttons added to the frame are grouped so that only one can be selected.

By default, when you add an option button to a frame, the option button's Value property is set to False. This means the button is not selected. If you want one of the option buttons on the frame to be selected when the form starts running, you can use the Properties window to set the Value property to True for that option button. As you've likely already figured out, only one option button in a frame group can have a Value property set to True at any time.

To add option buttons to a frame:

1. Make sure that the fraButtons frame is selected.

2. In the Toolbox, locate the OptionButton control (**Figure 2.23**).

3. Drag an instance of the OptionButton control onto fraButtons.

4. Position and size the option button (**Figure 2.24**).

5. Use the Properties window to set the option button's Name property to optOkOnly and its caption property to OK Only (**Figure 2.25**).

continues on next page

OPTION BUTTONS

6. Repeat the process of adding option buttons and setting their names and captions, using the values shown in **Table 2.3**.

When you have added the six option button listed in **Table 2.3,** your frame should look like the one shown in **Figure 2.26.**

7. Use the Properties window to set the Value property of optOKOnly to True.

8. Run the project to verify that the form starts with optOKOnly selected and that you can only select one option button at a time.

✔ Tip

- You don't actually have to drag and drop each option button onto the frame. An alternative procedure—which is faster because the option buttons that are created come "prefabricated," with many property settings—is to add one option button to the frame. After you have changed its properties, select the button. Then copy it by choosing Copy from the Edit menu or pressing Ctrl+C.

  Make sure that the destination frame is selected. Next, paste the copy of the control into the frame by choosing Paste from the Edit menu or pressing Ctrl+V.

  You will be asked whether you want to create a Control Array. Answer No. (Control arrays are covered in Chapters 4 and 5.)

  A copy of the control is added to the frame. You can proceed to modify its Name and Caption properties.

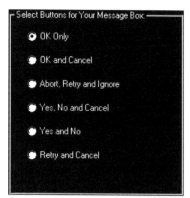

Figure 2.26 When you add option buttons, they should appear in a group.

Table 2.3

Name and Caption Values for fraButtons Option Buttons

NAME	CAPTION
optOKOnly	OK Only
optOKCancel	OK and Cancel
optAbortRetryIgnore	Abort, Retry, and Ignore
optYesNoCancel	Yes, No, and Cancel
optYesNo	Yes and No
optRetryCancel	Retry and Cancel

OPTION BUTTONS

Table 2.4

NAME	CAPTION
optCritical	Critical
optQuestion	Question
optExclamation	Exclamation
optInformation	Information
optNoIcon	No icon

Table title: **Name and Caption Values for fraIcons Option Buttons**

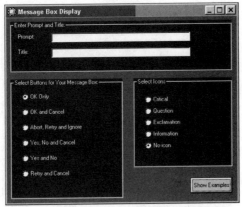

Figure 2.27 You should run your form to make sure that option-button groups start with the correct option button selected and that you can select only one at a time.

To add option buttons to the fraIcons frame:

1. Using the techniques explained in this section, add five option buttons to the fraIcons frame, with the name and caption property values listed in **Table 2.4**.

2. Use the Properties window to set the Value property of optNoIcon to True.

3. Run the project to make sure that only one option button in each frame can be selected at a time (**Figure 2.27**).

Adding a Button to Complete the Form

At this point, the form is almost complete. We lack only one thing: a button that the user can click to display the results of the choices she has made. (The Show Examples button you may have noticed in the illustrations is a way to access the examples that were explained earlier in this chapter.)

It's easy to add a command button: You've already done so several times.

To add a command button and complete the form:

1. Drag a CommandButton from the Toolbox onto the form (**Figure 2.28**).

2. Use the Properties window to set the button's name to cmdDisplayMsgBox and its caption to DISPLAY.

3. In the Properties window, set cmdDisplayMsgBox's default property to True, using the arrow selector in the right column (**Figure 2.29**).

   This sets things up so that pressing Enter has the same result as clicking the command button when the form is active and running.

4. Run the completed form to enjoy it in all its glory (**Figure 2.30**)!

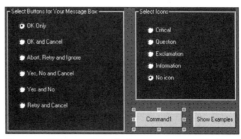

Figure 2.28 To complete the form, a command button that the user can click to display her choices is needed.

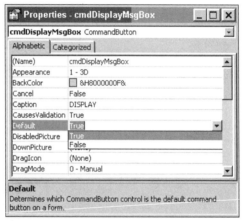

Figure 2.29 By setting a command button's Default property to True, you can activate the button by pressing Enter when the form is active and running.

Figure 2.30 Your form is completed and ready for wiring.

OPTION BUTTONS

If Statements

Your form is now ready to be wired, meaning that the user interface is in place. What is missing is the code that ties the elements of the user interface together and lets them achieve their purpose in life (which with our form, is to display varieties of MsgBox statements, in case you've lost track).

Before you get to this wiring, you need to understand If statements. *If statements* are used in code to allow the program to make decisions based on certain conditions. The form of the If statement that will be used in wiring the form is:

```
If condition1 Then
    first conditional block of statements
ElseIf condition2 Then
    second conditional block of statements
...
Else
    nth conditional block of statements
End If
```

The way this works is that VB first evaluates condition1. If it is true, the first conditional block of statements is executed (and that completes the execution of the If statement).

On the other hand, if condition1 is false, condition2 is evaluated. If condition2 is true, its statements are executed, and that is the end of the If statement. If it is false, the next ElseIf condition is evaluated, and so on.

If none of the conditional statements has been true, the conditional block following the Else clause is executed. You may want to leave out this final Else clause if you don't ever expect to fall through to it, because you believe that some condition will always be true. In this case, however, it's better practice to include the final Else clause and an error message that displays if its conditional block is executed.

Wiring the Form

Wiring the form involves two steps:

◆ Evaluating the buttons and icons selected by the user

◆ Displaying the message box based on the user's input and choices

The second step, displaying the message box, is something that you did earlier in this chapter. The only wrinkle is that the message box displays *variable* results depending on the user's input and choices.

All code that will be used to wire the form will be placed in the Click event of the button used to display results: cmdDisplayMsgBox.

To open the event procedure for adding code:

1. With your form open, right-click the Display command button.

2. From the pop-up menu, choose View Code (**Figure 2.31**).

   The Code Editor opens.

3. With the Code Editor open, choose cmdDisplayMsgBox from the Object list and Click from the Procedure list (**Figure 2.32**).

   You are now ready to start adding code to the Click event of the command button.

To determine the button selection:

1. Declare a variable, ButtonChoice, to hold the button selection, by typing the following line of code at the top of the event procedure:

   ```
   Dim ButtonChoice As Integer
   ```

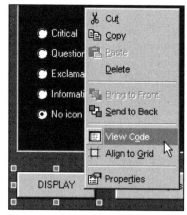

Figure 2.31 Choose View Code from the pop-up menu to open the Code Editor.

Figure 2.32 To add code to an object's Click event, in the Code Editor, choose the object from the Objects list and also choose Click from the Procedure list.

2. Below the declaration statement, add an If statement to determine the user's choice:

```
If optOkOnly.Value = True Then
        ButtonChoice = vbOKOnly
    ElseIf optOkCancel.Value = True
→ Then
        ButtonChoice = vbOKCancel
  ElseIf optAbortRetryIgnore.Value
→ = True Then
        ButtonChoice =
        → vbAbortRetryIgnore
    ElseIf optYesNoCancel.Value =
→ True Then
        ButtonChoice = vbYesNoCancel
    ElseIf optYesNo.Value = True Then
        ButtonChoice = vbYesNo
    ElseIf optRetryCancel.Value =
→ True Then
        ButtonChoice = vbRetryCancel
    End If
```

3. Although this code should cover all the bases in terms of possible user input, add an *Else* clause that covers the possibility of some unexpected error and ends the program:

```
...
Else
        MsgBox "Unexpected Error in
        → If statement!"
        End
...
```

To determine the icon selection:

1. Declare a variable, IconChoice, to hold the button selection, by typing the following line of code at the top of the event procedure right below the ButtonChoice declaration:

```
Dim IconChoice As Integer
```

continues on next page

2. Below the ButtonChoice block of code, skip a line, and add a comment by starting the line with an apostrophe:

```
'Determine Icon choice
```

3. Add an If statement to determine the user's choice:

```
If optCritical.Value = True Then
    IconChoice = vbCritical
ElseIf optQuestion.Value = True Then
    IconChoice = vbQuestion
ElseIf optExclamation.Value = True
→ Then
    IconChoice = vbExclamation
ElseIf optInformation.Value = True
→ Then
    IconChoice = vbInformation
ElseIf optNoIcon.Value = True Then
    IconChoice = 0
Else
    MsgBox "Abnormal Icon
    → Choice.Terminating."
    End
End If
```

To display the message box:

1. Following the icon display block, skip a line.

2. Enter a comment explaining the purpose of the code:

```
'Display the message box
```

3. Use the following code to display the message box:

```
MsgBox txtPrompt.Text, ButtonChoice
→ + IconChoice, txtTitle.Text
```

4. Run the program, and try various combinations of title, prompt, icons, and buttons to make sure that it is operating right (**Figures 2.33** and **2.34**).

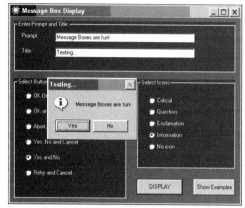

Figure 2.33 You can test the message-box display by trying different inputs.

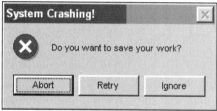

Figure 2.34 It is easy to create frightening message boxes for your applications!

✔ Tips

- It's important to test every possible input combination in an application like the message-box display, before releasing it to the public.

- Controls have a default property, which you can refer to by using shorthand to save time. The default property of the TextBox, for example, is Text. This means that the expression

  `txtPrompt.Text`

  is equivalent to
  `txtPrompt`

  Because Value is the default property for option buttons,
  `optQuestion.Value = True`

  is the same as
  `optQuestion = True`

  In this example, I've written it out the long way for clarity. But when you are reading code, if you see a reference to a control, you should know that the reference likely means the control's default property.

  You'll find the complete code for the Click event procedure in **Listing 2.2.**

Listing 2.2 Complete Click Event Code

```
Code                                                    _ □ x

Private Sub cmdDisplayMsgBox_Click()
    Dim ButtonChoice As Integer
    Dim IconChoice As Integer
    Dim Answer As Integer

    If optOKOnly.Value = True Then
        ButtonChoice = vbOKOnly
    ElseIf optOKCancel.Value = True Then
        ButtonChoice = vbOKCancel
    ElseIf optAbortRetryIgnore.Value = True Then
        ButtonChoice = vbAbortRetryIgnore
```

Code continues on next page

WIRING THE FORM

Listing 2.2 *continued*

```
┌─────────────────────────────────────────────────────────────────────┐
│ 🖳 Code                                                  _  □  ✕      │
├─────────────────────────────────────────────────────────────────────┤

      ElseIf optYesNoCancel.Value = True Then
          ButtonChoice = vbYesNoCancel
      ElseIf optYesNo.Value = True Then
          ButtonChoice = vbYesNo
      ElseIf optRetryCancel.Value = True Then
          ButtonChoice = vbRetryCancel
      Else
          MsgBox "Unexpected Error in If statement!"
          End
      End If

      'Determine Icon choice
      If optCritical.Value = True Then
          IconChoice = vbCritical
      ElseIf optQuestion.Value = True Then
          IconChoice = vbQuestion
      ElseIf optExclamation.Value = True Then
          IconChoice = vbExclamation
      ElseIf optInformation.Value = True Then
          IconChoice = vbInformation
      ElseIf optNoIcon.Value = True Then
          IconChoice = 0
      Else
          MsgBox "Abnormal Icon Choice. Terminating."
          End
      End If

      'Display the message box

      Answer = MsgBox(txtPrompt.Text, ButtonChoice + IconChoice, txtTitle.Text)
      If Answer = vbOK Then
          MsgBox "You clicked OK!"
      ElseIf Answer = vbCancel Then
          MsgBox "You clicked Cancel!"
      ElseIf Answer = vbAbort Then
          MsgBox "You clicked Abort!"
      ElseIf Answer = vbRetry Then
          MsgBox "You clicked Retry!"
      ElseIf Answer = vbIgnore Then
          MsgBox "You clicked Ignore!"
      ElseIf Answer = vbYes Then
          MsgBox "You clicked Yes!"
      ElseIf Answer = vbNo Then
          MsgBox "You clicked No!"
      Else
          MsgBox "No click detected!"
      End If
  End Sub
```

Evaluating the Response

You're almost there! The application is almost done. And it is not just any old application; rather, it is a handy-dandy, useful application that employs many important Visual Basic tools and techniques. I bet you didn't think you'd build anything quite so complex in such a hurry!

One thing remains to be done, however. When you use message boxes, you often want to know which button the user clicked. In programmer-speak, this is called *evaluating the response*. Ideally, different things happen in a real-world program when the user clicks Yes as opposed to No.

To find out which button was clicked and display this information:

1. Declare a variable to hold the response information at the top of the procedure, below the other two declarations:

```
Dim Answer As Integer
```

2. Rewrite the MsgBox statement as a function:

```
Answer = MsgBox(txtPrompt.Text,
→ ButtonChoice + IconChoice,
→ txtTitle.Text)
```

3. Write an If statement at the end of the Click procedure that tests the variable Answer and displays the result:

```
If Answer = vbOK Then
    MsgBox "You clicked OK!"
ElseIf Answer = vbCancel Then
    MsgBox "You clicked Cancel!"
ElseIf Answer = vbAbort Then
    MsgBox "You clicked Abort!"
ElseIf Answer = vbRetry Then
    MsgBox "You clicked Retry!"
```

continues on next page

```
ElseIf Answer = vbIgnore Then
    MsgBox "You clicked Ignore!"
ElseIf Answer = vbYes Then
    MsgBox "You clicked Yes!"
ElseIf Answer = vbNo Then
    MsgBox "You clicked No!"
Else
    MsgBox "No click detected!"
End If
```

Figure 2.35 You'll need to check all the button responses...

4. Run the program to make sure that every works.

This step involves clicking many buttons. Try clicking each kind of button at least once (**Figures 2.35** and **2.36**).

Figure 2.36 ...to make sure that the responses are being evaluated properly.

If everything is working right: congratulations! Your first significant Visual Basic application is complete.

Summary

In this chapter, you learned to:

- Work with message boxes and MsgBox syntax.

- Add buttons and icons to message boxes.

- Work with message-box constants.

- Understand message-box return values.

- Work with frames.

- Add labels and text boxes to a frame and form.

- Add groups of option buttons to a frame.

- Work with If statements and use them in code.

- Add code to a Click event to display a message box created based on user input.

- Evaluate user response to this dynamic message box.

EVALUATING THE RESPONSE

FORMS AND MODULES

In Chapters 1 and 2, you dove right in and built Visual Basic applications. In the course of doing this, you didn't worry too much about all the capabilities of the objects you used—just how to get them to do what you needed them to do. This is, in fact, characteristic of programming and creating applications in the real world.

The methodology used in the first two chapters was to first build the user interface. After the interface was complete it was wired, using relatively small amounts of code under the hood. This also is consistent with real-world development.

This chapter steps back and takes a somewhat different approach. The previous chapters used form modules without looking too closely at what you can do with them. This chapter—the first of three chapters that show you in more detail how to work with forms—explains how to work with form properties. Chapter 4 explains form events, and Chapter 5 tells you how to work with form methods.

Properties are fun and easy to use, so dig right in and go to it. Let's set some form properties today!

Form Properties

Properties represent characteristics of an object, such as a form. They can be used to set a characteristic. The property BackColor, for example, sets a form's color. Many properties also store—or, in programming jargon, *return*—the values they contain, so you can tap these values if necessary when your program is running. You might want to display a message box stating "Your form is red!"

The most common way to work with form properties is to set them at design time, using the Properties window. In addition, many properties can be set *dynamically* at run time, in response to a user action or program event. Some properties can be set *only* at run time in code and therefore do not appear in the Properties window.

You should know that many more form properties are available for your use than I will cover in this chapter. This best way to learn about the complete selection is to open the Properties window for an open form. Experiment with properties that interest you, and observe the consequences both in the Visual Basic design environment and when you run the form.

To view documentation for all form properties:

1. From the VB Help menu, choose Index.
   The MSDN Visual Studio Library application opens, with the Index tab active (**Figure 3.1**).

2. In the Active Subset list box, select *Visual Basic Documentation (**Figure 3.2**).

3. In the Type the Keyword to Find text box, enter `Form object` (**Figure 3.2**).

4. Click Display.
   The Form Object, Forms Collection page appears in the right pane (**Figure 3.3**).

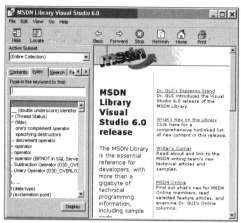

Figure 3.1 When you choose Index from the VB Help menu, the MSDN Visual Studio Library application opens with the Index tab active.

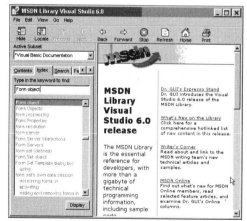

Figure 3.2 It is easier to find Visual Basic documentation if you restrict the index request to the Visual Basic documentation subset.

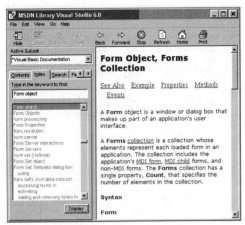

Figure 3.3 The Forms page provides an overview of information about forms.

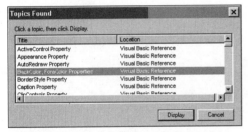

Figure 3.4 To view detailed information on any form property, select the property in the Topics Found dialog.

5. Click the Properties link at the top of the page.

The Topics Found dialog opens, displaying a list of all form properties (**Figure 3.4**).

6. Select the property you are interested in.

7. Click Display.

Form Property Preliminaries

Before we get started working with form properties, some preliminaries:

Me is a keyword used to refer to the currently active object. In other words, in the event code associated with a form, you do not need to reference the form by its name; you can use *Me* instead.

You should know a couple of pieces of good news.

First, the same properties that you work with when you work with forms are also used with many other objects. This means that when you understand how they work with forms, you also automatically understand how they work with many controls. The BackColor and ForeColor properties of the form, for example, set the color of the form background and text printed on the form, respectively. These properties are also available with Label controls (and many other controls) to set the background and text colors.

In the Code Editor, object properties and methods are invoked by referencing the object (a form, for example). Next, the dot operator (which looks like a period) is entered. Finally, the property or method is typed. For example:

```
' Property
Me.Caption = "I am a form!"


' Method
Me.Refresh
```

This discussion is jumping ahead a bit, but you should also know that you can stack object references in code by using the dot operator. To assign the contents of the TextBox txtUser to the variable UserInput from within a form event, for example, you can use the following code:

```
UserInput = Me.txtUser.Text
```

You will also be pleased to know that when you reference an object, such as a form, in the Code Editor and continue typing, you are automatically presented a list of possible properties and methods for you to invoke next (**Figure 3.5**). This helps you know what methods and properties are available.

Figure 3.5 When you invoke an object in the Code Editor followed by the dot operator, you'll see a drop-down list of available methods and properties.

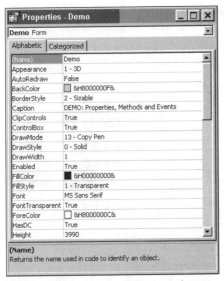

Figure 3.6 The Properties window is used to set properties at design time.

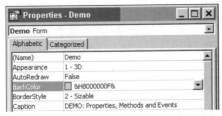

Figure 3.7 To change the background color, select the BackColor property.

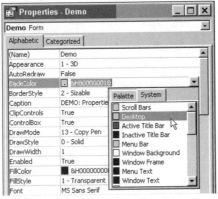

Figure 3.8 The System color list box allows you to choose one of the existing system colors.

BackColor and ForeColor Properties

The BackColor property is used to set the background color of a form. (It can also be used to determine the current background color of a form.)

The ForeColor property is used to set (or determine) the color of text and graphics on a form. It works the same way as the BackColor property. This property is less commonly used with forms than with objects such as Label controls.

To set a form's background color to a system color:

1. In the Visual Basic design-time environment, open a form.

2. With the form open, open the Properties window (**Figure 3.6**).

3. In the left column of the Alphabetic tab, select BackColor (**Figure 3.7**).

4. Click the down arrow on the right edge of the Properties window.

   The System color list box opens (**Figure 3.8**).

5. Select an available system color.

   This color now appears (as a swatch of color and as a series of hexadecimal numbers) in the right column of the Properties window. In addition, the background of the form changes to the color you selected.

To set a form's background color to a palette color:

1. With the System color list box open, select the Palette tab (**Figure 3.9**).

2. Select a color from the Palette color list box.

   This color now appears (as a swatch of color and as a series of hexadecimal numbers) in the right column of the Properties window. In addition, the background of the form changes to the color you selected.

Color Notation

To work with color in Visual Basic code, you'll need to know how color is *notated* (referred to).

Internally, Visual Basic colors are represented by hexadecimal—or base-16—numbers, which are shorthand for Red/Green/Blue (RGB) triplets. You can tell that a number is in hexadecimal format because it starts with &H. &H0000FF (or &HFF), for example, is pure red.

In this notation, the first two hexadecimal digits are the red component of the color; the next two are the blue component; and the final two are the green component. Each pair of hexadecimal numbers represents a decimal range of 0 to 255.

If you want to store an RGB value in a variable, the variable should be declared as a Long, which in Visual Basic terminology means a long integer.

You'll find the hexadecimal notation for colors selected in the Palette color list box in the right column of the Properties window.

You have several indirect ways to refer to RGB color values that you use. The easiest way is to use the built-in color constants. The constant vbRed, for example, is equivalent to &H0000FF (&HFF without the leading zeros), and the constant vbBlue means &HFF0000.

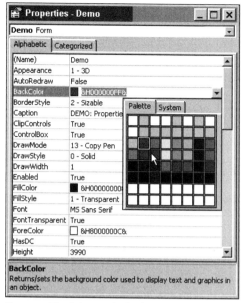

Figure 3.9 The Palette color list box allows you to choose colors from a palette.

Figure 3.10 It's easy to use the predefined color constants, which you can find by using the Object Browser.

Figure 3.11 System color constants are also available.

Using Visual Basic's Object Browser, you can find the list of color constants as the members of the ColorConstants class (**Figure 3.10**) of the VBRUN library. System color constants are also available; you can find them in the Object Browser as the members of the SystemColorConstants class in the VBRUN library (**Figure 3.11**).

For more information on using the Object Browser, see Chapter 10.

The BackColor Property in Code

It's not unusual to set the BackColor property in code. By changing the background color of a form (or other object) dynamically in response to a program event or user action, you are providing a visual cue that something has happened.

The mechanism for changing the BackColor property is to assign a valid color value to the form's BackColor property. For example:

```
frmDemo.BackColor = vbRed
```

The equivalent is:

```
frmDemo.BackColor = &HFF
```

To change the BackColor property dynamically:

1. Start a new Visual Basic project.

2. Use the Properties window to rename the default form in the project frmDemo.

3. Drag a Command Button from the Toolbox to the form.

4. Using the Properties window, change the name of the Command Button to cmdChangeCol and its caption to Change Color.

5. Right-click cmdChangeCol and choose View Code from the pop-up menu.

continues on next page

BackColor and ForeColor Properties

6. In the Code Editor, use the Object and Procedure lists to find cmdChangeCol's Click event procedure.

7. Within the Click event procedure, add a comment:

```
'Change form background to blue
```

8. Below the comment, assign the color blue to the BackColor property, using hexadecimal RGB color notation:

```
frmDemo.BackColor = &HFF0000
```

The complete event procedure should now read:

```
Private Sub cmdChangeCol_Click()
    'Change form background to blue
    frmDemo.BackColor = &HFF0000
End Sub
```

9. Run the project, and click the Change Color button to make sure that the form background turns blue (**Figure 3.12**).

To store a color value in a variable:

1. Add another Command Button to frmDemo.

2. Use the Properties window to name the button cmdChkCol, and give it the caption Check Color.

3. Using the Code Editor, in cmdChkCol's Click event procedure, add a declaration for the variable that will store the color value:

```
Dim formColorValue As Long
```

4. Below the declaration, add the statement that assigns the form's BackColor property to the variable:

```
formColorValue = frmDemo.BackColor
```

Figure 3.12 If the form background color changes to blue when you click the button, the dynamic property assignment worked.

Listing 3.1 cmdChkCol Event Procedure

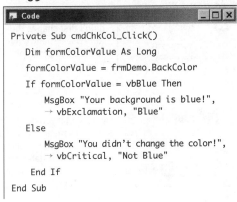

```
Private Sub cmdChkCol_Click()
   Dim formColorValue As Long
   formColorValue = frmDemo.BackColor
   If formColorValue = vbBlue Then
      MsgBox "Your background is blue!",
      → vbExclamation, "Blue"
   Else
      MsgBox "You didn't change the color!",
      → vbCritical, "Not Blue"
   End If
End Sub
```

The entire Click event procedure should now read:

```
Private Sub cmdChkCol_Click()
    Dim formColorValue As Long
    formColorValue = frmDemo.BackColor
End Sub
```

5. Run the project, and click the command button to make sure that you do not get any errors.

✔ Tips

- The Dim statement, which is short for Dimension, is used to declare a variable of a particular type. For more information on variable types, see Chapter 7.
- The Long variable type is shorthand for long integer. It is used to store color values, because the numbers used in representing a color can be greater than the maximum allowed in a regular integer variable.

To use the stored color value in a comparison:

1. In the cmdChkCol click event procedure, after the color assignment, add the following code:

```
If formColorValue = vbBlue Then
    MsgBox "Your background is
    → blue!", vbExclamation,
    → "Blue"
Else
    MsgBox "You didn't change the
    → color!", vbCritical,
    → "Not Blue"
End If
```

   The entire event procedure code is shown in **Listing 3.1**.

2. Run the project.

continues on next page

3. Test the code by first clicking the Check Color button *without* having changed the background form color to blue.

The message box saying the color is not blue displays (**Figure 3.13**).

4. Click OK.

5. Next, click the Change Color button. The form background is now blue!

6. Click the Check Color button. The Blue message displays (**Figure 3.14**).

Figure 3.13 If you didn't first change the form background color to blue, the program knows!

Figure 3.14 If you have already changed the background color to blue, the conditional statement is true, and this message box is displayed.

✔ Tips

■ Aren't you glad that you learned how to use message boxes in Chapter 2?

■ This code could be made shorter by comparing the BackColor property directly:

```
...
If frmDemo.BackColor = vbBlue Then
...
```

In other words, in this example, the formColorValue variable serves no purpose other than to illustrate a technique. In the real world, however, you often need to retain values in a variable after the object that they came from no longer exists.

BACKCOLOR AND FORECOLOR PROPERTIES

BorderStyle Property

A form's *BorderStyle property* determines the basic appearance and behavior of the window that the form creates when it is run. In other words, this property setting determines whether a form will be viewed as a general-purpose window, a dialog, or a tool-box-style window.

One key issue is whether a window is *sizable*. If a window is sizable, when the window is running, the user can change its size (usually by dragging the window border).

The BorderStyle property cannot be changed at run time. In other words, this property is usually set at design time in the Properties window. (In fact, a form's BorderStyle property is read-only at run time.)

The possible settings for a form's BorderStyle property are:

- **0 – None,** meaning no border or border-related elements. As you'll see in Chapter 5, this is the BorderStyle to use when creating a splash screen.

- **1 – FixedSingle,** a normal window, but resizable only with the Minimize and Maximize buttons, if they are present.

- **2 – Sizable,** a normal, resizable window. This is the default, and most common, setting.

- **3 – FixedDouble,** the setting used to create dialogs. If the BorderStyle property is set to FixedDouble, the dialog cannot be resized.

- **4 – FixedToolWindow,** which displays a nonsizable window with a Close button and reduced-size title bar text. Unlike the previous settings, FixedToolWindow forms do not appear as icons in the Windows Taskbar.

- **5 – SizableToolWindow,** like FixedToolWindow but sizable.

To create a dialog:

1. Make sure the form that you want to use as a dialog is open in the Visual Basic design-time environment.

2. Open the Properties window.

3. In the left column of the Properties window, select BorderStyle.

4. From the pull-down menu in the right column, choose 3 – FixedDouble (**Figure 3.15**).

5. Run the form to view it as a dialog (**Figure 3.16**).

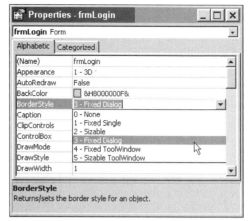

Figure 3.15 To create a dialog, set the BorderStyle property to FixedDouble.

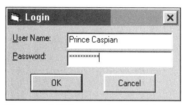

Figure 3.16 Dialogs can be closed, but they cannot be resized.

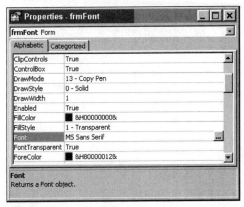

Figure 3.17 You can change the font for an object by using the Properties window.

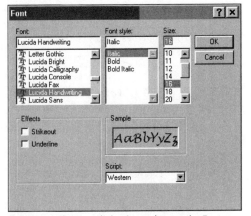

Figure 3.18 The Font dialog is used to set the Font object's Name, Size, and Style properties.

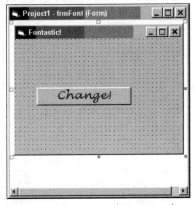

Figure 3.19 The Command Button text has changed to reflect your font choice.

Font Property

The *Font property* is itself both a property and an *object*—meaning that the Font object has properties you can set, such as Name and Size. You could set the Font property of a form as follows:

```
frmFont.Font.Name = "Arial"
frmFont.Font.Size = 12
```

When you set the Font property of a form, you are also setting the default Font property for objects such as Command Buttons and Labels when they are *seated* on the form. An object, such as a control, is seated on another object, such as a form, when the first object is placed on the second object. Another way of saying this is that the second object is the container for the first object. Forms can act as containers, and some—but not all— Visual Basic controls can also be containers.

You can change the Font property for a particular control, of course, without changing the property for other contained controls.

To set the Font property for a form:

1. With a form open, select Font in the Properties window (**Figure 3.17**).

   MS San Serif is the default font for most objects.

2. Click the small button with ellipses on the right side of the Properties window.

   The Font dialog opens (**Figure 3.18**).

3. Select a font and size.

4. Click OK.

5. Using the Toolbox, drag a Command Button into the form.

   Its caption is in the font face and size you selected (**Figure 3.19**).

✔ Tip

■ The Font dialog displays only fonts that are available on your system.

To change the font while a program is running:

1. Use the Properties window to change the Command Button's name to cmdChange.

2. Using the Code Editor, in the Command Button's Click event, enter code to change the text displayed by the Command Button (**Figure 3.20**):

```
Me.cmdChange.Caption = "XYZ"
```

3. Next, change the font name to Wingdings and the font size to 15 points:

```
Me.cmdChange.Font.Name = "Wingdings"
Me.cmdChange.Font.Size = 15
```

The complete code for the Click event is shown in **Listing 3.2**.

4. Run the program.

The button appears with the original caption, font, and size (**Figure 3.21**).

5. Click the button to test the program.

The Command Button is displayed with the new font choice (**Figure 3.22**).

✔ Tip

■ The form in this example, frmFont, is part of the 03ch project on this book's companion Web site. To run this form, you need to set the StartUp Object to frmFont in the Project Properties dialog (**Figure 3.23**).

Listing 3.2 Changing the Font Object

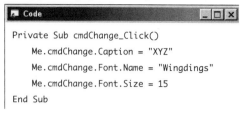

```
Private Sub cmdChange_Click()
    Me.cmdChange.Caption = "XYZ"
    Me.cmdChange.Font.Name = "Wingdings"
    Me.cmdChange.Font.Size = 15
End Sub
```

Figure 3.20 Font properties can also be changed dynamically in code.

Figure 3.21 Until the Click event is activated, the font retains its old characteristics.

Figure 3.22 When the user clicks the Command Button, the font changes as specified.

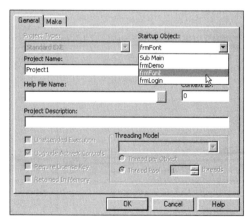

Figure 3.23 The StartUp object—opened when the project is run—is specified in the Project Properties dialog.

FONT PROPERTY

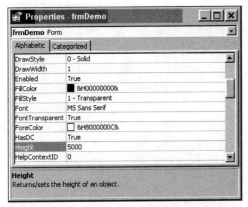

Figure 3.24 A form's Height and Width properties can be used in the Properties window to size a form.

Height and Width Properties

A form's height and width properties can be used—you guessed it!—to set the height and width of the form. You can set these properties at design time, using the Properties window or set them dynamically in code at run time.

The unit of measurement used for a form's height and width property is twip. A *twip* is a screen-independent unit designed to ensure that the size and placement of elements is the same on all systems, regardless of display size. A twip is equal to 1/20 of a printer's point. (OK, you know and I know that some twip thought up the term.)

Height and width properties are read and write at run time. You can not only set them dynamically but also use them to determine the size of a form, if necessary.

To set a form's height with the Properties window:

1. With the form open, open the Properties window.

2. Select the Height property in the left column of the Properties window.

3. In the right column, enter a valid height in twips (**Figure 3.24**).

✔ Tips

- The form Width property can be set in exactly the same fashion.

- Because the twips unit of measure is so unintuitive, trial and error may be the best way to find appropriate settings. One trick that helps: You can read the current size of a form in the design-time environment by looking at the Height and Width property values in the Properties window.

- To position a form precisely, you need to use two other properties: Left and Top, which specify (again, in twips) the position of the top-left corner of a form.

To size a form dynamically at run time:

1. Add to the form a Command Button named cmdBigger and captioned Bigger.

2. Add another Command Button named cmdSmaller and captioned Smaller.

3. Using the Code Editor, add code to cmdBigger's Click event, moving the form to the top-left corner of the screen:

   ```
   Me.Top = 0
   Me.Left = 0
   ```

4. Add code to cmdBigger's Click event to make the form large:

   ```
   Me.Height = 10000
   Me.Width = 15000
   ```

5. Using the Code Editor, add code to cmdSmaller's Click event to move the form to the top-left corner of the screen and to make the form reasonably small:

   ```
   Me.Top = 0
   Me.Left = 0
   Me.Height = 5000
   Me.Width = 3000
   ```

6. Run the project.

7. Click the Bigger button to make the form bigger (**Figure 3.25**) and the Smaller button to make the form smaller (**Figure 3.26**).

✔ Tip

- The complete code for the two event procedures is in **Listing 3.3**.

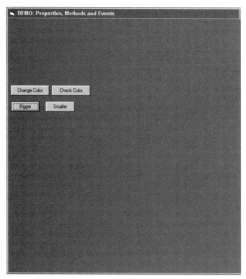

Figure 3.25 You can also use these properties at run time to dynamically make a form larger...

Figure 3.26 ...or to make a form smaller.

Listing 3.3 Sizing a Form

```
Private Sub cmdBigger_Click()
    Me.Top = 0
    Me.Left = 0
    Me.Height = 10000
    Me.Width = 15000
End Sub
Private Sub cmdSmaller_Click()
    Me.Top = 0
    Me.Left = 0
    Me.Height = 5000
    Me.Width = 3000
End Sub
```

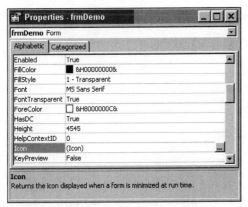

Figure 3.27 The Icon property is used to assign an icon to a form.

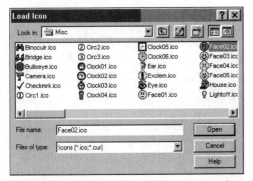

Figure 3.28 Using the Load Icon dialog, you can select an icon file of the type *.ico or *.cur.

Figure 3.29 When an icon is loaded, it appears in a form's caption bar.

Icon and Picture Properties

The Icon property sets the icon—or small graphic—that appears in a form's caption bar. This, of course, occurs provided that the form's BorderStyle property is set so that the form and window have a caption bar. The icon also represents the form in the Windows Taskbar.

The picture property is used to set a graphic that appears as a form background.

To add an icon to a form:

1. With the form open, in the Properties window, select the Icon property (**Figure 3.27**).

2. Click the ellipsis on the right side of the Properties window.
   The Load Icon dialog opens (**Figure 3.28**).

3. Select an icon file.

4. Click Open.
   The icon now appears in the form's caption bar (**Figure 3.29**).

5. Run the form.

6. Minimize the running window.
   You see the icon that you selected in the Windows Taskbar (**Figure 3.30**).

Figure 3.30 The icon is used to represent a running form in the Windows Taskbar.

To set a background graphic:

1. With the form open, in the Properties window, select the Picture property (**Figure 3.31**).

2. Click the ellipsis on the right side of the Properties window.

The Load Picture dialog opens (**Figure 3.32**).

3. Select a graphics file.

4. Click Open.

The Picture property in the Properties window now indicates a graphic file type *(Metafile)*, for example (**Figure 3.33**)— and the graphic appears in the form background (**Figure 3.34**).

To delete the background graphic:

1. In the Properties window, select the Picture property.

2. Click the right column (not the ellipsis).

3. Press the Delete key.

The Picture property value changes to (none) and the graphic is deleted from the form.

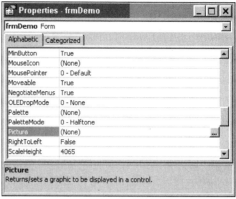

Figure 3.31 The Picture property is used to select a background graphic for a form.

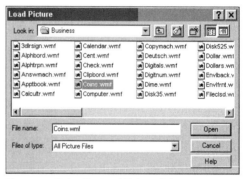

Figure 3.32 Using the Load Picture dialog, you can select a graphic file.

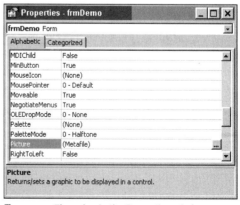

Figure 3.33 The value in the Properties window indicates the graphic file type.

Figure 3.34 When a graphic file has been loaded as the value of a form's Picture property, the graphic appears as the form background.

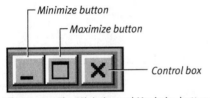

Figure 3.35 The Minimize and Maximize buttons and the control box are important aspects of a form's appearance and functionality.

Figure 3.36 When the control box is removed from a form, the user can no longer access the Control menu.

Window Appearance Properties

Besides the BorderStyle property, explained earlier in this chapter, the appearance and behavior of form-based windows is controlled by the MaxButton, MinButton, and ControlBox properties. Note that if the BorderStyle property is set so that the form cannot have Minimize and Maximize buttons and a control box—to 0 – None, for example—changes you make in the MaxButton, MinButton, and ControlBox properties have no impact.

The Maximize button—which appears at the right end side of a form's caption bar (**Figure 3.35**)—is used to maximize a running form.

The Minimize button—also at the right end of the caption bar (**Figure 3.35**)—is used to minimize a running form.

The control box is the box that contains an X, located to the right of the Minimize and Maximize buttons in the caption bar (**Figure 3.35**).

In addition to determining whether a control box is present in a running form, the ControlBox property is used to determine whether the form has a *Control menu*. A Control menu, if present, is accessed by clicking the form icon in the caption bar. The Control menu contains system-generated choices such as resizing and closing the window (**Figure 3.36**).

To remove the Maximize button:

1. With the form open, in the Properties window, select MaxButton.

2. From the drop-down list in the right column, choose False.

   When you run the form, it will not have a Maximize button.

To remove the Minimize button:

1. In the Properties window, select MinButton.

2. From the drop-down list in the right column, choose False.

   When you run the form, it will not have a Minimize button.

To remove the control box and Control menu:

1. In the Properties window, select ControlBox.

2. From the drop-down list in the right column, choose False.

   When you run the form, it will not have a control box or a Control menu.

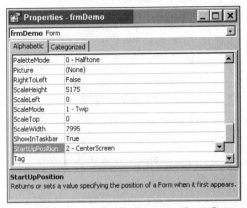

Figure 3.37 Set the StartUpPosition to 2 - CenterScreen to have a window start in the middle of the screen.

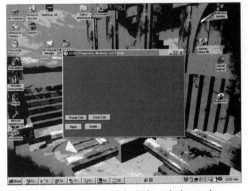

Figure 3.38 Centering initial windows helps make applications well organized and attractive.

StartUpPosition Property

The *StartUpPosition property* determines the position of a form when it first runs. (Normally, after a form is running, the user can move it.)

To set a form to start in the middle of the screen:

1. With the form open, in the Properties window, select StartUpPosition.

2. In the right column of the Properties window, select 2 – CenterScreen (**Figure 3.37**).

3. Run the project.

   The window based on the form appears in the center of the screen (**Figure 3.38**).

Summary

In this chapter, you learned to:

- Find documentation on all form properties.

- Use the Me keyword.

- Set form background and foreground colors in the Properties window and in code.

- Work with hexadecimal RGB color notation.

- Use the built-in Visual Basic color constants.

- Change color properties dynamically.

- Store a color value in a variable.

- Set a form's BorderStyle property.

- Set the properties of a form's Font object.

- Use a form's Height and Width properties.

- Size a form dynamically at run time.

- Add an icon to a form.

- Add a background graphic to a form.

- Set the MinButton, MaxButton, and ControlBox properties.

- Set a form to start in the center of the screen.

THE FORM LIFE CYCLE: EVENTS

In Visual Basic, event procedures are placeholders for your code. You do not have to place any code in any event procedure, but if you do, the code is processed when the event is *fired*. An event is fired—or triggered—in one of three ways:

◆ By an action taken by a user, such as clicking an object

◆ By an instruction that you've placed in your code

◆ By the system

You need to understand events for two reasons. The first is that events represent the life cycle of an object such as a form. When a form is loaded, for example, an event is fired, and when a form is unloaded another event goes off. Without understanding the sequence of events related to an object—that is, the object's life cycle—and what user action triggers what event, you will not really know how to work with the object.

Understanding the second reason why events are important requires going back in time. In the bad old days, before programs ran in windowing environments, programs were—by and large—*linear*. That means they started at one place and ended at another.

Event-Driven Programming

A Visual Basic program is usually not linear. Typically, program code responds to user events—and you have no way to know what event the user will trigger next. The user might click a button, or she might resize a form; you have no way to know. This means that organizing a program requires managing events and knowing which events require programmatic response.

The big three characteristics of a Visual Basic object are *properties* (form properties, or attributes, were covered in Chapter 3), *events* (explained in this chapter), and *methods* (which cause an object to do something, as explained in Chapter 5).

Topics covered in this chapter include:

◆ Creating form events, which represent the complete life cycle of how a form lives and dies

◆ Using the Immediate window

◆ Adding code to event procedures

Table 4.1

Form Events: Birth Sequence

EVENT	CATEGORY	WHEN TRIGGERED AND HOW USED
Initialize	Birth Sequence	First event triggered when an instance of a form is created. You can use the form's Initialize event to set the starting values of data that will be used by the form.
Load	Birth Sequence	Loads a copy of a form, but doesn't make it visible. You can use this event for initialization code and for reading form properties.
Resize	Birth Sequence, User Interaction	Occurs when the form is first displayed or when the form is resized.
Activate	Birth Sequence	Occurs as part of the birth sequence and when a form becomes the active window. This event can occur only when a form is visible.
Gotfocus	Birth Sequence, User Interaction	Occurs as part of the birth sequence and when the form receives the focus, meaning that it becomes the window that receives keyboard and mouse input.
Paint	Birth Sequence, User Interaction	Occurs as part of the birth sequence and when a window has been resized or uncovered (hence causing the form to require "painting").

Creating Form Events

Form events fall into three categories, as shown in **Tables 4.1** through **4.3**. These categories are form birth, user interaction with a running form, and form death. The birth and death events in **Tables 4.1** and **4.3** are shown in the order in which they are fired.

In addition to the invocation triggers shown in **Tables 4.1** to **4.3**, you can invoke all form event procedures in your code. If you place Form_Click in code, for example, the form's Click event will be fired. Beware, however, of creating circular event logic. If you place a call to the LostFocus event in the GotFocus event and a call to the GotFocus event in the LostFocus event (see **Listing 4.1**), you will have created an infinite loop when you run your form. The form will keep on running (actually, blinking) until the Visual Basic environment runs out of stack space (a form of memory) or until you pull the plug on your computer.

Table 4.2

Form Events: Selected User Interactions

EVENT	CATEGORY	WHEN TRIGGERED AND HOW USED
Click	User Interaction	User clicks in form.
MouseMove	User Interaction	User moves mouse over form.
Resize	User Interaction	Form is resized.

Table 4.3

Form Events: Death Sequence

EVENT	CATEGORY	WHEN TRIGGERED AND HOW USED
QueryUnload	Death Sequence	First event in the form death sequence; gives the programmer a chance to put in code canceling the unload (see "Unloading a Form" later in this chapter).
Unload	Death Sequence	Form is about to be removed from the screen.
Terminate	Death Sequence	All references to the form are removed from the computer's memory.

Listing 4.1 Self-Referencing Event Procedures in an Infinite Loop

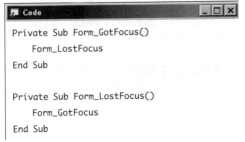

```
Private Sub Form_GotFocus()
    Form_LostFocus
End Sub

Private Sub Form_LostFocus()
    Form_GotFocus
End Sub
```

To view documentation for all form events:

1. Choose Index from the VB Help menu.

   The MSDN Visual Studio Library application opens, with the Index tab active (**Figure 4.1**).

2. In the Active Subset list box, select *Visual Basic Documentation (**Figure 4.2**).

3. In the Type the Keyword to Find text box, enter Form object (**Figure 4.2**).

4. Click Display.

   The Form Object, Forms Collection page displays in the right pane (**Figure 4.3**).

5. Click the Events link at the top of the page.

   The Topics Found dialog opens, displaying a list of all form events (**Figure 4.4**).

6. Select the event you are interested in.

7. Click Display.

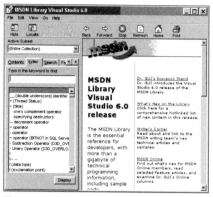

Figure 4.1 When you choose Index from the VB Help menu, the MSDN Visual Studio Library application opens, with the Index tab active.

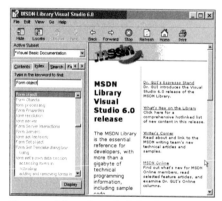

Figure 4.2 It is easier to find Visual Basic documentation if you restrict the index request to the Visual Basic documentation subset.

Figure 4.3 The Forms page provides an overview of information about forms.

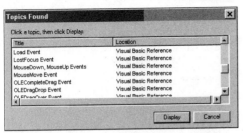

Figure 4.4 To view detailed information on any form event, select the event in the Topics Found dialog.

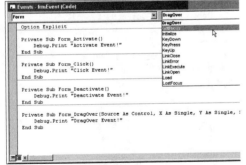

Figure 4.5 The form that will be used to show event firing order is called frmEvent.

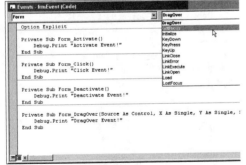

Figure 4.6 When you choose Form from the Code Editor's Object list, all the form's event procedures appear in the Procedure list.

Using the Immediate Pane

The Immediate Pane—sometimes referred to by old-timers as the Debug window—is used for help in debugging as a program is running in the Visual Basic design-time environment.

You can use this pane to display the value of program variables or simply to display text when the program reaches a certain point. In this section, I'll show you how to use the latter facility—which is kind of a glorified MsgBox statement used for debugging—to trace the order in which events are fired.

This technique is handy for getting a grip on the life cycle of forms (and other objects). With full information about the order in which events are fired, you will know in which event procedure to place your code.

Generally, the Immediate Pane opens automatically when you place code that references the Debug object in your program.

The Print method of the Debug object causes a *string* of text—text delimited by straight quotes—to be displayed in the Immediate pane. (For more information on *methods*, which are ways of telling an object to do something, see Chapter 5.)

To add Debug.Print statements to track events:

1. Start a new project.

2. Using the Properties window, name the default form frmEvent and caption it Event Madness (**Figure 4.5**).

3. Open the Code Editor.

4. In the Object list, select Form.

   The Procedure list now displays all the event procedures associated with the form (**Figure 4.6**).

continues on next page

5. In turn, right-click each event procedure that you would like to track in the Procedure list.

As you click an event procedure in the list, the beginning and ending lines of code of the procedure are created in the Code Editor. For example:

```
Private Sub Form_Activate()

End Sub
```

6. Within the event procedure *framework*, add code that invokes the Print method of the Debug object with a text string that says what event was fired:

```
Debug.Print "Activate Event!"
```

The complete event procedure now looks like this:

```
Private Sub Form_Activate()
    Debug.Print "Activate Event!"
End Sub
```

7. Repeat this process for all the events you want to track.

The complete form code for tracking the events shown in **Tables 4.1** to **4.3** is shown in **Listing 4.2**.

To witness events from birth events being fired:

◆ Run the form.

The Immediate Pane opens, showing events in the order in which they were fired (**Figure 4.7**).

✔ Tip

■ The Immediate Pane is an example of a Tool window style. You can get the same effect in your own projects by setting a form's BorderStyle property to 5 — Sizable ToolWindow.

Figure 4.7 The Immediate Pane showing the form load sequence.

Listing 4.2 Form Events Being Fired

```
Option Explicit

Private Sub Form_Activate()
    Debug.Print "Activate Event!"
End Sub

Private Sub Form_Click()
    Debug.Print "Click Event!"
End Sub

Private Sub Form_Deactivate()
    Debug.Print "Deactivate Event!"
End Sub

Private Sub Form_GotFocus()
    Debug.Print "GotFocus Event!"
End Sub

Private Sub Form_Initialize()
    Debug.Print "Initialize Event!"
End Sub

Private Sub Form_Load()
    Debug.Print "Load Event!"
End Sub

Private Sub Form_LostFocus()
    Debug.Print "LostFocus Event!"
End Sub

Private Sub Form_MouseMove(Button As Integer,
→ Shift As Integer, X As Single, Y As Single)
    Debug.Print "MouseMove Event!"
End Sub
```

Code continues on next page

Figure 4.8 The Immediate Pane showing events in response to user actions.

Figure 4.9 The Immediate Pane showing the form unload sequence.

To watch user interaction events:

◆ Click the form and move the mouse around. The Immediate pane displays the order in which events were fired (**Figure 4.8**).

To view the form shutdown events:

◆ Close the form by clicking the form's control box. The Immediate pane displays the form's death sequence (**Figure 4.9**).

✔ Tip

■ When the form closes, the Immediate pane may also close. In that case, to view its most recent contents, choose Immediate Window from the View menu.

Listing 4.2 *continued*

```
Private Sub Form_Paint()
    Debug.Print "Paint Event!"
End Sub

Private Sub Form_QueryUnload(Cancel As Integer, UnloadMode As Integer)
    Debug.Print "QueryUnload Event!"
End Sub

Private Sub Form_Resize()
    Debug.Print "Resize Event!"
End Sub

Private Sub Form_Terminate()
    Debug.Print "Terminate Event!"
End Sub

Private Sub Form_Unload(Cancel As Integer)
    Debug.Print "Unload Event!"
End Sub
```

USING THE IMMEDIATE PANE

Using the Form Load Event

It's easy and fun to work with events when you understand how they are triggered!

To see how simple it really is, write a program that uses the form's Load event—and the form properties explained in Chapter 3—to store the position and size of the form. Later, when the form has loaded, the user can resize the form to her heart's content. But when she clicks anywhere on the form, it is restored to its original size and position.

This program actually involves three steps:

◆ Declaring the variables that will "remember" the size and position of the form at the form level, rather than within an event procedure. That way, the variables will be available to both the form event procedures that use them: form_click and form_load. The question of the availability of a variable is called the *scope* of a variable (or, sometimes, *scoping a variable*). It is explained in more detail in Chapter 9.

◆ Adding code to the form's Load event to "remember" the form's initial position and size. (You could set the initial form position and size in the Visual Basic design-time environment by using Properties window and the Form Designer, although in a larger program, it could also be set in code.)

◆ Adding code to the form's Click event to restore the original size and position settings.

For the complete code for all three procedures, see **Listing 4.3**.

To declare form-level variables:

1. With frmEvent active in the Visual Basic design-time environment, open the Code Editor.

Listing 4.3 Remembering and Restoring a Form to Its Original Size and Position

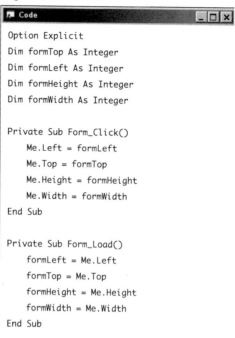

```
Option Explicit
Dim formTop As Integer
Dim formLeft As Integer
Dim formHeight As Integer
Dim formWidth As Integer

Private Sub Form_Click()
    Me.Left = formLeft
    Me.Top = formTop
    Me.Height = formHeight
    Me.Width = formWidth
End Sub

Private Sub Form_Load()
    formLeft = Me.Left
    formTop = Me.Top
    formHeight = Me.Height
    formWidth = Me.Width
End Sub
```

2. Scroll to the top of the Code Editor.

3. Make sure that (General) is selected in the Objects list and (Declarations) is selected in the Procedures list.

4. If you enabled the Require Variable Declaration checkbox, as explained in Chapter 1, add the declarations right below the Option Explicit statements. If you did not enable the Require Variable Declaration checkbox, add the declarations at the top of the Code Editor.

5. You should add a variable declaration for each of the four form position and size properties: Top, Left, Height, and Width. Here are the declarations:

```
Option Explicit
Dim formTop As Integer
Dim formLeft As Integer
Dim formHeight As Integer
Dim formWidth As Integer
```

These variables are now available—and retain their values—in any form procedure.

To store the form position and size:

1. In the Code Editor, choose Form from the Objects list.

2. Choose Load from the Procedures list. The form's Load event procedure framework is created:

```
Private Sub Form_Load()

End Sub
```

3. Add *assignment* statements to the event procedure:

```
formLeft = Me.Left
formTop = Me.Top
formHeight = Me.Height
formWidth = Me.Width
```

continues on next page

Each assignment statement stores a current form property value in the variable to the left of the equal sign. formLeft, for example, now contains the value of the form's Left property.

To restore the form position and size:

1. In the Code Editor, choose Form from the Objects list.

2. Choose Click from the Procedures list.

   The form's Click event procedure framework is created:

   ```
   Private Sub Form_Click()

   End Sub
   ```

3. Add assignment statements to the procedure that transfer the stored variable values back to the form properties:

   ```
   Me.Left = formLeft
   Me.Top = formTop
   Me.Height = formHeight
   Me.Width = formWidth
   ```

   These statements take the "remembered" values from the variables that are holding the form's original position and size, and set the form's properties equal to them, thereby restoring the original form position and size.

4. To see this in action, run the form.

   Note the position and size of the form when it first loads.

5. With the form running, resize it (a wide, thin shape is shown in **Figure 4.10**).

6. Click the form.

   It returns to its original size and position (**Figure 4.11**).

Figure 4.10 You can test the event code by changing the shape of the form.

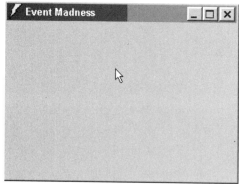

Figure 4.11 When you click it, the form returns to its original size and position.

Listing 4.4 Does the User Really Want to Close the Window?

```
Code                              _ □ ×
Private Sub Form_QueryUnload(Cancel As
→ Integer, UnloadMode As Integer)

    Dim Answer As Integer

    Answer = MsgBox("Do you really want to
→ close this window?", vbYesNo +
→ vbQuestion, "Events!")

    If Answer = vbYes Then
        Cancel = False
    Else
        Cancel = True
    End If
End Sub
```

Unloading a Form

A form's QueryUnload event is the first event fired in the form's death process. You can use the event to stop the process of unloading the form.

It's easiest to think of this as canceling the termination process, because the mechanism is to set the QueryUnload event procedure parameter named Cancel to True. (A *parameter* is a variable that is passed to a procedure when the procedure is invoked.)

Using the QueryUnload event in this fashion in combination with a MsgBox statement is very common. It's the mechanism for asking your users, "Are you sure you really want to close this window?"

Listing 4.4 contains the complete QueryUnload code.

To check whether the user really wants to close the form:

1. In the Code Editor, choose Form from the Objects list.

2. Choose QueryUnload from the Procedures list.

   The QueryUnload event procedure framework is created:

   ```
   Private Sub Form_QueryUnload(Cancel
   → As Integer, UnloadMode As Integer)

   End Sub
   ```

3. Within the event framework, declare a variable to hold the user's response:

   ```
   Dim Answer As Integer
   ```

   continues on next page

4. Using the MsgBox statement (explained in Chapter 2), find out whether the user really wants to close the window:

```
Answer = MsgBox("Do you really want
→ to close this window?", vbYesNo +
→ vbQuestion, "Events!")
```

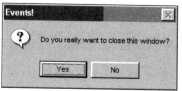

Figure 4.12 You can use the QueryUnload event to find out whether the user really does want to close a window.

5. If the user clicks Yes, continue the process of unloading the form (Cancel = False). If the user clicks No, meaning, "I don't want to unload the window," cancel the process (Cancel = True):

```
If Answer = vbYes Then
    Cancel = False
Else
    Cancel = True
End If
```

6. Run the form.

7. Close the form.

The message box from the QueryUnload event procedure appears (**Figure 4.12**).

8. If you click Yes, the form is unloaded; if you click No, the form remains running on the screen.

UNLOADING A FORM

Summary

In this chapter, you learned to:

- The form life cycle: how forms are born, how they live, and how they die.

- The order in which form events are fired.

- How to find documentation for all form events.

- How to use the Immediate pane.

- How to place Debug statements to observe events being fired.

- How to declare form-level variables.

- How to "remember" initial form properties.

- Restoring initial form properties from variables.

- Using the QueryUnload event to find out whether a user really does want to close a window.

Working with Forms and Modules

Methods are a way of telling an object to do something. I explained in Chapter 4 that the Print method of the Debug object causes text to be displayed in the Immediate Pane.

Invoking the methods of the form object is the easiest way to get forms—and the windows based upon them—to do things. You can think of a form's methods as a way to put the form through its tricks.

This chapter explains how to work with some of the most commonly used form methods. You learn how to load and unload forms by using code.

So far, the programs in *Visual Basic: Visual QuickStart Guide* have placed code in the event procedures within the form *module*. This chapter introduces another kind of Visual Basic module: the *code module*, which consists entirely of program code and does not have an object (such as a form) associated with it.

The forms you have worked with so far are instances of Visual Basic's default stand-alone form, representing what is called the Single Document Interface (or SDI for short). You can also have another kind of form interface, called the Multiple Document Interface (or MDI). In an MDI application—Microsoft Word is an example—it is typical to have many child forms of the same kind (think of word processing documents) and one parent form that is used to organize the children.

In this chapter, I show you the basics of creating an MDI application.

Using Form Methods

Form methods are used to manipulate a form, typically to affect the way the form appears, but sometimes more radically. The Show method, for example, causes the form module, with all its controls, properties, and code, to be loaded into memory and displayed on the screen.

Form methods are invoked by naming the form (or using the Me keyword) followed by the dot operator, followed by the Method. To load and display frmFirst, for example:

```
frmFirst.Show
```

In some cases, using a form's methods has exactly the same results as setting a form property. You make a form invisible on the screen by invoking its Hide method:

```
Me.Hide
```

or by setting its Visible property to False:

```
Me.Visible = False
```

Table 5.1 shows some commonly used form methods.

To view documentation for all form methods:

1. From the VB Help menu, choose Index. The MSDN Visual Studio Library application opens, with the Index tab active (**Figure 5.1**).

2. In the Active Subset list box, select *Visual Basic Documentation (**Figure 5.2**).

3. In the Type the Keyword to Find text box, enter Form object (**Figure 5.2**).

Table 5.1

Commonly Used Form Methods	
METHOD	FUNCTIONALITY
Circle	Displays a circle on the form using supplied parameters for position, appearance, and so on.
Hide	Makes a form invisible on the screen without unloading it from memory.
Move	Moves a form on the screen the specified amount and direction.
Print	Displays text on the form.
Refresh	"Paints" the form.
Show	Loads the form into memory (if it isn't already loaded) and displays it on the screen.

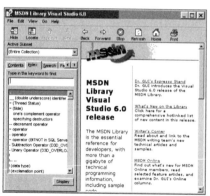

Figure 5.1 When you choose Index from the VB Help menu, the MSDN Visual Studio Library application opens, with the Index tab active.

Figure 5.2 It is easier to find Visual Basic documentation if you restrict the index request to the Visual Basic documentation subset.

Figure 5.3 The Forms page provides an overview of information about forms.

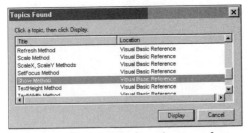

Figure 5.4 To view detailed information on any form event, select the event in the Topics Found dialog.

4. Click Display.

The Form Object, Forms Collection page displays in the right pane (**Figure 5.3**).

5. Click the Methods link at the top of the page.

The Topics Found dialog opens, displaying a list of all form methods (**Figure 5.4**).

6. Select the method you are interested in.

7. Click Display.

✔ **Tip**

■ If the MSDN Library CD-ROM is not loaded, you will be prompted for it before this documentation can be retrieved.

Using Code Modules

So far, all the examples in *Visual Basic: Visual QuickStart Guide* have involved forms. *Forms* are objects—or *modules*—that are displayed on the screen and that contain program code.

Code modules are modules that consist entirely of code. They do not have a representation on the screen.

As you'll see in this section, a procedure named Main in a code module can be used to kick off projects. In addition, it's good programming practice to place code that will be shared by many forms in a single code module.

To add a code module to a project:

1. Right-click in the Project Explorer.

2. From the pop-up menu, choose Add.

3. From the pop-up menu below Add, choose Module.

   The Add Module dialog opens, with an empty code module selected (**Figure 5.5**).

4. Click Open.

   The code module is added to your project and appears in the Project Explorer.

✔ Tip

■ You can also open the Add Module dialog by choosing Add Module from the Project menu.

Sub Main

As you or I do when beginning a research task, Visual Basic projects need to start *somewhere*.

A Visual Basic project can be set to start from one of the project's forms. If the project has only one form and no other modules, the only choice is to start the project by loading the single form.

Another choice is to start the project from a code module. This is often the best choice.

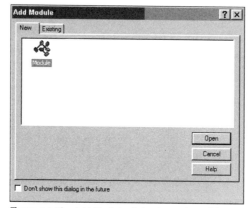

Figure 5.5 The Add Module dialog is used to add a code module to a project.

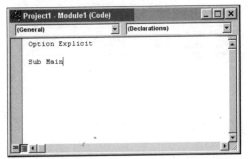

Figure 5.6 To begin a Main procedure, type Sub Main in the Code Editor.

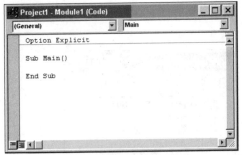

Figure 5.7 After you press Enter, Visual Basic automatically completes the procedure's framework for you.

For one thing, some Visual Basic programs don't display any forms. For another, you might want your program to handle multiple forms or to do some processing before any form is opened (or after the last form has been closed). In any of these cases, the best bet is to start the program from a code module—not a form.

The way the Visual Basic rule book is written, if you want to start your project from a code module, you must have a procedure in the module named *Main*. (There can be only one procedure named Main in your project.)

To add a Main procedure:

1. Right-click your new code module in the Project Explorer.

2. From the pop-up menu, choose View Code. The Code Editor opens.

   Unlike form modules, code modules do not have any prefabricated event procedures. You can verify this by checking the Procedures list, which will be empty.

3. At the top of the Code Editor, just below the Option Explicit directive, type the following on a new line (**Figure 5.6**):

   ```
   Sub Main
   ```

4. Press the Enter key.

   Visual Basic automatically closes the procedure for you (**Figure 5.7**).

   You have successfully created a Main procedure. Here's the framework code:

   ```
   Sub Main()

   End Sub
   ```

✔ Tip

- The word *Sub* is short for *subroutine*, which is an older way of saying "procedure."

To name the code module:

1. Right-click the code module in the Project Explorer.

2. From the pop-up menu, choose Properties.

   The Properties window opens, with the code module selected (**Figure 5.8**). You'll see that a code module has only one property, Name.

3. Name the code module mdlMain by typing in the right column of the Name property display in the Properties window.

   The code module now appears with its new name in the Project Explorer (**Figure 5.9**).

To start the project from Sub Main:

1. From the Project menu, choose Properties.

   The Project Properties dialog opens (**Figure 5.10**).

2. From the StartUp Object drop-down menu, choose Sub Main (**Figure 5.10**).

3. Click OK.

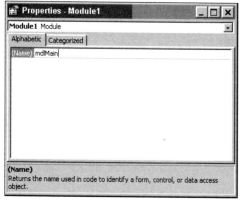

Figure 5.8 A code modules has only one property: its name.

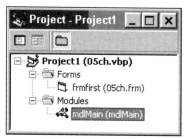

Figure 5.9 Module names are displayed in the Project Explorer.

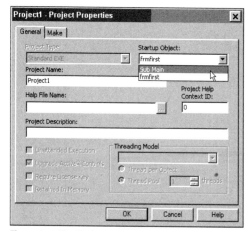

Figure 5.10 The Project Properties dialog is used to set the Startup Object.

Listing 5.1 Conditionally Displaying a Modal Form

```
Code                              _ □ ✕

Option Explicit
Sub Main()
    Dim Answer As Integer
    Answer = MsgBox("Do you want to load the
    → form?", vbYesNo + vbQuestion,
    → "Fooling with forms...")
    If Answer = vbYes Then
        frmFirst.Show vbModal
        MsgBox "What's my mode?"
    Else
        MsgBox "Maybe tomorrow!"
    End If
End Sub
```

Opening and Closing Forms

So far, we have a project starting from Sub Main. But Sub Main contains no code. So the program doesn't display any windows—or do anything at all.

To load and display a form from Sub Main, the form's Show method is used. For example:

```
frmFirst.Show
```

Forms displayed using the Show method can be modal or modeless. A *modal* form waits for the user to close the form before continuing with program execution.

You can use the MsgBox statement (explained in Chapter 2) to conditionally display a form depending on the user's input.

The complete code for conditionally displaying a modal form is shown in **Listing 5.1**.

To display a form if the user clicks Yes:

1. Make sure there is a form named frmFirst in your project.

2. In the Sub Main procedure, add a variable declaration to store the MsgBox return:

   ```
   Dim Answer As Integer
   ```

3. Add code to display the message box:

   ```
   Answer = MsgBox("Do you want to load
   → the form?", vbYesNo + vbQuestion,
   → "Fooling with forms...")
   ```

4. Add code to display the form if the user clicks Yes and to display a "consolation" message if the user clicks No:

   ```
   If Answer = vbYes Then
       frmFirst.Show
   Else
       MsgBox "Maybe tomorrow!"
   End If
   ```

continues on next page

OPENING AND CLOSING FORMS

5. Run the project.

The message box is displayed (**Figure 5.11**).

6. If the user clicks Yes, the form is displayed (**Figure 5.12**). If the user clicks No, the "Maybe tomorrow!" message box (but not the form) is displayed (**Figure 5.13**).

To display a modal form and test modality:

1. Add a MsgBox statement immediately following the call to the form's Show method:

```
MsgBox "What's my mode?"
```

2. Run the project.

3. Click Yes to display the form.

The "What's my mode?" message box is displayed along with the form (**Figure 5.14**). This is the way a modeless form works.

4. Stop the project.

5. Change the line of code that shows the form so that it includes the vbModal constant:

```
frmFirst.Show vbModal
```

6. Run the project again.

This time, the "What's my mode?" message box does is not displayed until the form has been closed (**Figure 5.15**).

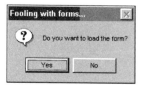

Figure 5.11 It's easy to conditionally display a form, depending on the user's selection.

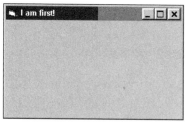

Figure 5.12 The form is displayed using its Show method if the user clicks Yes.

Figure 5.13 The form is not displayed if the user clicks No.

Figure 5.14 Code following the form's Show method is processed right away if the form is modeless.

Figure 5.15 If the form is modal, subsequent code is not processed until the form is closed.

OPENING AND CLOSING FORMS

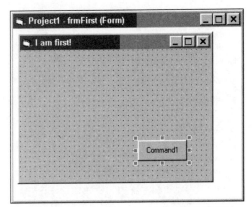

Figure 5.16 It is common to close a form in response to a user event.

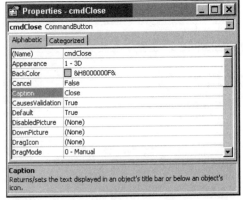

Figure 5.17 You can easily add a Close button to your forms.

Closing a Form

If the user clicks the control box on a form or chooses Close from the form's built-in Control menu, the form closes. (For that matter, you can close a form running in the Visual Basic design-time environment by stopping the project from running.)

What if you need to close a form without using an existing mechanism—as part of the response to a user action, for example?

The Unload statement is used to close a form, meaning to remove it from the display and unload it from memory.

To close a form when a button is clicked:

1. Use the Toolbox to add a Command Button to the form (**Figure 5.16**).

2. Use the Properties window to caption the button Close and name it cmdClose (**Figure 5.17**).

3. Right-click the Command Button.

4. From the pop-up menu, choose View Code to open the Code Editor.

5. From the Objects List, choose cmdClose.

6. From the Procedures List, choose Click. Visual Basic creates a Click event procedure framework:

    ```
    Private Sub cmdClose_Click()

    End Sub
    ```

7. Add an Unload statement to the procedure:

    ```
    Private Sub cmdClose_Click()
        Unload Me
    End Sub
    ```

8. Run the project.

9. Click the Close button to make sure that the form unloads.

Navigating Between Forms

Suppose that you have a project that displays one form, frmFirst, and you want to respond to a user action by opening a second form.

It is easy to use the Show method to open a second form.

To open a new form in response to a user action:

1. Add a Command button to the first form.

2. Use the Properties window to set its caption to Show Form and its name to cmdShowTwo (**Figure 5.18**).

3. Choose Add Form from the Project menu to add a new form to the project.

4. Use the Properties window to set the new form's caption to I am second! and its name to frmSecond (**Figure 5.19**).

5. With the first form active, open the Code Editor.

6. From the Objects list, choose cmdShowTwo.

7. From the Procedures list, choose Click. Visual Basic creates the Click event procedure framework:

```
Private Sub cmdShowTwo_Click()

End Sub
```

8. Add a line of code that invokes frmSecond's Show event to the procedure, which now should read:

```
Private Sub cmdShowTwo_Click()
    frmSecond.Show
End Sub
```

9. Run the project.

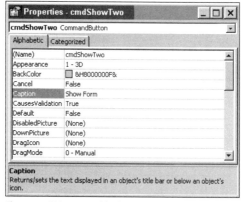

Figure 5.18 You can add a button that displays a second form to the first form.

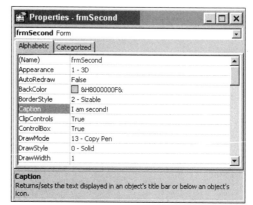

Figure 5.19 The second form uses properties set in the Properties window.

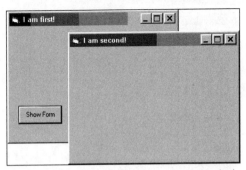

Figure 5.20 The second form's Show event is invoked in the Command button Click procedure on the first form.

Listing 5.2 Showing a New Instance of an Old Form

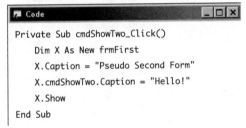

```
Private Sub cmdShowTwo_Click()
    Dim X As New frmFirst
    X.Caption = "Pseudo Second Form"
    X.cmdShowTwo.Caption = "Hello!"
    X.Show
End Sub
```

10. Click the Show Form button.

The second form is displayed (**Figure 5.20**).

✔ **Tip**

■ You cannot show a modal form from a modeless form. In other words, to invoke a modal second form, the first form must also be modal.

Opening a New Instance of the First Form

Suppose that you want to do something slightly different: You want your application to be able to open a new form, but you just don't want to have to create a new form in Visual Basic each time a new form is to be displayed. Ideally, you'd like to be able to open new *instances* of the same old form, perhaps with some properties changed a little.

You can easily do this by:

◆ Declaring a variable that stores a new instance of your original form.

◆ Changing some of the properties of the form instance represented by the variable.

◆ Showing the new form instance.

The complete code for this process is shown in **Listing 5.2**.

To open a new instance of the first form:

1. In the cmdShowTwo Click event procedure, add a line of code to declare a new form instance:

   ```
   Dim X As New frmFirst
   ```

2. Change some of the properties of the new form instance:

   ```
   X.Caption = "Pseudo Second Form"
   X.cmdShowTwo.Caption = "Hello!"
   ```

3. Show the new form instance:
   ```
   X.Show
   ```

4. Run the project.

5. Click the Show Form button.

   A copy of the form with the property changes opens (**Figure 5.21**).

✔ Tip

■ You can keep opening new instances of the form (**Figure 5.22**). Each new instance inherits code and those properties that you haven't altered from the original form.

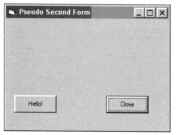

Figure 5.21 You can open a new form that is an instance of an existing form.

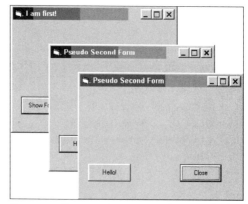

Figure 5.22 Many new instances can be opened using the same procedure.

NAVIGATING BETWEEN FORMS

Positioning Forms

In your applications, you will often want to position a form. You might want to set the initial position of a form, or you might want to move the form in response to a user action.

You can initially center a form on the screen by using its StartUpPosition property. If you want to use some position other than screen center, however, or if you want to position a form in relationship to another form, you'll need to use a little code.

One way to position a form is to set its Left, Top, Width, and Height properties (see Chapter 3 for more information on setting properties in code). You can set one form's position properties by using another form's position properties. For example, in a second form:

```
Me.Left = frmFirst.Left + 1000
```

Another technique is to use the second form's Move method.

The Move method applies to a form (if the form is omitted, the current form is assumed). When the Move method call is processed, the form is moved to the specified position and dimensions. It accepts four rather familiar parameters:

- ◆ Left, which is required

- ◆ Top, which is optional

- ◆ Width, which is optional

- ◆ Height, which is required

To position a second form in relation to a first form, apply the Move method to the second form, using parameters that refer to the first form.

To center one form on another:

1. Open a project, and name the default form frmFirst.

2. From the Project menu, choose Add Form to add a second form to the project.

3. Change the name of the second form to frmSecond and its caption to I am second!

4. Add a Command button to the first form.

5. Add code to the Command button's Click event to display the second form (as explained in "Navigating Between Forms" earlier in this chapter).

6. Make sure that the second form is open.

7. Right-click the second form.

8. From the pop-up menu, choose View Code to open the Code Editor.

9. Choose Form from the Object list.

10. Choose Load from the Procedures list.

11. Add to the second form's Move method a call that centers it in relationship to the first form (the complete event procedure is shown in **Listing 5.3**):

```
Me.Move frmFirst.Left +
→ (frmFirst.Width - Me.Width) \ 2,
→ frmFirst.Top +
→ (frmFirst.Height - Me.Height) \ 2
```

12. Run the project.

13. Click the button to display the second form.

The second form is centered in relation to the first form (**Figure 5.23**).

Listing 5.3 Centering a Form on Another

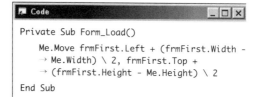

```
Private Sub Form_Load()
    Me.Move frmFirst.Left + (frmFirst.Width -
    → Me.Width) \ 2, frmFirst.Top +
    → (frmFirst.Height - Me.Height) \ 2
End Sub
```

Figure 5.23 You can use a form's Move method with parameters that relate to another form to position the first form in connection to the second form.

✔ Tip

■ In this example, the second form is centered against the full height of the first form, including title bar and form border. It's often the case that what you really want to do is center the second form in the *client* area of the first form. To achieve this, substitute ScaleWidth and ScaleHeight properties for Width and Height.

Listing 5.4 Printing Text on a Form

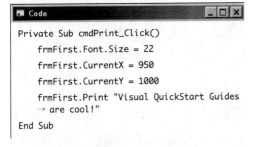

```
Private Sub cmdPrint_Click()
    frmFirst.Font.Size = 22
    frmFirst.CurrentX = 950
    frmFirst.CurrentY = 1000
    frmFirst.Print "Visual QuickStart Guides
    → are cool!"
End Sub
```

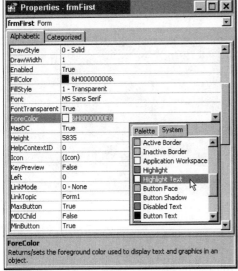

Figure 5.24 A form's ForeColor property is used to set the color for text that is printed on the form.

Drawing on Forms

You can set many things about the appearance of a form by setting the form's properties as explained in Chapter 3. You can also place controls on a form, and the design using the controls (see Chapter 6 for more information).

Another possibility is to use form methods such as Print and Circle to "paint" directly on the form. **Listing 5.4** provides an event procedure that displays text on a form.

To print text on a form:

1. Use the Properties window to set the form's BackColor property to red.

2. Use the Properties window to set the form's ForeColor property to white (**Figure 5.24**).

   Actually, you can use any color combination for the BackColor and ForeColor properties. But note that the ForeColor property is use to print the text. If the ForeColor and BackColor properties are the same, you will not see any text displayed.

3. Add to the form a Command button named cmdPrint and captioned Print.

4. In the Code Editor, locate cmdPrint's Click event procedure.

5. In the Click event procedure, add a line of code to size the font that will be used (you can also name the font if you don't want to use the default):

   ```
   frmFirst.Font.Size = 22
   ```

6. Use the form's CurrentX and CurrentY properties to specify where the text will be printed:

   ```
   frmFirst.CurrentX = 950
   frmFirst.CurrentY = 1000
   ```

continues on next page

7. Use the Print method to display text on the form:

```
frmFirst.Print "Visual QuickStart
Guides are cool!"
```

8. Run the form.

The text appears on the form in the position and size you specified (**Figure 5.25**).

Refreshing the Form

Suppose that you think your users may get tired of always seeing the statement about how cool Visual QuickStart Guides are displayed on the form.

You can easily use the form's Refresh method to return it to the state it was in which before the text was printed.

To remove the text:

1. Add to the form a Command button named cmdRefresh and captioned Refresh.

2. Use the Code Editor to locate cmdRefresh's Click event procedure.

3. Add code to the event procedure to invoke the form's Refresh method:

```
Private Sub cmdRefresh_Click()
    frmFirst.Refresh
End Sub
```

4. Run the form.

5. Click the Print button to display the text.

6. Click the Refresh button to remove the text.

Drawing Circles

You can use a form's Circle method to draw circles on a form. The code in **Listing 5.5** draws concentric circles on a form—like a target or bull's eye—using colors that are randomly generated (**Figure 5.26**).

Figure 5.25 Using the Print method, you can specify text that will be displayed on a form.

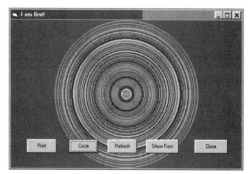

Figure 5.26 You can use the Circle method to draw circles on a form.

Listing 5.5 Drawing Circles on a Form

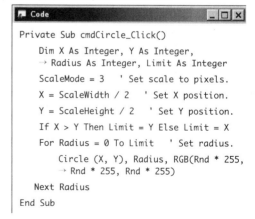

```
Private Sub cmdCircle_Click()
    Dim X As Integer, Y As Integer,
    ⇾ Radius As Integer, Limit As Integer
    ScaleMode = 3   ' Set scale to pixels.
    X = ScaleWidth / 2   ' Set X position.
    Y = ScaleHeight / 2   ' Set Y position.
    If X > Y Then Limit = Y Else Limit = X
    For Radius = 0 To Limit   ' Set radius.
        Circle (X, Y), Radius, RGB(Rnd * 255,
        ⇾ Rnd * 255, Rnd * 255)
    Next Radius
End Sub
```

Figure 5.27 Choose MDI Form to open the Add MDI Form dialog.

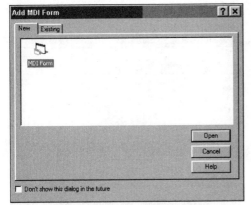

Figure 5.28 Accept the default new MDI form to add an MDI parent to your project.

Figure 5.29 The icon for the MDI form in the Project Explorer shows a parent and child form (as opposed to the single form representation for an SDI form).

MDI Applications

So far, the forms I have shown you have been *Single Document Interface* (SDI), or stand-alone. The other kind of form is *Multiple Document Interface* (MDI).

In an MDI application, there is one MDI—or parent—form. There can be many MDI child forms, and there can be more than one type of child form. But all the children must fit in the *client* space of the parent MDI form, meaning the form area exclusive of title bar, toolbars, and border.

There are many well-known MDI applications. You have probably used some of them, such as Microsoft Word. Because more powerful computers are easily able to open multiple instances of SDI applications, however, the MDI form has somewhat fallen out of favor in the user interface design crowd.

To create an MDI application:

1. Start a new Visual Basic project.

2. Right-click in the Project Explorer.

3. From the pop-up menu, choose Add Form, and then choose MDI Form (**Figure 5.27**).
   The Add MDI Form dialog opens (**Figure 5.28**).

4. Make sure that MDI Form is selected.

5. Click Open.
   The MDI form is added to your project. Note that in the Project Explorer, the icon for the MDI form is different from that for a regular form: It shows a larger form and a small child, rather than a single form representation (**Figure 5.29**).

continues on next page

6. Use the Properties window to name the form mdiParent and caption it I am the parent! (**Figure 5.30**).

7. Use the Properties window to rename the standard form in the project, naming it frmChild and captioning it I am a child... (**Figure 5.31**).

8. With frmChild selected, in the Properties window, scroll down the list of properties and select MDIChild.

9. Using the drop-down list on the right side of the Properties window, set the MDIChild property to True (**Figure 5.32**).

The icon for frmChild changes in the Project Explorer to represent a child form in an MDI application (**Figure 5.33**).

10. With mdiParent selected, open the Code Editor.

11. From the Object list, choose MDIForm.

12. From the Procedures list, choose Click.

13. Add code to the Click event procedure to open a new instance of the child form when the user clicks the parent form:

```
Private Sub MDIForm_Click()
    Dim X As New frmChild
    X.Show
End Sub
```

14. Run the project.

15. Click the form as many times as you want.

Figure 5.30 It's a good idea to name MDI forms starting with an mdi prefix so that they can clearly be identified.

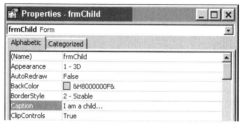

Figure 5.31 MDI child forms should be named with the standard frm prefix.

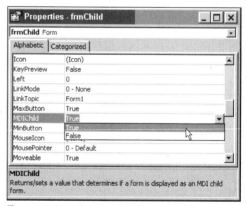

Figure 5.32 Standard forms become MDI children when their MDIChild property is set to True at design time.

Figure 5.33 When you change a standard form to an MDI child, its iconic representation changes in the Project Explorer.

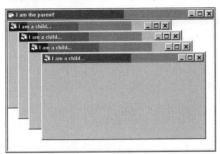

Figure 5.34 Most MDI applications allow users to open many children within the client area of the parent MDI form.

✔ Tips

■ MDI child forms should be named with the standard frm prefix.

■ Standard forms become MDI children when their MDIChild property is set to True at design time.

Each time you click, a new child form is displayed (**Figure 5.34**). Note that the child forms cannot be moved out of the parent's client area.

MDI APPLICATIONS

Summary

In this chapter, you learned to:

- ◆ Display and hide forms.
- ◆ Find documentation for all form methods.
- ◆ Work with code modules.
- ◆ Create a Sub Main procedure.
- ◆ Select a StartUp object.
- ◆ Conditionally display a form.
- ◆ Display modal and modeless forms.
- ◆ Unload forms.
- ◆ Open a form in response to a user request.

- ◆ Open multiple instances of the same form.
- ◆ Position forms.
- ◆ Center one form on another.
- ◆ Print text on a form.
- ◆ Refresh a form.
- ◆ Draw circles on a form.
- ◆ Create a Multiple Document Interface (MDI) application.

CONTROLS: DESIGNING THE FORM

So far, we've mainly worked with forms. Forms, the basis for application windows and dialogs, provide the underlying structure of most Visual Basic user interfaces. But controls, which are placed on forms, are the meat and potatoes of form behavior and appearance. They determine application response to most user actions.

Like forms, controls have properties, events, and methods. (A control's properties, events, and methods are called its *interface*.) You should understand each control's interface to work with that control.

In quite a few cases, control interfaces work the same way as form interfaces. Placing code in a Click event, for example, is for the most part no different for a control than for a form. It is also pretty much true that a BackColor property is a BackColor property, whether the property belongs to a control or a form. All this is by way of saying that the things you have learned about form properties, events, and methods will largely carry over to controls.

Chapters 6 through 11 explain how to use many of the 31 controls that ship with the Learning Edition of Visual Basic. Chapter 16 explains how to work with the database controls that ship with the Learning Edition.

To start with, this chapter explains a bit more about exactly what kind of beast a Visual Basic control is. Next, I show you how to add all the Visual Basic Learning Edition controls to a project Toolbox.

You learn how to use the Components dialog to add controls to a project or remove controls from a project.

Finally, I explain how to work with three "lightweight" controls that affect the appearance of forms: the Image, Shape, and Line controls.

What Is a Control?

It may help you when working with controls to understand a bit more about what controls are and what they are not.

Controls are compiled programs with special characteristics, which I'll explain in a minute. Most controls are written in C, C++, or Visual Basic 6. You will not be able to create controls by using the Learning Edition of Visual Basic: the Professional or Enterprise Edition is required. (Creating controls with Visual Basic, although not especially difficult, is beyond the scope of *Visual Basic: Visual QuickStart Guide*.)

Controls are objects that combine code with visual parts. In this sense, they are like forms, which also combine code and a visual representation. Unlike forms, however, they require a *container*—that is, an object (such as a form or other control) that *seats* the control. It is worth noting that controls, including those written in Visual Basic, can be deployed in any application with containers capable of seating ActiveX controls, such as Microsoft's Access, Excel, Word, and Visual C++ and Borland-Inprise's Delphi.

Developers work with controls in one way; then they are distributed as part of a VB project and used by end users in a completely different fashion. If you are creating a control, you must create what amounts to two applications: one for the developer and one that sets run-time behavior of the control when it is included in a larger project.

The developer part of the control includes an icon for the Toolbox. In addition, the control has a visual representation when it is placed on a container, such as a form. But most important, the control has properties, events, and methods, which are collectively known as the control's interface. A creator of controls is responsible for the programming that enables the interface: for making sure that properties appear in the Properties window, that events are fired when they are supposed to be fired, and much more.

The user of an application that includes a control doesn't see this internal scaffolding. The user's interaction with the control depends on the interface settings that the application developer (not the control developer) has made and on code added by the developer.

When you use the Learning Edition of Visual Basic, you are using the interfaces provided by controls that have been developed for you. You need to know how to place the control on a container and how to use the control's interface. You do not need to know the mechanism that created this interface. But understanding that the scaffolding is there—and that someone created it—may help you work with controls.

WHAT IS A CONTROL?

A Learning Edition Controls Project

The Leaning Edition of Visual Basic ships with 31 controls. You can start a new project with all these controls preloaded in the Toolbox.

To open a project with all Learning Edition controls preloaded:

1. From the File menu, choose New Project.
   The New Project dialog opens (**Figure 6.1**).

2. Select VB Learning Edition Controls.

3. Click OK.
   A new project opens, with all the Learning Edition controls preloaded in the Toolbox (**Figure 6.2**).

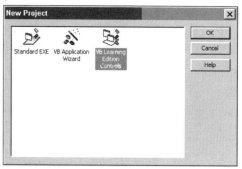

Figure 6.1 You can use the New Project dialog to open a project that has preloaded all Learning Edition controls.

Figure 6.2 All 31 controls are preloaded into the project's Toolbox.

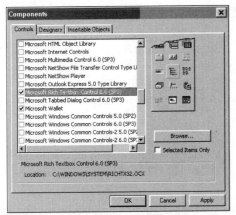

Figure 6.3 The Components dialog is used to add and remove controls.

Figure 6.4 Controls added in the Components dialog appear in your Toolbox.

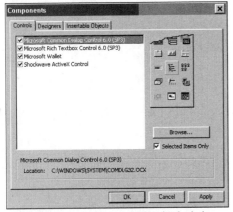

Figure 6.5 If Selected Items Only is checked, the Controls tab of the Components dialog displays only loaded controls.

Adding and Removing Controls

Controls can most easily be added to and removed from your project Toolbox via the Components dialog.

To add a control to your Toolbox:

1. From the Project menu, choose Components, or right-click the Toolbox and choose Components from the pop-up menu.

   The Controls tab of the Components dialog opens (**Figure 6.3**).

2. Place a check mark in the box next to the control you want to add.

   The RichTextBox control is being added in **Figure 6.3**.

3. Click Close, or click Apply and close the Components dialog when you are through adding controls.

   The control you elected to add appears in your Toolbox (**Figure 6.4**).

✔ Tips

- If Selected Items Only is checked (**Figure 6.5**), the Components dialog shows only the controls that are already loaded in your project Toolbox.

- Controls that you add can be provided by Microsoft as part of Visual Basic—RichTextBox, for example—or they can be provided by a third-party developer. Many, many ActiveX controls are available either for purchase or as free downloads.

- The Controls tab of the Components dialog shows ActiveX controls that have been properly included in your system Registry. You can also use the Browse button in the Components dialog to add ActiveX controls (.ocx files) that have not yet been registered.

- If no additional controls are selected, your Toolbox nonetheless includes a set of 20 controls (**Figure 6.6**). With the exception of the OLE control, this minimal set of controls cannot be removed from a project. In other words, these controls are built into Visual Basic. They are sometimes referred to as the Visual Basic *intrinsic* controls.

To remove a control from your project Toolbox:

1. Open the Components dialog.

2. Clear the checkbox next to the control you want to remove from your project.
   The RichTextBox control is being removed in **Figure 6.7**.

3. Click Close (or click Apply).
   The control no longer appears in your Toolbox.

Figure 6.6 The intrinsic controls cannot be removed from your Toolbox.

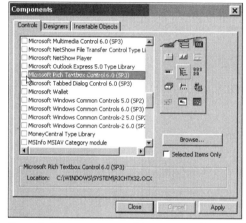

Figure 6.7 To remove a control from your Toolbox, clear the checkbox next to the control listing in the Components dialog.

Figure 6.8 Double-click the Image control—or drag and drop it—to place it on an open form.

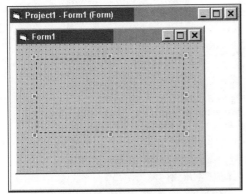

Figure 6.9 Use the Image control's handles to size and position the control.

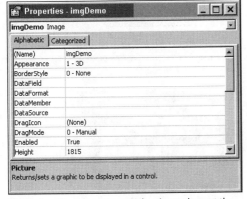

Figure 6.10 The Properties window is used to set the Image control's properties at design time.

Image Control

The Image control is used to display a picture. Along with the Shape and Line controls, the Image control is termed a *lightweight* control. These controls are primarily used decoratively. They do not consume much in the way of resources, but they are also not very powerful—hence, lightweight.

The Image control's smarter younger brother is the PictureBox control. The PictureBox control can do everything the Image control can do. (It is, however, a true heavyweight when it comes to consuming system resources.) In addition, it can be used to seat other controls and supports some advanced events and methods.

For everyday use, sometimes a lightweight is best. There's lots you can do with the Image control.

To add an Image control to a form:

1. Make sure that the Toolbox and a form are open.

2. In the Toolbox (**Figure 6.8**), double-click the Image control to place a copy on the form.

   You can also drag the Image control into the form.

3. Using its handles, size and position the Image control in the form (**Figure 6.9**).

To set the Picture property at design time:

1. With the Image control selected, open the Properties window.

2. Set the Image control's name to imgDemo (**Figure 6.10**).

continues on next page

3. Set the Image control's Stretch property to True.

This causes the picture that you place in the Image control to resize to fit the control (rather than vice versa).

4. Select the Picture property (**Figure 6.11**).

5. Click the ellipsis button on the right side of the Properties window.

The Load Picture dialog opens (**Figure 6.12**).

6. Select a file.

7. Click Open.

The picture file is loaded into the Image control (**Figure 6.13**).

8. Run the project.

The form now appears to be decorated with the picture (**Figure 6.14**).

To set the Picture property at runtime:

1. With the form containing the Image control open, open the Code Editor.

2. Choose the form from the Objects List.

3. From the Procedures List, choose Load.

4. Add code that assigns the value of the LoadPicture function to the Picture property of the Image control.

The file location of the picture is the argument of the LoadPicture function. For example:

```
Private Sub Form_Load()
    imgDemo.Picture = LoadPicture
    → (App.Path + "\Hozcirar.wmf")
End Sub
```

Figure 6.11 A picture is loaded into the Image control via the Picture property.

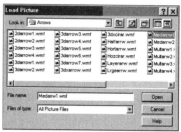

Figure 6.12 The button next to the Picture property opens the Load Picture dialog, which is used to select a picture file from your file system.

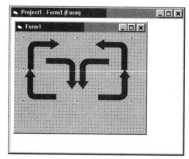

Figure 6.13 The picture file has been loaded into the Image control.

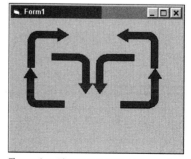

Figure 6.14 The Image control decorates the form when it is run.

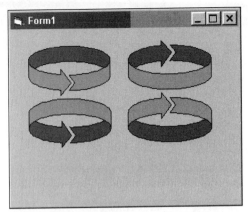

Figure 6.15 Pictures can be assigned to an Image control in code at run time.

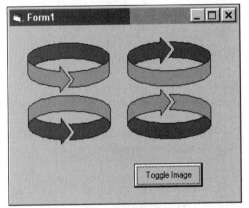

Figure 6.16 The picture is displayed until the Image control's Picture property is changed.

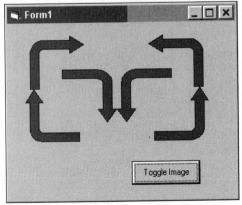

Figure 6.17 The Image control's Picture property can be changed dynamically, depending on user input.

5. Run the project.

The picture file you assigned to the Image control appears (**Figure 6.15**).

✔ Tip

■ For this code to work, the picture file must be located as specified. In the example, `App.Path` invokes the Path property of the application object, which specifies the directory used to run a Visual Basic project. In other words, the example assumes that these graphic files are sitting in the same directory as the project and form files.

You could also specify a file location absolutely. For example:

```
imgDemo.Picture = LoadPicture
  → ("C:\Graphics\Hozcirar.wmf")
```

To let the user toggle to a new picture:

1. Add a Command Button to the form.

2. Use the Properties window to name the button `cmdToggle` and caption it `Toggle`.

3. From the Objects list, choose cmdToggle.

4. From the Procedures list, choose Click.

5. Add code to the button's Click event to change the loaded picture when the button is clicked:

```
Private Sub cmdToggle_Click()
    imgDemo.Picture = LoadPicture
    → (App.Path + "\Medarrw1.wmf")
End Sub
```

6. Run the project.

The initial picture is displayed (**Figure 6.16**).

7. Click Toggle.

The new image is displayed (**Figure 6.17**).

IMAGE CONTROL

111

Shape Control

The Shape control doesn't support any events and is used entirely for decorative purposes, names drawing a shape on a form. **Table 6.1** shows the kinds of shapes you can create with the Shape control.

To add a circle to a form:

1. With the form and the Toolbox open, locate the Shape control in the Toolbox (**Figure 6.18**).

2. Double-click the Shape control (or drag and drop it) to place it on the form.

3. Use the Shape control's handles to size and position the control (**Figure 6.19**).

4. Use the Properties window to set the BackStyle of the form to 1 - Opaque (**Figure 6.20**).

   This causes the background of the shape to be visible against the form.

5. In the Properties window, set the Shape's BackColor property to vbRed.

6. In the Properties window, set the Shape's Shape property to 3 - Circle (**Figure 6.20**).

7. Run the project.

   A red circle appears on the form (**Figure 6.21**).

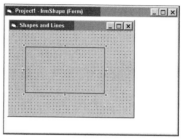

Figure 6.18 The Shape control is represented in the Toolbox by an icon portraying different shapes.

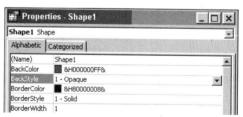

Figure 6.19 When a Shape control is placed on a form, it can be sized and positioned by means of its handles.

Figure 6.20 The Shape control's Shape property determines what kind of shape it is.

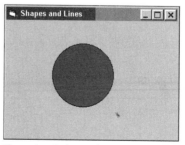

Figure 6.21 A shape whose background is opaque appears solid when the form that contains it is run.

Table 6.1

Shape Property Settings
SETTING
0 - Rectangle
1 - Square
2 - Oval
3 - Circle
4 - Rounded Rectangle
5 - Rounded Square

Figure 6.22 Lines can be easily drawn on a form.

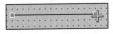

Figure 6.23 Using their handles, you can position and size lines as you like.

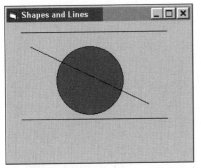

Figure 6.24 A Line control can be positioned above or below another control, such as the Shape control shown here.

Line Control

Although lines don't *do* anything, they are important parts of user interface design. Properly positioned lines separate areas of a form and divide functional areas.

You can use the Properties window to set line size and position, but it is probably easier to just draw lines on the form.

To draw lines on a form:

1. With form and the Toolbox open, locate the Line control in the Toolbox (**Figure 6.22**).

2. Double-click the Line control (or drag and drop it) to add it to the form.

    When the Line control has been added to the form, it appears with a handle at either end (**Figure 6.23**).

    When your mouse pointer gets close to a Line handle, it turns into a crosshair (**Figure 6.23**).

3. Using the crosshair, size and position the line any way you want.

4. Draw as many lines as you want on the form.

5. Run the form to view your lines (**Figure 6.24**).

LINE CONTROL

Summary

In this chapter, you learned to:

- Start a project with all the Visual Basic Learning Edition controls already loaded.

- Add a control to your project's Toolbox.

- Remove a control from the Toolbox.

- Work with the Image control.

- Work with the Shape control.

- Work with the Line control.

CONTROLS THAT ACCEPT USER INPUT

Some of the most important controls are those that accept user input. There are many kinds of user input. You may need to know whether something is on or off, for example. This kind of Boolean choice is best represented by the CheckBox control: it is either checked, or it is not.

If the user is supposed to choose one of several items, OptionButton controls may work well. These controls present a familiar radio button interface, which can easily be set to allow the user to make only one choice from a group of items.

Another possibility along the same lines (but with a different interface) is to allow the user to make a choice from a list, using either the ListBox or ComboBox control.

The key principle is that the choice of control should be in harmony with the nature of the input that the user is asked to make. (The general topic of organizing the ways users interact with your programs is called *user interface architecture*.)

This chapter explains how to accept user input by using CheckBox, OptionButton, ListBox, and ComboBox controls. Generally, you'll find that a bit of code is needed to *do* anything with the user input that you have accepted. I'll show you the basics of processing the user input that you have generated and how to combine these controls into an effective user interface architecture.

Checkboxes

In this section, I show you how to add several checkboxes to a form.

The *Value property* of the CheckBox control is the property that sets (or reads) the check-box. There are three possible values: Unchecked, Checked, and Grayed. In code, you can use either the numerical equivalent or a built-in constant to set or check for these values (**Table 7.1**).

When your program is running, you'll be able to determine the *state*, meaning, have they been checked, unchecked, or grayed by the user. In a real-life program, the next actions your code would take would depend on the check button state.

To add checkboxes to a form:

1. With your form open, select the CheckBox control in your Toolbox (**Figure 7.1**).

2. Double-click the CheckBox (or drag and drop it) to position it on the form.

   The CheckBox has the default caption Check1 (**Figure 7.2**).

3. Use the Properties window to change the CheckBox's name to chkSpam and its caption to Can we add you to our junk email list? (**Figure 7.3**).

Table 7.1

CheckBox Value Settings		
BUILT-IN CONSTANT	NUMERICAL EQUIVALENT	MEANING
vbUnchecked	0	The CheckBox is unchecked.
vbChecked	1	The CheckBox is checked.
vbGrayed	2	The CheckBox is grayed, or disabled, so the user cannot click it, with a check in place.

Figure 7.1 In your Toolbox, the CheckBox control looks like, well, a checked box.

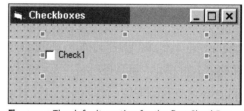

Figure 7.2 The default caption for the first CheckBox you place on a form is Check1.

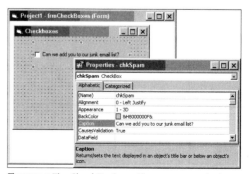

Figure 7.3 The CheckBox's caption appears as text next to the checkbox.

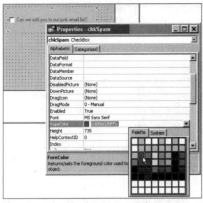

Figure 7.4 The CheckBox's ForeColor property changes the color used to display text.

Figure 7.5 If you set a CheckBox's Value property to 1 - Checked in the Properties window, when your program runs, your checkbox will be checked.

Figure 7.6 If you set a CheckBox's Value property to 0 - Unchecked in the Properties window, when your program runs, your checkbox will be unchecked.

4. In the Properties window, change chkSpam's ForeColor property to red, so that the text it displays will appear more distinctive (**Figure 7.4**).

5. Using the Properties window, change chkSpam's Value property to 1 - Checked (**Figure 7.5**).

This makes chkSpam start with the initial value of vbChecked.

6. Add another CheckBox control to the form.

7. Use the Properties window to name the new CheckBox chkPrize, set its caption to Check to receive free tee-shirt!, and set its Value property to 0 - Unchecked (**Figure 7.6**).

To add a procedure that will determine the state of the checkboxes:

1. Using the Toolbox, add a Command Button to the form.

2. Using the Properties window, set the Command Button's name to cmdShow and its caption to Show CheckBox Values (**Figure 7.7**).

3. Add a Label control to the form.

   The Label will be used to display the checkbox states.

4. Use the Properties window to name the Label lblDisplay and to delete its caption.

   When the program first runs, you will not see any text displayed in lblDisplay.

5. Use the Code Editor to add the code shown in **Listing 7.1** to cmdShow's Click event.

   This code creates a variable, strDisplay. The state of each checkbox is determined, with an appropriate value assigned to strDisplay. Finally, strDisplay is assigned as the caption of the Label lblDisplay.

6. Run the program.

7. Click the checkboxes to change their state.

8. Click cmdShow, and an appropriate message regarding checkbox state appears (**Figure 7.8**).

Listing 7.1 Determining Checkbox State

```
Code                                    _□X
Private Sub cmdShow_Click()
    Dim strDisplay As String
    If chkSpam = vbChecked Then
        strDisplay = "You want spam email!"
    ElseIf chkSpam = vbUnchecked Then
        strDisplay = "No spam for you!"
    End If
    If chkPrize = vbChecked Then
        strDisplay = strDisplay & " Your
→ shirt is on its way!"
    ElseIf chkPrize = vbUnchecked Then
        strDisplay = strDisplay & " No shirt
→ for you!"
    End If
    lblDisplay.Caption = strDisplay
End Sub
```

Figure 7.7 You can add a command button that will display the state of the checkboxes when it is clicked.

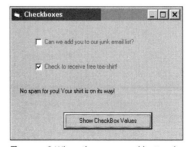

Figure 7.8 When the command button is clicked, the label will display checkbox state information.

Listing 7.2 Graying and Ungraying a Checkbox

```
Code                                    _ □ ×

Private Sub cmdGray_Click()
    If cmdGray.Caption = "Gray" Then
        chkPrize.Value = vbGrayed
        cmdGray.Caption = "UnGray"
    Else
        chkPrize.Value = vbUnchecked
        cmdGray.Caption = "Gray"
    End If
End Sub
```

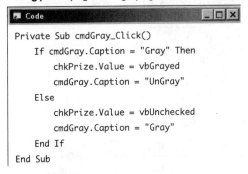

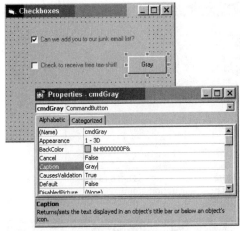

Figure 7.9 You can add a button to allow users to gray a button on the fly.

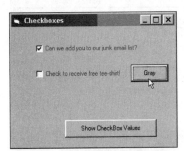

Figure 7.10 A command button can be used to gray and ungray a checkbox.

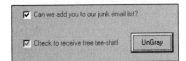

Figure 7.11 A grayed checkbox does not accept user clicks.

Graying a Checkbox

Graying a checkbox denies your users the right to change its state. It's easy to dynamically gray checkboxes.

To gray a checkbox dynamically:

1. Add a button to your form.

2. Use the Properties window to name the button cmdGray and caption it Gray (**Figure 7.9**).

3. Using the Code Editor, add the code shown in **Listing 7.2** to cmdGray's Click event.

   This procedure grays the chkPrize checkbox if it is not gray and ungrays it if it is gray. It also appropriately changes the caption of cmdGray.

4. Run the program.

5. Click the Gray button (**Figure 7.10**). The check box becomes grayed (**Figure 7.11**).

Option Buttons

Use option buttons when you want your user to make a single choice from a list of possibilities.

It's an important part of the option button user interface that users can select only one option button in a list of option buttons at any time.

Fortunately, this is taken care of for you automatically. If you add several option buttons (called an *option button group*) to a container (such as a form) and run the project, you'll find that you can select only one of the buttons.

Most of the time, you'll want to have more than one group of option buttons on a form. To do so, you add an intermediate control to the form for each option button group. The usual choice is a Frame control. If you add several Frames, and then add a group of option buttons to each Frame, only one item in each group can be selected.

To add option groups:

1. With an open form, select the Frame control in the Toolbox (**Figure 7.12**).

2. Double-click the Frame control (or drag and drop it) to add it to the form.

3. Add a second frame (for a second group of option buttons) to the form (**Figure 7.13**).

4. Use each frame's handles to size and position the frame.

5. Using the Properties window, name the top frame fraModel and caption it What Model would you like? (**Figure 7.14**).

6. Using the Properties window, name the bottom frame fraColor and caption it Choose a Color (**Figure 7.15**).

Figure 7.12 The Frame control is used as the container for groups of option buttons.

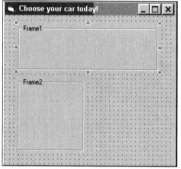

Figure 7.13 Each frame is used to contain —or host—an option group.

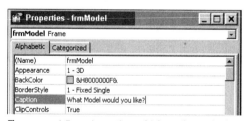

Figure 7.14 A Frame's caption, which can be set in the Properties window, appears in the top-left corner of the frame.

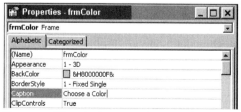

Figure 7.15 When the frame contains an option group, the frame's caption is often used to identify the choice the user will be making.

Figure 7.16 The Toolbox is used to add an OptionButton to a frame.

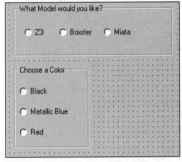

Figure 7.17 Each frame is used to group related option buttons.

Figure 7.18 The OptionButton in each group whose Value property is set to True will initially be selected when a project is run.

Table 7.2

Option Button Names and Captions		
GROUP	NAME	CAPTION
fraModel	optZ3	Z3
fraModel	optBoxster	Boxster
fraModel	optMiata	Miata
fraColor	optBlack	Black
fraColor	optMetBlue	Metallic Blue
fraColor	optRed	Red

7. In the Toolbox select the OptionButton control (**Figure 7.16**).

8. Double-click (or drag and drop) the OptionButton control to add three OptionButtons to each frame, using the name and caption values specified in **Table 7.2**.

   The form now appears to have two groups of option buttons, arranged by topic (**Figure 7.17**).

9. Using the Properties window, in each group, choose the button that you want to be selected initially by setting its Value property to True.

   Figure 7.18 shows setting the Value property of the optBoxster option button in the fraModel group to True so that it is initially selected.

✔ Tip

- One reason why all controls of the same sort should be named with the same prefix (opt for OptionButtons, for example) is so that they will be positioned contiguously in the Properties Window drop-down list and the Code Editor's Objects list. Imagine how hard it would be to find option buttons in a group if they were named randomly.

OPTION BUTTONS

To determine which option buttons were selected:

1. Add a Command button named cmdChoice and captioned Display Choice! to the form to display the user's choice of option buttons (**Figure 7.19**).

2. Use the Code Editor to add a variable declaration that will hold a description of the button selected for each group (the complete event procedure code is shown in **Listing 7.3**):

```
Dim CarAnswer As String, ColorAnswer
→ As String
```

3. For each option group, add an If statement that determines which option button's Value property is True and adds the corresponding text string to the appropriate variable:

```
If optZ3.Value = True Then
    CarAnswer = "Z3"
ElseIf optBoxster.Value = True Then
    CarAnswer = "Boxster"
ElseIf optMiata.Value = True Then
    CarAnswer = "Miata"
End If
```

4. Add a MsgBox statement that uses the group variables to display a message depending on the user's selections (for information about the & character, which is the *string concatenation operator*, see the "String Concatenation" sidebar):

```
MsgBox "You selected a " & CarAnswer
→ & " in " & ColorAnswer & ".",
→ vbExclamation, "Your car will be
→ delivered tomorrow!"
```

Listing 7.3 Finding Which Option Button Was Selected

```
Private Sub cmdChoice_Click()
    Dim CarAnswer As String,
    → ColorAnswer As String
    If optZ3.Value = True Then
        CarAnswer = "Z3"
    ElseIf optBoxster.Value = True Then
        CarAnswer = "Boxster"
    ElseIf optMiata.Value = True Then
        CarAnswer = "Miata"
    End If
    If optBlack.Value = True Then
        ColorAnswer = "Black"
    ElseIf optMetBlue.Value = True Then
        ColorAnswer = "Metallic Blue"
    ElseIf optRed.Value = True Then
        ColorAnswer = "Red"
    End If
    MsgBox "You selected a " & CarAnswer & "
    → in " & ColorAnswer & ".",
    → vbExclamation, "Your car will be
    → delivered tomorrow!"
End Sub
```

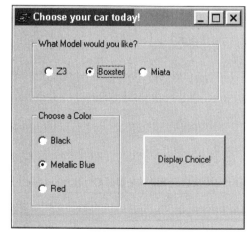

Figure 7.19 A Command button's Click event can be used to display the user's choice of option buttons.

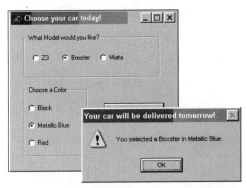

Figure 7.20 A text string indicating the user's choice is displayed after testing each option button's Value property.

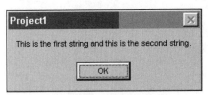

Figure 7.21 String concatenation means joining alphanumeric strings.

String Concatenation

Concatenation simply means adding two things by placing the second after the first. 1 concatenated with 2, for example, would be 12. In other words, the second thing has been joined with the first thing. (Note that the string "1" is different from the number 1, although the two may be processed and evaluate to the same thing.)

Strings (short for text strings) are lengths of alphanumeric characters. These can be stored in a Visual Basic string variable or placed between quotation marks (sometimes called string literals).

When you concatenate two strings, you are forming a new string that places the second concatenated string after the first string. String variables can be concatenated with other string variables, or with string literals, in any combination.

5. Run the program.

6. Make a choice in each group of option buttons.

7. Click Display Choice!

A message box appears with your choice: a Boxster in metallic blue, for example (**Figure 7.20**).

Concatenation in Visual Basic

Visual Basic has two string concatenation operators, which are used to indicate that a string concatenation should occur. These operators are & and +. Functionally, the two operators are almost the same. It is better practice, however, to use &, which is used only for concatenation, as opposed to +, which is also used to add.

You may find this easier to understand as part of an example.

To declare two string variables:

```
Dim strVar1 As String, strVar2 As String
```

To assign text strings to each variable:

```
strVar1 = "This is the first string"
strVar2 = "this is the second string."
```

To concatenate the first string variable with the string literal "and" and the second string variable, display the results in a message box (**Figure 7.21**):

```
MsgBox strVar1 & " and " & strVar2
```

Option Button Arrays

If you've had a look at the example in the preceding section, you can see that you can determine which option was selected by checking the Value property of each distinctly named option button. Although this works, it quickly gets cumbersome when you have more than two or three options. You must write code to check each option button's value, using the name of the option button. There ought to be a better way, and fortunately, there is!

An *array* is used to store objects of similar type and access them by using an *index*. You could have an array of integer numbers, for example. It's common to start an array's index with 0 rather than 1. So suppose that our array has three *elements*: the numbers 1, 3, and 5. The number 1 would be the value of the first array element; 3, the value of the second array element; and 5, the value of the third element. To access these array elements in code, you would use the array index (in Visual Basic, an array's index is indicated with parentheses):

```
array(0) = 1
array(1) = 3
array(2) = 5
```

Put this way, you can see that the array in this simple example functions as a single-column lookup table. You should file away for future reference the concept of a multidimensional array, in which at least one pair of coordinates is required to identify (and access) the array value.

It's a good thing that you can store more than just integer numbers in an array. In Visual Basic, you can have arrays of many types of objects, including real numbers (that is, numbers that include a decimal place), text strings, and objects (such as forms and controls).

Listing 7.4 Using Option Button Arrays

```
Code                                    _ □ ×
Private Sub cmdSubmit_Click()
    Dim I As Integer
    Dim strSecurity As String, strType As
    → String
    For I = 0 To 2
        If optSecurity(I).Value = True Then
            strSecurity = optSecurity(I).
            → Caption
        End If
        If optOrdType(I).Value = True Then
            strType = optOrdType(I).Caption
        End If
    Next I
    MsgBox "Your order: " & strSecurity
    → & " - " & strType, vbInformation,
    → "Order Information"
End Sub
```

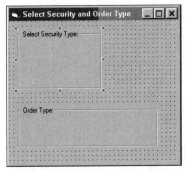

Figure 7.22 Arrays of option button controls can be added to container controls, such as frames.

Figure 7.23 The first option button in an array is added to the frame normally.

Arrays of controls turn out to be particularly useful in Visual Basic, because they simplify the coding involved in wiring bunches of essentially identical controls.

In the case of option buttons, you can refer to each member of the option button control array by using its index—optDecision(0), optDecision(1), and so on.

The next step is replacing the explicit use of the array index with an integer variable. You can use a loop to check all the OptionButton controls in the array in one fell swoop, without having to refer to each control using an individual name.

Let's have a look at this in practice! **Listing 7.4** shows the complete event procedure that determines which option buttons in two different option button arrays were selected.

To add option button arrays:

1. Using the Frame control, draw two frames on a control (**Figure 7.22**).

2. Add an OptionButton to the first frame.

3. Use the Properties window to name the option button optSecurity and caption it Stock (**Figure 7.23**).

4. Click the newly created OptionButton control to select it.

5. With the control selected, copy it by choosing Copy from the Edit menu or by pressing Ctrl+C.

continues on next page

6. Click the frame that will be used to contain the option button array (**Figure 7.24**).

7. Choose Paste from the Edit menu, or press Ctrl+V, to paste the copied control into the frame.

A message box appears, noting that you already have a control named "optSecurity" and asking whether you want to create a control array (**Figure 7.25**).

8. Click Yes.

The new control appears in the top-left corner of the frame.

9. Use the mouse to position the control in the frame.

10. Use the Properties window to change the caption of the second element of the option button array to Bond.

11. Making sure that the frame is selected, choose Paste from the Edit menu, or press Ctrl+V, to add another control array element to the frame.

This time, you will not see a message asking whether you want to create a control array, because it has already been created.

12. Position the new control in the frame.

13. Use the Properties window to change the caption of the third element to Mutual Fund.

You'll notice that the Properties window lists the three elements of the option button control array as optSecurity(0), optSecurity(1), and optSecurity(2) (**Figure 7.26**).

14. Add an option button to the second frame.

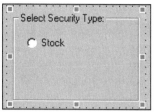

Figure 7.24 Before pasting a control to start a control array, you must make sure that the destination container is selected.

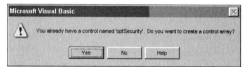

Figure 7.25 When you first copy a control into a container, you will be asked whether you want to create a control array.

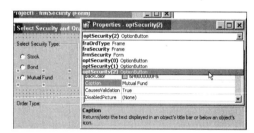

Figure 7.26 Visual Basic has automatically named control array elements for you.

Figure 7.27 New control array elements appear in the top-left corner of the frame and must be positioned appropriately.

15. Use the Properties window to change its name to `optOrdType` and its caption to `Sell at Market`.

16. Select the control.

17. Select the frame that will be the container for the control array.

18. Paste the copy of the control into the frame.

19. When you are asked whether you want to start a control array, click Yes.

A copy of the control is pasted in the top-left corner of the frame (**Figure 7.27**).

20. Position the new control.

21. Use the Properties window to caption it `Sell with a limit`.

22. Paste a new copy of the control into the frame.

23. Position the copy of the control.

24. Use the Properties Window to caption it Buy.

You'll find in the Properties window that this control array has three elements: optOrdType(0), optOrdType(1), and optOrdType(2).

To determine the user's choices:

1. Add a command button to the form
   (**Figure 7.28**).

   This button is used to display the options
   that have been selected when the user
   clicks it.

2. Use the Properties window to name
   the button cmdSubmit and caption it
   Submit Order.

3. Set the initial values that you want to
   be selected in each control array by using
   the Properties window to set that array
   element's Value property to True
   (**Figure 7.29**).

4. In the Code Editor, choose cmdClick
   from the Objects List and Click from the
   Procedures List.

   The Click event procedure framework is
   created for you.

5. Within the Click event procedure, declare
   an array index variable:

   ```
   Dim I As Integer
   ```

6. Declare holding variables to store the
   caption values of the array elements:

   ```
   Dim strSecurity As String,
   → strType As String
   ```

7. Create a loop that counts through all
   three array elements:

   ```
   For I = 0 To 2
   ...
   Next I
   ```

8. Within the loop, assign an option array's
   Caption string to the holding variables
   when the Value property for a particular
   element is True:

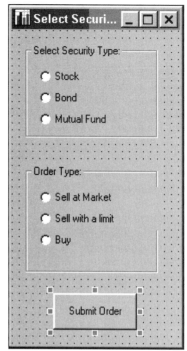

Figure 7.28 A command button will be
used to display the user's choice of
options.

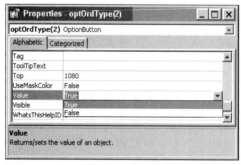

Figure 7.29 The option control array element with its
Value property set to True will be initially selected.

✔ Tip

■ You can use the OptionButton's Click event
  for processing the user's choices, rather
  than using the Click event of a separate
  control, such as a command button.

OPTION BUTTON ARRAYS

Figure 7.30 A message box is used to display the user's choices.

```
If optSecurity(I).Value = True Then
    strSecurity =
    → optSecurity(I).Caption
End If
If optOrdType(I).Value = True Then
    strType = optOrdType(I).Caption
End If
```

9. After the loop is processed, add a MsgBox statement to display the results:

```
MsgBox "Your order: " & strSecurity
→ & " - " & strType, vbInformation,
→ "Order Information"
```

10. Run the project.

11. Make a choice in each group of option buttons.

12. Click Submit Order.

Your choices are displayed in a message box (**Figure 7.30**).

For...Next Statements

A *For...Next statement* is one way to set up a loop in Visual Basic.

A *For loop* uses a variable called a counter that increases or decreases in value during each repetition of the loop. In its simplest, default form, the For loop counter increases by 1 each time the loop is passed through.

The syntax of the For loop is (the brackets indicate an optional part):

```
For counter = start To end [Step increment]
...
Next [counter]
```

When it first encounters a For loop, Visual Basic sets the counter equal to start. It next tests whether counter is greater than end. If so, Visual Basic exits the loop.

Assuming that the loop hasn't been exited, VB then executes the statements within the loop. Usually, these statements make some use of counter to iterate through an array.

When VB hits the Next statement (which ends the loop), it increments the counter by 1 (or by increment, if it's specified in the For statement). Execution control is passed back to the For statement, and the incremented counter is compared with end. If the counter is still less than end, the statements are executed once more, and so on.

List Boxes

Another approach for letting users choose among several options is the ListBox control.

The ListBox presents a series of items in a box. Depending on how you've drawn the control, arrows may be used to access list items that are not visible on the screen.

Items in a list box are selected by clicking them. You can tell that an item has been selected if it is highlighted.

Unlike an option button group, you can set up a list box so that more than one choice can be made.

To add a ListBox to a form:

1. With your form open, select the ListBox control in the Toolbox (**Figure 7.31**).

2. Double-click the ListBox control (or drag and drop it) to add it to the form.

   The ListBox appears on the form with its default name, List1 (**Figure 7.32**).

3. Use the Properties window to name the ListBox control (lstBBQ, for example).

   Its new name now appears on the form (**Figure 7.33**).

To add items to a ListBox by using the Properties window:

1. With the ListBox selected, open the Properties window.

2. Select the List property (**Figure 7.34**).

3. Click the arrow in the right column of the Properties window.

   A text box opens in the Properties window.

4. Type a list item.

5. Press Enter.

6. To add the next list item, click the arrow in the right column again.

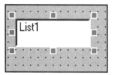

Figure 7.31 The ListBox, which allows users to make choices from a list, is part of many user interfaces.

Figure 7.32 When you draw a ListBox on a form, it will appear with its default name, List1.

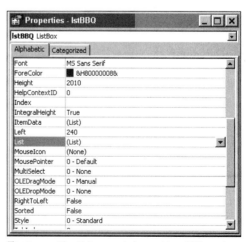

Figure 7.33 When you change the name of the ListBox control, the new name appears in the ListBox at design time.

Properties - lstBBQ	
lstBBQ ListBox	

Alphabetic	Categorized
Font	MS Sans Serif
ForeColor	&H80000008&
Height	2010
HelpContextID	0
Index	
IntegralHeight	True
ItemData	(List)
Left	240
List	(List)
MouseIcon	(None)
MousePointer	0 - Default
MultiSelect	0 - None
OLEDragMode	0 - Manual
OLEDropMode	0 - None
RightToLeft	False
Sorted	False
Style	0 - Standard

Figure 7.34 The List property is used to add items to a ListBox.

Figure 7.35 The items added via the Properties window appear in the ListBox in the order in which they were entered.

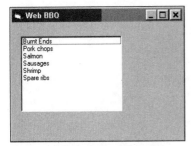

Figure 7.36 If the ListBox's Sorted property is set to True, then items in the list box will be alphabetized when the project is run.

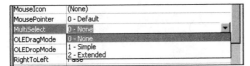

Figure 7.37 To enable multiselection, set the MultiSelect property to 1 - Simple or 2 - Extended.

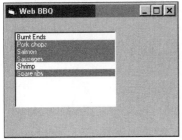

Figure 7.38 If the MultiSelect property has been set, users can highlight more than one item.

7. Type the next list item.

8. Press Enter.

9. Repeat this process until all your list items have been entered.

The list items that you entered appears in the ListBox in the order in which you entered them (**Figure 7.35**).

To sort a ListBox:

1. With the ListBox selected, use the Properties window to highlight the ListBox's Sorted property.

2. Click the arrow on the right side of the Properties window to set the Sorted property to True.

When you run the list box, the items in it are sorted alphabetically (**Figure 7.36**).

To enable multiselection:

1. Use the Properties window to highlight the ListBox's MultiSelect property.

2. Set the MultiSelect property to 1 - Simple or 2 - Extended (**Figure 7.37**).

3. Run the project.

You now can multiselect items in the ListBox (**Figure 7.38**).

✔ Tip

■ In a simple multiselect, a mouse click or a press of the spacebar selects—and deselects—items. In an extended multi-select, you can use the Shift key combined with the mouse to select blocks of items, and the Ctrl key and mouse to select and deselect items within a selected block.

To add items to a ListBox using code:

◆ Using the Code Editor, place statements that invoke the ListBox's AddItem method in an event where they will be executed.

Add the following code to the form's Load event. For example:

```
Private Sub Form_Load()
    lstBBQ.AddItem
    → "Roast Suckling Pig"
    lstBBQ.AddItem "Red Peppers"
    lstBBQ.AddItem "Lobsters"
    lstBBQ.AddItem "Filet Mignon"
    lstBBQ.AddItem "Tofu"
End Sub
```

The new items appear in the list box when the form is run (**Figure 7.39**).

Figure 7.39 You can use the ListBox's AddItem method to add items in code.

✔ Tips

■ It's often easier to add items in code than by using the Properties window.

■ It's very common to track items in an array, and use a loop to add all the items in the array to a list box.

To determine whether any list items are selected:

1. Use the Properties window to make sure that the ListBox's MultiSelect property is set to 0 - None.

2. Add to the form a command button named cmdSelect and captioned Any Selected?

Listing 7.5 Displaying a Selected Item

```
Code                                    _ □ ✕

Private Sub cmdSelected_Click()
    If lstBBQ.ListIndex = -1 Then
        lblSelected.Caption = "No item
        → selected!"
    Else
        lblSelected.Caption = lstBBQ.List
        → (lstBBQ.ListIndex)
    End If
End Sub
```

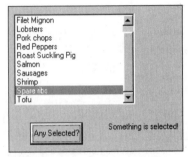

Figure 7.40 If the ListBox's ListIndex property equals -1, nothing is selected.

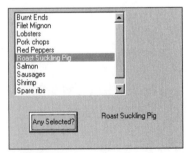

Figure 7.41 The List and ListIndex properties are used to return the text of a selected item.

3. Using the Code Editor, add code that checks whether lstBBQ.ListIndex = -1 (meaning that nothing is selected) and adds an appropriate message to the label:

```
Private Sub cmdSelected_Click()
    If lstBBQ.ListIndex = -1 Then
        lblSelected.Caption = "No
        → item selected!"
    Else
        lblSelected.Caption =
        → "Something is selected!"
    End If
End Sub
```

4. Run the project.

When you click the button, the message that displays depends on whether an item is selected (**Figure 7.40**).

To display a single selected item:

1. Make sure the ListBox's MultiSelect property is set to 0 - None.

2. Using the Code Editor, edit the cmdSelected Click event code so that if something is selected, it is displayed:

```
lblSelected.Caption = lstBBQ.List
→ (lstBBQ.ListIndex)
```

3. Run the project.

If you select an item in the list and click the Any Selected button, the selected item is displayed (**Figure 7.41**).

✔ Tip

■ lstBBQ.ListIndex returns the index of the currently selected item in the list box. The List property returns the text of the item with the specified index. The complete code for the revised event procedure is shown in **Listing 7.5**.

To display multiple selected items:

1. Use the Properties window to make sure that the MultiSelect property of lstBBQ is set to 1 - Simple or 2 - Extended.

2. Add to the form a command button named cmdMulti and captioned Multiple Selection.

3. Add to the form a new ListBox named lstMulti (**Figure 7.42**).

4. Use the Code Editor to add code to cmdMulti's Click event procedure that starts by making sure that cmdMulti is empty:

   lstMulti.Clear

5. Next, add a For loop that runs through the items in lstBBQ:

   ```
   For I = 0 To lstBBQ.ListCount - 1
   Next I
   ```

6. Within the For loop, add code that adds each selected item in lstBBQ to lstMulti:

   ```
   If lstBBQ.Selected(I) Then
       lstMulti.AddItem lstBBQ.List(I)
   End If
   ```

7. Run the project.

8. Select some items in lstBBQ.

9. Click Multiple Selection.

   The items that you clicked now appear in the second list box (**Figure 7.43**).

Figure 7.42 The items selected in one ListBox are added to a new ListBox named lstMulti.

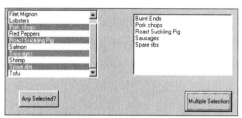

Figure 7.43 When you select multiple items and click the Multiple Selection button, all selected items are transferred to the new ListBox.

Listing 7.6 Adding Selected Items to a New ListBox

```
Code                                    _ □ ✕
Private Sub cmdMulti_Click()
    Dim I  As Integer
    lstMulti.Clear
    ' If an item is selected, add it to lstMulti
    For I = 0 To lstBBQ.ListCount - 1
        If lstBBQ.Selected(I) Then
            lstMulti.AddItem lstBBQ.List(I)
        End If
    Next I
End Sub
```

✔ **Tip**

■ A ListBox's ListCount property is the number of items in the box; the index of list items runs from 0 to ListCount - 1.

The complete code for the event procedure is shown in **Listing 7.6**.

Comments

Comments are added to code to help explain what is going on.

In Visual Basic, any line of code starting with a straight apostrophe is a comment. For example:

```
' I am a comment
' ********************************
' Program by Harold Davis.
```

Listing 7.6 has one comment:

```
' If an item is selected, add it to
→ lstMulti
```

Visual Basic ignores comments when it processes code, so you don't have to worry that adding comments will make your programs slower.

Although a good program should be written so that it is clear without explanation, if an explanation is needed, it is far better to put in a (possibly extraneous) comment than to leave a reader of your code guessing. Who knows? The person reading your code may be you at some point in the future.

LIST BOXES

Combo Boxes

A ComboBox control is like a ListBox combined with a TextBox. The user can choose an item from the ComboBox list or, alternatively, type in his own text.

There are three styles of ComboBoxes, which you set at design time by using the Properties window to set the Style property of the ComboBox to the appropriate value.

The *drop-down* ComboBox (Style = 0 - Dropdown Combo) is the default. In this style of ComboBox, the user can enter text directly, as in a TextBox, or click the arrow on the right side of the ComboBox to open a list of choices, which are inserted into the text portion of the box when selected (**Figure 7.44**).

A *simple* ComboBox (Style = 1 - Simple Combo) displays the list of items all the time, with no need for the user to click an arrow (**Figure 7.45**). You should be sure to draw the box large enough to hold the items that you want to display. A vertical scroll bar is inserted automatically if there are more list items than can be displayed in the space you've provided. In this style of ComboBox, like the drop-down ComboBox, the user can enter her own text rather than selecting a list item.

The *drop-down list* ComboBox (Style = 2 - Dropdown List) is actually a ListBox in disguise (**Figure 7.46**). This style of ComboBox behaves exactly like a ListBox, except that the list is not displayed until the arrow is clicked. The user *cannot* enter text. This style of ComboBox is used in place of a ListBox when screen real estate is tight.

To add a ComboBox to a form:

1. With your form open, select the ComboBox control in the Toolbox (**Figure 7.47**).

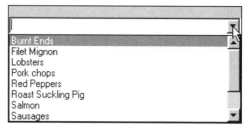

Figure 7.44 A drop-down ComboBox allows the user to enter text or make selections from a list of items by clicking the arrow.

Figure 7.45 A simple ComboBox works like a drop-down ComboBox, except that the list of items is always visible.

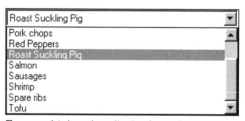

Figure 7.46 A drop-down list ComboBox is a space-saving version of a ListBox.

Figure 7.47 A ComboBox is added to a form via the Toolbox.

Listing 7.7 A Click Event Procedure That Adds All Items in a ListBox to a ComboBox

```
Private Sub cmdFillCombo_Click()
    Dim I As Integer
    For I = 0 To lstBBQ.ListCount - 1
        cmbBBQ.AddItem lstBBQ.List(I)
    Next I
End Sub
```

Figure 7.48 A drop-down ComboBox cannot be sized vertically on a form.

Figure 7.49 The Properties window is used to set the ComboBox's Style property.

Figure 7.50 A button captioned Fill Combo will be used to load ListBox items into the ComboBox.

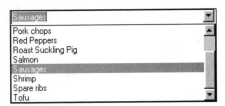

Figure 7.51 All the items that were in the ListBox have been loaded into the ComboBox.

2. Double-click (or drag and drop) the ComboBox to add it to the form.

In the default state, a ComboBox's Style property is set to drop-down, and it cannot be sized vertically on a form (**Figure 7.48**).

3. If you want to change the ComboBox's Style setting, use the Properties window to select the new setting (**Figure 7.49**).

4. Using the Properties window, name the ComboBox cmbBBQ.

To fill the ComboBox in code:

1. Add a command button to the form named cmdFillCombo and captioned Fill Combo (**Figure 7.50**).

2. Using the Code Editor, add code that loops through the existing ListBox and adds each ListBox item to the ComboBox (see **Listing 7.7**).

3. Run the project.

4. Click Fill Combo.

The items that were in the ListBox are added to the ComboBox (**Figure 7.51**).

✔ Tips

■ You can use the ComboBox's List property in the Properties window to add Combo list items manually.

■ You can use essentially the same code to add items from an array of text strings.

To display the ComboBox text:

1. Use the Toolbox to add a Label to the form.

   The Label will be used to display text that the user enters (or that she selects from the list of items).

2. Use the Properties window to change the Label's name to lblCombo and to delete its caption.

3. Make sure that the ComboBox's Style property is set to 0 or 1.

4. Open the Code Editor.

5. From the Objects list, choose cmbBBQ.

6. From the Procedures list, choose LostFocus.

   The LostFocus event is fired when the user moves to another control.

7. Within the LostFocus event framework, add code to display the ComboBox text in the label:

   ```
   Private Sub cmbBBQ_LostFocus()
       lblCombo.Caption = "Combo box
       → text is: " & cmbBBQ.Text
   End Sub
   ```

8. Run the project.

9. Click Fill Combo to load items into the ComboBox.

   When the ComboBox is first loaded, no text is displayed (**Figure 7.52**).

10. Double-click a list item to add it to the ComboBox's text area.

11. Press the Tab key to move to another control.

    The ComboBox text is displayed (**Figure 7.53**).

12. Go back to the ComboBox.

13. This time, enter text (Fried Chicken, for example).

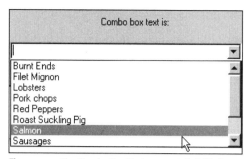

Figure 7.52 The ComboBox Text property is initially empty.

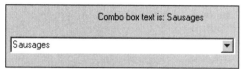

Figure 7.53 The ComboBox's LostFocus event is used to display the ComboBox's text.

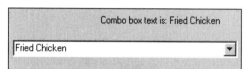

Figure 7.54 Text can be selected from the list or entered via the keyboard.

Listing 7.8 Displaying ComboBox Text, and Adding ComboBox Text to the List of Items

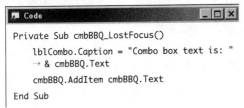

```
Private Sub cmbBBQ_LostFocus()

    lblCombo.Caption = "Combo box text is: "
    → & cmbBBQ.Text

    cmbBBQ.AddItem cmbBBQ.Text

End Sub
```

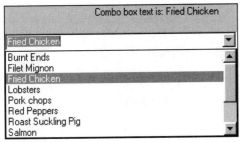

Figure 7.55 You can add the current ComboBox text to the list of items.

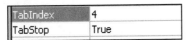

Figure 7.56 The TabIndex property determines where a control is positioned in the tab order.

14. Tab away from the ComboBox.

The text that you entered is displayed (**Figure 7.54**).

To add text entered in the ComboBox to the list of items:

1. Add the following line of code to the ComboBox's LostFocus event (see **Listing 7.8**):

```
cmbBBQ.AddItem cmbBBQ.Text
```

2. Run the project.

3. Fill the ComboBox.

4. Enter some text in the ComboBox's text area.

5. Tab away from the ComboControl.

The text that you entered is added to the list of items in the ComboBox (**Figure 7.55**).

Setting the Tab Order

Professional forms and dialogs need to be designed with the tab order in mind.

The tab order is the order in which controls receive the focus when the Tab key is used to navigate around a form.

Controls that cannot accept user input—such as a Frame or a Label—are not included in the tab order (because they never receive focus). In addition, a control that would otherwise be in the tab order can be removed from it by using the Properties window to set the control's TabStop property to False.

Controls that are in the tab order are ordered by their TabIndex. The lower the TabIndex, the earlier the control is in the tab order navigation. The first control in the tab order has a TabIndex of 0.

To change a control's position in the tab order, use the Properties window to change the control's TabIndex property (**Figure 7.56**).

Summary

In this chapter, you learned to:

- Add a CheckBox control to a form.
- Determine the state of checkboxes.
- Gray a checkbox.
- Add option groups to a frame.
- Determine which option in a group was selected.
- Concatenate two strings.
- Add option button arrays to a container.
- Determine the user's selection from an option button array.

- Code a For...Next loop.
- Work with ListBox controls.
- Determine the user's selections from ListBox controls.
- Display multiple ListBox selections.
- Use comments in code.
- Work with ComboBox controls.
- Set the TabIndex for a control.

STATUS BARS, TOOLBARS, AND TABBED DIALOGS

8

Status bars—implemented in Visual Basic via the StatusBar control—usually run along the bottom of an application window and provide information about the current status of the application.

Toolbars—implemented in Visual Basic with the Toolbar control—provide the user with access to an application's functionality via clickable buttons. Toolbars are often placed across the top of an application window but can also run along the sides or bottom. (Dockable toolbars are also quite popular but are not easily achieved with the Toolbar control. You can purchase third-party controls that allow you to easily add this functionality to your applications.)

Tabbed dialogs are a convenient and familiar visual interface metaphor for presenting groups of related material. The Learning Edition of Visual Basic ships with two Tab controls (described in this chapter). These two controls differ slightly, so I'll show you how to work with only the better of the two.

Status bars, toolbars, and tabbed dialogs together form the kernel of modern user interfaces. These controls are easy to add to your forms in Visual Basic. When you use them, your applications can have a sophisticated look and feel!

Property Pages

So far, I've shown you how to change control properties by using the Properties window, which is part of the Visual Basic design-time environment. Property pages—tabbed dialogs, with each tab representing a page of related properties uniquely associated with a control (**Figure 8.1**)—are another mechanism for working with properties in VB at design time.

It's important to understand that not all controls have property pages. In particular, the controls you have worked with up to this point in *Visual Basic: Visual QuickStart Guide*—all intrinsic VB controls—do come equipped with property pages.

In addition, for those controls that do have property pages, not all properties are accessible through them. Usually, control property pages represent a way to manipulate properties beyond those present in the Properties window (although there can be some overlap, with property settings appearing both in property pages and in the Properties window).

You can take your choice among a number of ways of opening a control's property pages.

To open a control's property pages directly:

To open the property pages, *do one of the following*:

◆ With a control selected, from the View menu, choose Property Pages.

◆ With a control selected, press Shift+F4.

◆ Right-click the control, and choose Properties from the pop-up menu.

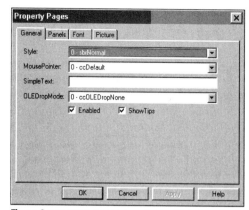

Figure 8.1 property pages are a tabbed interface for many of a control's properties—with each page representing a grouping of related properties.

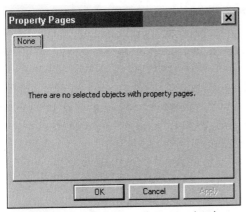

Figure 8.2 Many controls do not have associated property pages.

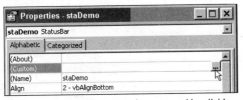

Figure 8.3 property pages can be accessed by clicking the ellipsis on the right side of the control's (Custom) property in the Properties window.

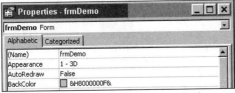

Figure 8.4 The (Custom) property appears in the Properties window only if the control has property pages.

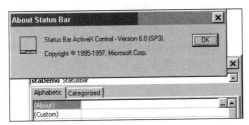

Figure 8.5 Controls with a (Custom) property usually also have an (About) property, which provides authorship and version information.

✔ Tip

- If the control has no property pages, the first two approaches cause an empty property pages dialog to open, displaying the statement "There are no selected objects with property pages" (**Figure 8.2**). Right-clicking a control that has no property pages and then choosing Properties from the pop-up menu opens the Properties window.

To open a control's property pages from the Properties window:

1. Open the Properties window.

2. From the drop-down list at the top of the Properties window, select the control.

3. From the top of the Alphabetic properties list, choose the (Custom) property (**Figure 8.3**).

4. Click the ellipsis on the right side of the Properties window.

   The property pages for the control open.

✔ Tips

- Objects that do not have associated property pages do not have a (Custom) property in the Properties window (**Figure 8.4**).

- The (About) property is also not one that all controls have. Clicking (About), if it is present, provides authorship and version information about the control (**Figure 8.5**).

PROPERTY PAGES

Status Bars

Status bars give your applications that well-dressed look. In addition, the status bar can be a good place to put information that helps users of your application keep track of program options they have selected.

One kind of application interface that almost cried out for a status bar is the Multiple Document Interface (see Chapter 5).

Because the StatusBar control is not an intrinsic control, it may not be preloaded in your Toolbox. Before showing you how to use the StatusBar control, I'll show you how to add it to your Toolbox, if it isn't present.

You can configure a StatusBar as one long panel. But it's more usual to create a StatusBar that consists of a group of panels. In large part, working with StatusBars means working with the panel objects of the StatusBar.

To add the StatusBar control to your Toolbox:

1. Check to see whether the StatusBar control appears in your Toolbox.

   Figure 8.6 shows the Toolbox for a default Visual Basic project with no StatusBar control.

2. If the StatusBar is not loaded, from the Project menu, choose Components, or right-click the Toolbox and choose Components from the pop-up menu.

   The Components dialog opens (**Figure 8.7**).

3. In the Controls tab, scroll down until you see Microsoft Windows Common Controls 6.0.

4. Check the box next to Microsoft Windows Common Controls 6.0 to enable this group of controls.

Figure 8.6 The StatusBar control is not preloaded in the default Visual Basic project.

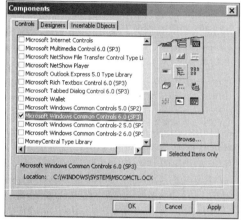

Figure 8.7 Enable the Windows Common Controls in the Components dialog to add the StatusBar to your Toolbox.

Figure 8.8 When the StatusBar has been added to your project via the Components dialog, it appears in the Toolbox.

Figure 8.9 It's easy to draw a StatusBar the width of a fixed-size form.

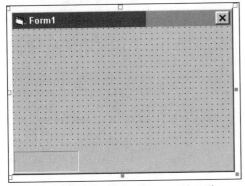

Figure 8.10 By default, a status bar runs along the bottom of the form.

Figure 8.11 You can change the StatusBar's alignment by setting its Align property in the Properties window.

5. Click Apply or OK to close the Components dialog.

The Windows Common Controls, including the StatusBar, are added to your Toolbox (**Figure 8.8**).

✔ Tip

- You may notice in **Figure 8.7** that Microsoft Windows Common Controls 6.0 is listed as SP3. SP3 is short for Service Pack 3, which was the most recent Visual Basic Service Pack at the time this book went to press. You should always make sure that you are working with the current Visual Basic Service Pack, which can be downloaded for free from www.microsoft.com/vb/.

To add a StatusBar to a form:

1. Use the Properties window to set the BorderStyle of your form to 1 - Fixed Single (**Figure 8.9**).

It's easier to construct a status bar for a form when the user can't change the size of the form (although code can be added that resizes the status bar when a user resizes the form).

2. With the form open, double-click the StatusBar control in the Toolbox to add it to the form.

The StatusBar now appears along the bottom of the form, with one panel (**Figure 8.10**).

3. Use the Properties window to name the StatusBar "staDemo" (**Figure 8.11**).

✔ Tip

- Note that the Align property of the StatusBar is set to the default, 2 - vbAlignBottom. If you wanted to run a status bar along the top or sides of a form, you would change this property.

To configure the first panel:

1. Open the property pages for the StatusBar.

2. Click the Panels tab (**Figure 8.12**).

   The default panel Style property setting is 0 -sbrText, meaning that the panel displays text. We will use this panel to show whether Caps Lock is on.

3. Use the drop-down list to set the Style property to 1 -sbrCaps (Figure **8.12**).

   See **Table 8.1** for the possible panel Style values.

4. The Text property is ignored unless the Style property is set to 0 -sbrText, so leave the Text field empty.

5. In the ToolTip Text field, enter Is the Caps Lock key on?

   This text is displayed when the user runs her mouse across the panel.

6. Click Apply or OK.

7. Run the project.

   The panel displays CAPS in bold if Caps Lock is on; otherwise, CAPS is grayed. In addition, the ToolTip text you specified is displayed (**Figure 8.13**).

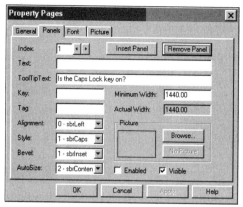

Figure 8.12 The Panels tab of the StatusBar property pages is used to configure the StatusBar panels.

Figure 8.13 CAPS appears in bold if Caps Lock is enabled.

Table 8.1

Panel Style Property Values

Value and Constant	Description
0 - sbrText	Default; panel displays text.
1 - sbrCaps	Displays CAPS in bold when Caps Lock is enabled and grayed when disabled.
2 - sbrNum	Displays NUM in bold when Num Lock is enabled and grayed when disabled.
3 - sbrIns	Displays INS in bold when Insert mode is enabled and grayed when disabled.
4 - sbrScrl	Displays SCRL in bold when Scroll Lock is enabled and grayed when disabled.
5 - sbrTime	Displays the current time, using the system format.
6 - sbrDate	Displays the current date, using the system format.
7 - sbrKana	Displays KANA in bold when Scroll Lock is enabled and grayed when disabled.

STATUS BARS

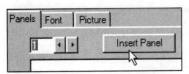

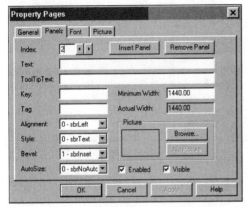

Figure 8.14 The Insert Panel button is used to add panels to the StatusBar.

Figure 8.15 The Index buttons are used to navigate between panels.

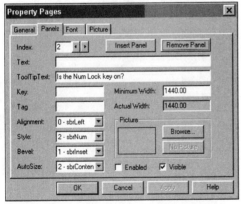

Figure 8.16 If the Style is set to 2 - strNum, NUM appears in bold is Num Lock is engaged.

To add StatusBar panels:

1. With the Panels tab of the StatusBar property pages open, click the Insert Panel button (**Figure 8.14**).

   A new panel is added, but the panel shown is still the first panel.

2. Click the right arrow to the right of the Index box to move to the second panel.

   The Index box now shows the panel index to be 2 (**Figure 8.15**).

3. Set Style property of the second panel to 2 - sbrNum (**Figure 8.16**).

4. Set the ToolTip Text field to Is the Num Lock key on?

5. Click Apply or OK.

   When you run the project, the second panel displays NUM in bold when Num Lock is enabled and NUM in gray if it is not.

To add a text panel:

1. Click the Insert Panel button to add another panel.

2. Click the arrow button to the right of the Index box to move to the third panel.

3. Leave the third panel's Style property set to the default, 0 - sbrText (**Figure 8.17**).

4. Set the panel Alignment property to 1 - sbrCenter.

   This aligns the text in the middle of the panel.

5. Add text to display in the Panel's Text property—for example, Hello, Panel fans!

6. Add ToolTip text for the panel—for example, Your text can go here!

7. Click Apply or OK.

8. Run the project.

   The text you specified is displayed in the panel.

9. Pause your mouse over the panel.

   The ToolTip text you specified appears (**Figure 8.18**).

Time and Date Panels

You can easily add panels that display the current time and date.

To add time and date panels:

1. Click the Insert Panel button to add another panel.

2. Click the arrow button to the right of the Index box to move to the fourth panel.

3. Change the fourth panel's Style property to 5 - sbrTime (**Figure 8.19**).

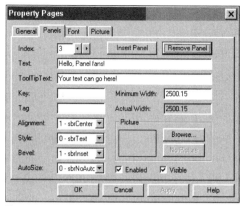

Figure 8.17 A panel's Alignment property determines where on the panel contents appear.

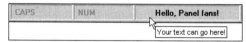

Figure 8.18 You can use the 0 - sbrText panel Style setting to send text messages to users.

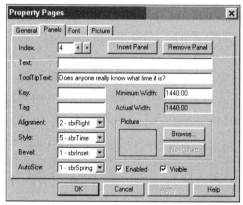

Figure 8.19 If the Style property is set to 5 -sbrTime, the current time displays in the panel.

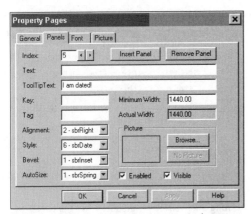

Figure 8.20 If the Style property is set to 6 -sbrDate, the current date displays in the panel.

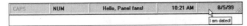

Figure 8.21 The five StatusBar panels display different information.

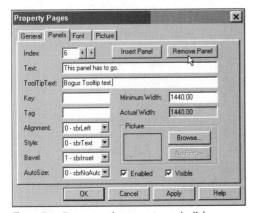

Figure 8.22 To remove the current panel, click Remove Panel.

4. Set the panel Alignment property to 2 -sbrRight.

   This aligns the time in the right of the panel.

5. Add ToolTip text for the panel—for example, Does anyone really know what time it is?

6. Click Apply.

7. Click the Insert Panel button to add another panel.

8. Click the arrow button to the right of the Index box to move to the fifth panel.

9. Change the fourth panel's Style property to 6 - sbrDate (**Figure 8.20**).

10. Set the panel Alignment property to 2 -sbrRight.

    This aligns the time in the right of the panel.

11. Add ToolTip text for the panel—for example, I am dated!

12. Click OK.

13. Run the project.

    The StatusBar displays all five panels (**Figure 8.21**).

To remove a panel:

1. In the Panels tab of the StatusBar property pages, use the Index field and tabs to navigate to the panel you want to remove.

2. Click the Remove Panel button (**Figure 8.22**).

   The panel is removed, and you return to the first panel.

STATUS BARS

Now You See It, Now You Don't!

Many interfaces allow the user to decide whether she wants to see a status bar. This is called *toggling the status bar*. It is most easily achieved in code, via the Visible property of the StatusBar object. A StatusBar whose Visible property is set to True is drawn on the screen. If the Visible property is set to False, although the StatusBar is present in memory it is not apparent on the screen.

To toggle a StatusBar:

1. Use the Code Editor to add code to a user-initiated Click event (the form Click event is shown in **Listing 8.1**) that sets the StatusBar Visible property to False if it is True and True if it is false (in other words, the current state is reverse).

2. Run the project. You see the status bar.

3. Click the form. The status bar disappears.

4. Click the form again. The status bar reappears.

Resizing the Status Bar

So far, the StatusBar has been placed on a form that the user cannot resize. Things get a bit more complex if we allow the user to resize the form—and expect the status bar to still occupy the entire inside bottom width of the form.

With a bit of trial and error, it's pretty easy to add code that accomplishes this. The example works with the five panel StatusBar developed earlier in this section and assumes that the middle (third) panel that is used to display text is the only panel that will shrink or expand when the user changes the width of the form.

The code that handles resizing the StatusBar panels is placed in the Resize event of the form, which is fired every time the user changes the size of the form. That code is shown in **Listing 8.2**.

Listing 8.1 Toggling a StatusBar

```
Private Sub Form_Click()
    If staDemo.Visible = True Then
        staDemo.Visible = False
    Else
        staDemo.Visible = True
    End If
End Sub
```

Listing 8.2 Resizing a StatusBar When the User Resizes a Form

```
Private Sub Form_Resize()
    If frmDemo.Width < 6300 Then
        frmDemo.Width = 6300
        'Use trial and error to find this
        'number
    End If

    staDemo.Panels(3).Width = _
        frmDemo.ScaleWidth - _
        (staDemo.Width -
        ➝ staDemo.Panels(3).Width)
End Sub
```

STATUS BARS

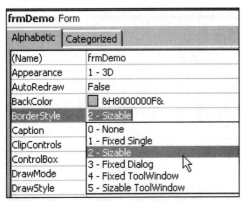

Figure 8.23 Before the user can resize a window, the form must be set so that it is resizable.

Figure 8.24 The status bar extends horizontally with the form.

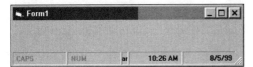

Figure 8.25 The status bar contracts only up to a point.

✔ Tip

■ The exact form width that works depends on the dimensions of your form and the panels in the status bar. It is best found by trial and error by adding the command

```
debug.print frmDemo.Width
```

to your code. This shows the current value for the form width in the Immediate Window when you run the project.

To resize the StatusBar along with the form:

1. Use the Properties window to set the form's BorderStyle to 2 -Sizable (**Figure 8.23**).

2. Use the Code Editor to add to the form's Resize event code that makes the width of the third panel whatever interior form width has not been used by the rest of the panel:

```
staDemo.Panels(3).Width =
→ frmDemo.ScaleWidth -
→ (staDemo.Width -
→ staDemo.Panels(3).Width)
```

3. The code the resizes the third panel works if the user makes the form bigger, but runs into problems if the form gets small enough that the fourth and fifth panels disappear. So add code to make sure this cannot happen:

```
If frmDemo.Width < 6300 Then
    frmDemo.Width = 6300
    'Use trial and error to find
    'this number
End If
```

4. Run the project.

5. Elongate the form.

   The StatusBar's third panel expands horizontally with the form (**Figure 8.24**).

6. Shrink the width of the form.

   You'll see that the third panel shrinks with the form but doesn't shrink beyond the point you set in code (**Figure 8.25**).

Toolbars

Toolbars are used to present buttons to the user. Generally, the user can click toolbar buttons instead of choosing menu items.

The Toolbar control that ships with Visual Basic includes a great deal of user interface capability. This control is a pretty powerful piece of work!

To add buttons to a toolbar, you need to use it in conjunction with a linked ImageList control, which functions as a kind of image library. The ImageList control is added to your form and used to store images, but it is invisible at run time to the users of your application.

You often see a toolbar and a StatusBar forming an interface together, particularly as part of a Multiple Document Interface application.

To add a toolbar to your form:

1. Make sure that the Toolbar control is loaded in your Toolbox.

    If it is not, follow the procedure in "To add the StatusBar control to your Toolbox" earlier in this chapter. (The Toolbar is also included in the Microsoft Windows Common Controls group.)

2. Make sure that a form is open.

3. Double-click the Toolbar control in your Toolbox (**Figure 8.26**).

    A toolbar is added to the form.

4. Use the Toolbar property pages to set the toolbar's BorderStyle to 1 - ccFixedSingle (**Figure 8.27**).

5. Use the Properties window to name the toolbar "tbrDemo" (**Figure 8.28**).

6. Run the project.

    You see the toolbar aligned at the top of the form (**Figure 8.29**).

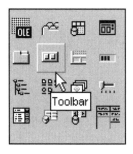

Figure 8.26 Double-click the Toolbar icon in the Toolbox to add it to your form.

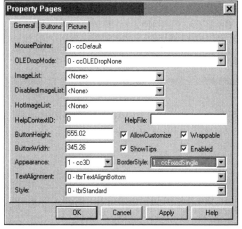

Figure 8.27 Setting the toolbar's border to FixedSingle means that all the toolbar will be visible on a form, even if it has no buttons.

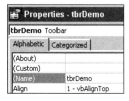

Figure 8.28 The Properties window is used to name the toolbar.

Figure 8.29 When the project is run, the toolbar appears along the top of the form.

Figure 8.30 Double-click the ImageList control to add it to your form.

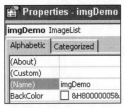

Figure 8.31 The ImageList appears at design time on your form but does not show at run time.

Properties - imgDemo

imgDemo ImageList

Alphabetic	Categorized
(About)	
(Custom)	
(Name)	imgDemo
BackColor	&H80000005&

Figure 8.32
The Properties window is used to name the ImageList.

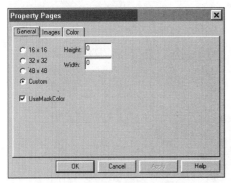

Figure 8.33 When the property pages for the ImageList opens, the General tab is selected.

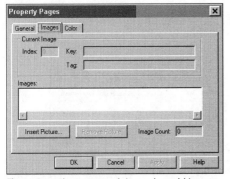

Figure 8.34 The Images tab is used to add images.

To add an ImageList to your form:

◆ Double-click the ImageList control in the Toolbox (**Figure 8.30**).

It is added to your form (**Figure 8.31**).

✔ Tips

■ Although you can see a representation of the ImageList control on a form at design time, this control does not appear visually at run time. It functions as a behind-the-scenes image librarian.

■ The ImageList is part of the same controls group as the Toolbar, so if the Toolbar is loaded in your Toolbox, you also have the ImageList control ready to be used.

To load the ImageList with images:

1. Use the Properties window to change the name of the ImageList to imgDemo (**Figure 8.32**).

2. Open the property pages for the ImageList.

   You see the General tab (**Figure 8.33**).

3. Click the Images tab (**Figure 8.34**).

continues on next page

4. Click Insert Picture.

The Select Picture dialog opens (**Figure 8.35**).

5. Select an image file.

6. Click Open.

A representation of the image you selected appears in the Images tab (**Figure 8.36**).

7. Repeat the process of adding an image as many times as you want.

8. When you have the correct number of images in the ImageList (**Figure 8.37**), click OK.

✔ Tips

■ After you have loaded images into the ImageList, you can no longer change the size of those images in the control (**Figure 8.38**). You have to remove all the images before you can change the image size. So it really pays to figure out what size image you want to use before you start loading them into the control.

■ This section shows icon files being loaded into the ImageList. It's normal to use smaller graphics for toolbars.

■ Visual Basic ships with a large library of pictures—including icon files and button bitmaps—that you can use in a toolbar. You'll find these files in C:\Program Files\ Microsoft Visual Studio\Common\ Graphics. If you didn't install these files when you installed Visual Basic, you may have to rerun the installation program to get them installed.

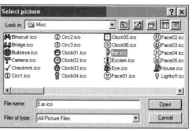

Figure 8.35 Picture files are inserted from the file system.

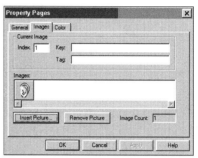

Figure 8.36 The Images tab shows the image that has been added to the ImageList library.

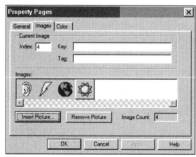

Figure 8.37 All the pictures in the ImageList library are displayed in the Images tab.

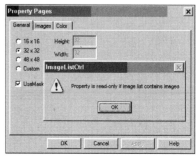

Figure 8.38 You cannot resize images after they have been added to the ImageList.

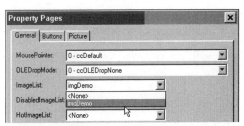

Figure 8.39 The ImageList property of the toolbar is used to link an ImageList with the toolbar.

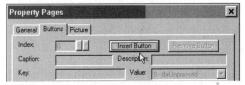

Figure 8.40 The Buttons page is used to add pictures to the toolbar.

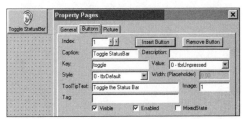

Figure 8.41 Pictures are linked to the toolbar by their order in the ImageList.

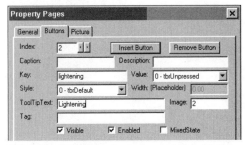

Figure 8.42 Each picture in the ImageList is added as a button to the toolbar.

Figure 8.43 All the buttons that have been added are present on the toolbar when the project is run.

To link the toolbar to the ImageList:

1. Open the property pages for the toolbar.

2. In the General tab, use the drop-down list to set the ImageList property to the name of the ImageList (imgDemo) (**Figure 8.39**).

To add buttons to the toolbar:

1. With the property pages for the toolbar open, select the Buttons tab (**Figure 8.40**).

   Notice that the Index field is grayed.

2. Click Insert Picture.

   The Index field is now active.

3. In the Image field, put the number of the picture in the ImageList (1 for the first ImageList picture, and so on).

4. Tab away from the field.

   A button with first ImageList picture appears in the toolbar (**Figure 8.41**).

5. Add a caption if you want text to appear on the button—for example, `Toggle StatusBar`.

6. Add a name to the Key field that will be used to reference the button in code— for example, `toggle`.

7. Add ToolTip text, if you want—for example, `Toggle the Status Bar`.

8. Click Apply.

9. Click Insert Picture, and repeat the process for the second button (**Figure 8.42**).

10. Repeat the process for each of the buttons that will be in the toolbar.

11. Run the project.

    Your toolbar, with all the buttons you added, appears along the top of the form (**Figure 8.43**).

TOOLBARS

To customize a running toolbar:

With the form running, double-click the toolbar.

The Customize Toolbar dialog opens (**Figure 8.44**).

To add code to toolbar buttons:

1. Open the Code Editor.

2. From the Objects List, choose Toolbar.

3. From the Procedures List, choose ButtonClick.

4. Add to the toolbar's ButtonClick event code that uses the Key property of each button to take an action. The action will depend on what button was clicked (see **Listing 8.3**).

   Clicking the toggle button, for example, toggles the StatusBar. And clicking the lightning button causes the phrase "Thunder and lightning!" to appear in the third panel of the StatusBar (**Figure 8.45**).

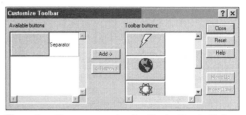

Figure 8.44 Users can customize the toolbar to their own taste.

Figure 8.45 The ButtonClick event of the toolbar is used to initiate actions when buttons are clicked. Individual buttons are identified by their Key property.

Listing 8.3 Wiring a Toolbar

```
Private Sub tbrDemo_ButtonClick(ByVal Button As MSComctlLib.Button)
    ' Use the Key property with the SelectCase statement to specify
    ' an action.
    Select Case Button.Key
    Case Is = "toggle"        ' Toggle status bar
        If staDemo.Visible = True Then
            staDemo.Visible = False
        Else
            staDemo.Visible = True
        End If
    Case Is = "lightening"        ' Display text
        staDemo.Panels(3).Text = "Thunder and lightening!"
    Case Is = "earth"        ' Display text
        staDemo.Panels(3).Text = "The earth is our mother!"
    Case Is = "sun"          ' Display text
        staDemo.Panels(3).Text = "Sunshine is good for all living things!"
    End Select
End Sub
```

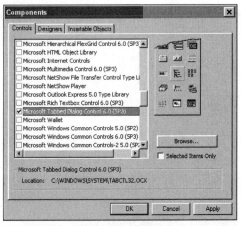

Figure 8.46 The SSTab is identified in the Components dialog as the Microsoft Tabbed Dialog Control.

Tab Controls

Tab controls are used to create tabbed dialogs. In a tabbed dialog, the user clicks a tab to open different pages.

You can use tabbed dialogs not only to save space but also to intelligently group related controls, with each group on its own page.

An example of a tabbed dialog that you've seen in this chapter is the property pages interface.

Visual Basic Learning Edition ships with two Tab controls. The TabStrip control is part of the Microsoft Windows Common Controls 6.0 group. The other Tab control, the SSTab, is listed in the Components dialog as Microsoft Tabbed Dialog Control 6.0.

The SSTab was originally written by Sheridan Software, and it is easier to use than the TabStrip (though, frankly, when you've seen one Tab control, you've pretty much seen them all). In this section, I'll walk you through the basics of using the SSTab.

To add the SSTab to your Toolbox:

1. From the Project menu, choose Components.
   The Controls tab of the Components dialog opens.

2. Check the Microsoft Tabbed Dialog Control checkbox (**Figure 8.46**).

3. Click OK or Apply to close the dialog.
   The SSTab is added to your Toolbox.

Select Case Statements

The Select Case statement is used extensively in Visual Basic code. This statement causes execution to branch depending on the first Case condition it encounters that evaluates to True.

Anything that can be written using Select Case statements can also be written using If statements—and vice versa. The great virtue of Select Case statements is that—compared with a series of nested If statements—they are easy to read. It's much easier to determine what is really going on. When code is clear, it is less prone to bugs.

Is Operator

The Is operator is used to determine whether two objects are the same. If A and B are objects, A Is B evaluates to True if they are the same and False if they are not.

To add the SSTab to a form:

1. With your form open, double-click the SSTab in the Toolbox (**Figure 8.47**).

   The SSTab is added to your form (**Figure 8.48**).

2. Use the SSTab's handles to position and size the tab control.

To configure the Tab control:

1. Use the Properties window to change the name of the Tab control to tabDemo (**Figure 8.49**).

2. Open the property pages for tabDemo (**Figure 8.50**).

   You'll find a great many configuration options.

Changing Tab Names

When you add a SSTab to the form, it comes by default with three tabs, named Tab 0, Tab 1, and Tab 2. You will certainly want to change these names. Also, you can easily use the Tab's property pages to add new tabs.

To change the default tab names:

1. Open the General tab of tabDemo's property pages.

   Tab 0 is the current tab.

2. Change the TabCaption to whatever you want—for example, Yes (**Figure 8.51**).

3. Click Apply.

4. Click the right arrow below Current Tab to move to Tab 1.

5. Change the TabCaption for the second tab to whatever you ant—for example, No.

Figure 8.47 Double-click the SSTab to add it to your form.

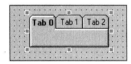

Figure 8.48 When the Tab control has been added to your form it can be sized and positioned.

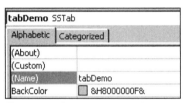

Figure 8.49 The Properties window is used to name the Tab.

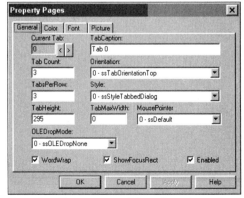

Figure 8.50 There are many Tab configuration options available in its property pages.

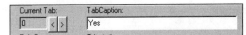

Figure 8.51 The TabCaption property changes the name of a tab.

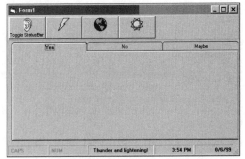

Figure 8.52 You can click between the tab pages.

6. Click Apply.

7. Click the right arrow below Current Tab to move to Tab 2.

8. Change the TabCaption for the third tab to whatever you want—for example, Maybe.

9. Click OK.

10. Run the project.

All three tabs are displayed with their new captions (**Figure 8.52**).

Adding Controls to the Tab Pages

Adding controls to the tab pages in the design-time environment is a simple matter of clicking a tab and drawing the control on the tab. Controls placed on different tabs in this fashion are referred to in code in the normal fashion.

To add controls to tab pages:

1. Add a TextBox control to the first tab page, the Yes tab.

2. Use the Properties window to name the TextBox txtStory.

3. In the Properties window, set the MultiLine property of txtStory to True (**Figure 8.53**).

   The text box now can display many lines of text.

4. Use the drop-down box next to the Text property in the Properties window to add some text to txtStory (**Figure 8.54**).

   The text entered in the Properties window appears on the Yes tab in the design environment (**Figure 8.55**) and when you run the form (**Figure 8.56**).

5. Stop the form from running so as to return to the design-time environment.

6. Click the No tab to add a control to that tab.

7. Add a Command Button to the No tab.

8. Use the Properties window to name the Command Button cmdClear and caption it Clear.

9. Use the Code Editor to add to the cmdClear Click event code that will clear txtStory:

```
Private Sub cmdClear_Click()
    txtStory.Text = ""
End Sub
```

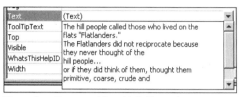

Figure 8.53 If a TextBox's MultiLine property is True, the TextBox displays many lines of text.

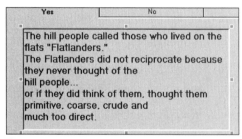

Figure 8.54 You can add multiple lines of text to a MultiLine TextBox via the Text drop-down list in the Properties window.

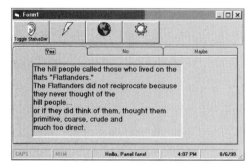

Figure 8.55 Text entered in the Properties window appears on the first tab at design time...

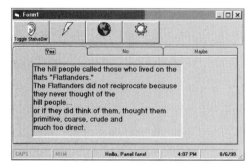

Figure 8.56 ...and also appears on the tab at run time.

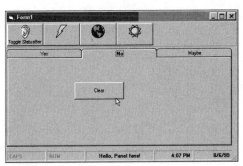

Figure 8.57 You can click a tab to see the controls on a tab page.

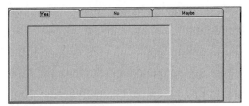

Figure 8.58 Controls on one tab page can reference the controls on another tab page.

10. Click the Yes tab.

11. Run the project.
The Yes page of the Tab control appears.

12. Click the No tab.
You see the Clear button (**Figure 8.57**).

13. Click the Clear button to clear the text on the Yes tab.

14. Click the Yes tab.
The text is cleared (**Figure 8.58**).

Summary

In this chapter, you learned to:

- Work with property pages.
- Add the StatusBar control to your Toolbox.
- Add a StatusBar to a form.
- Configure StatusBar panels.
- Use different panel styles.
- Add text to a panel.
- Add time and date panels.
- Toggle a status bar.

- Resize a status bar.
- Add a Toolbar control.
- Add an ImageList control.
- Work with the ImageList control.
- Link a Toolbar and an ImageList.
- Add buttons to the toolbar.
- Add code to the toolbar buttons.
- Use the Select Case statement.
- Work with the SSTab control.

TAB CONTROLS

THE COMMON DIALOG CONTROL

9

The Common Dialog control is used to provide familiar Windows dialogs for your users. Essentially, this control provides an easy way for you to use dialogs that are already built into the Windows operating system.

You can use seven dialogs (plus a few variants) with the control. Each dialog is invoked with a call in code to a different method of the common dialog control. The dialogs are:

- **Color,** invoked with the ShowColor method, which allows the user to select a color.

- **Font,** invoked with the ShowFont method, which allows the user to select a font.

- **Help,** invoked with the ShowHelp method, which starts the Windows Help Engine.

- **Open,** invoked with the ShowOpen method, which lets the user choose a file to open from the file system.

- **Print,** invoked with the ShowPrint method, which displays the Print or Print Options dialog.

- **Save,** invoked with the ShowSave method, which lets the user select a file name and location.

It is important to understand that the dialogs invoked with the different methods of the Common Dialog control don't actually *do* anything. Rather, they present a familiar interface that lets the user select something. It is up to you to do the wiring necessary to make something happen with the user's selection.

Each of the dialogs that the control presents can be configured with property pages or with property assignments in code. The results—what the dialog displays—are the same either way. It probably makes more sense to do all the work in code, however, because some code is necessary no matter when you use the Common Dialog control.

In this chapter, I'll show you how to configure the common Color dialog by using the control's Property Pages. (As I've said, it does take code to actually change an object's color by using the dialog's results.)

The rest of the examples in the chapter use code and not Property Pages to configure the common dialogs.

Next, I'll show you how to use code to change the underlying font for text in a RichTextBox control. (The RichTextBox control is like the TextBox control but with extended font and formatting capabilities.) You'll also learn how to change the properties of selected text in the RichTextBox.

Finally, I'll show you the code needed to use the file Open and Save dialogs to get file names from the user and to open and save the contents of the RichTextBox control to the Windows file system.

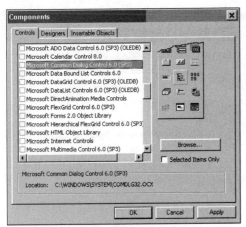

Figure 9.1 The Components dialog is used to add the Common Dialog control to your Toolbox.

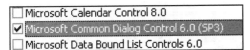

Figure 9.2 Enable the Common Dialog control to add it to your project.

Figure 9.3 Double-click the Common Dialog control to add it to your form.

Figure 9.4 The Common Dialog control cannot be resized and does not display at run time.

The Common Dialog Control

If the Common Dialog control has not already been loaded in your Toolbox, you need to add it. When the control is loaded in the Toolbox, you can add it to a form.

To add the Common Dialog control to your Toolbox:

1. From the Project menu, choose Components.

   The Components dialog opens (**Figure 9.1**).

2. In the Controls tab, scroll down to he Microsoft Common Dialog Control 6.0.

3. Check the checkbox on the left side of the dialog to enable the control (**Figure 9.2**).

4. Click OK, or click Apply and Close.

   The Common Dialog control is added to your Toolbox.

To add the Common Dialog control to a form:

1. Select the Common Dialog control in the Toolbox (**Figure 9.3**).

2. Double-click to add the control to your form (**Figure 9.4**).

✔ Tips

- The Common Dialog control cannot be resized and does not display at run time. It doesn't matter where you put it on a form—so place it where it won't get in your way when you are drawing other controls on the form.

- Enabling CancelError provides a way to determine whether the user clicked Cancel in the dialog—something you may want to know so that you can take additional programmatic steps.

THE COMMON DIALOG CONTROL

The Color Dialog

The Color dialog can be used to obtain a color selection from the user. You can use the color obtained from the user to reset the color for any object that has a color property that can be set dynamically (at run time, for example).

In this section, I show you how to use the Color dialog to obtain a color value that is used to set the BackColor property of a form. In other words, the user can reset the form's color as often as she wants.

The complete code for the event procedure that changes the form's BackColor property is shown in **Listing 9.1**.

To add a button to invoke the Color dialog:

1. Double-click the CommandButton control in the Toolbox to add it to the form.

2. Use the Properties window to change its caption to Change Color and its name to cmdColor (**Figure 9.5**).

3. Position and size the command button on the form (**Figure 9.6**).

To set the Color dialog using Property Pages:

1. Make sure that a Common Dialog control has been added to the form, and accept the Common Dialog control's default name, CommonDialog1.

2. Right-click the Common Dialog control, and choose Properties from the pop-up menu.

   The Common Dialog Property Pages opens (**Figure 9.7**).

3. Check the CancelError checkbox.

4. Click OK.

Listing 9.1 Using ShowColor

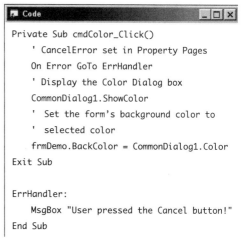

```
Private Sub cmdColor_Click()
    ' CancelError set in Property Pages
    On Error GoTo ErrHandler
    ' Display the Color Dialog box
    CommonDialog1.ShowColor
    ' Set the form's background color to
    ' selected color
    frmDemo.BackColor = CommonDialog1.Color
Exit Sub

ErrHandler:
    MsgBox "User pressed the Cancel button!"
End Sub
```

Figure 9.5 The Properties window is used to name and caption the command button that will launch the Color dialog.

Figure 9.6 When the command button has been added to the form, it can be positioned and sized.

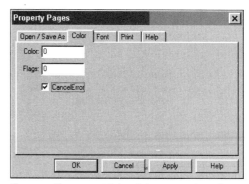

Figure 9.7 You can set Color dialog properties using the Common Dialog control's Property Pages.

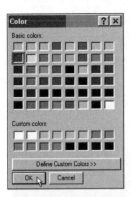

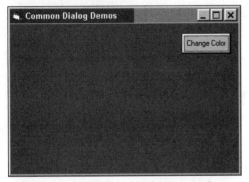

Figure 9.8 The Color dialog allows the user to select a color.

Figure 9.9 The color selected by the user sets the BackColor property of the running form.

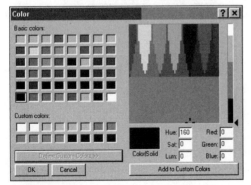

Figure 9.10 The user can access the Custom Color dialog through the Color dialog.

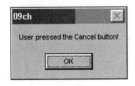

Figure 9.11 You can add code to detect user cancellation of the dialog.

To invoke the Color dialog:

1. Open the Code Editor.

2. Choose cmdColor from the Objects List.

3. Choose Click from the Procedures List. The cmdColor Click event procedure is created.

4. Add a line of code that processes errors: On Error GoTo ErrHandler

5. Add a line of code that displays the Color dialog:

   ```
   CommonDialog1.ShowColor
   ```

6. Change the form's BackColor property depending on the color selected:

   ```
   frmDemo.BackColor =
   → CommonDialog1.Color
   ```

7. Add code to handle error processing:

   ```
   Exit Sub
   ErrHandler:
       MsgBox "User pressed the Cancel
       → button!"
   ```

8. Run the project.

9. Click Change Color. The Color dialog opens (**Figure 9.8**).

10. Select a color.

11. Click OK. The form's color changes (**Figure 9.9**).

✔ Tips

■ The user can expand the Color dialog to select custom colors by clicking Define Custom Colors in the Color dialog (**Figure 9.10**).

■ The error-handling portion of the procedure is used to see whether the user clicked Cancel (**Figure 9.11**).

The Font Dialog

In this section, I show you how to use the Font dialog to change the overall font for text entered in a RichTextBox control.

The RichTextBox control is an extended version of the TextBox control. You can use the RichTextBox to achieve a great deal of formatting and to open and save files in Rich Text Format (RTF).

The complete event procedure code for invoking the Font dialog is shown in **Listing 9.2.**

To add a button to invoke the Font dialog:

1. Double-click the CommandButton control in the Toolbox to add it to the form.

2. Use the Properties window to change its caption to Change Font and its name to cmdFont.

3. Position and size the command button on the form (**Figure 9.12**).

Figure 9.12 The Change Font button will be used to change the RichTextBox's font.

Listing 9.2 Using ShowFont

```
Private Sub cmdFont_Click()
    ' Set Cancel to True
    CommonDialog1.CancelError = True
    On Error GoTo ErrHandler
    ' Set the Flags property
    CommonDialog1.Flags = cdlCFBoth
    ' Display the Font dialog box
    CommonDialog1.ShowFont
    RichTextBox1.Font.Name = CommonDialog1.FontName
    RichTextBox1.Font.Size = CommonDialog1.FontSize
    RichTextBox1.Font.Bold = CommonDialog1.FontBold
    RichTextBox1.Font.Italic = CommonDialog1.FontItalic
    Exit Sub

ErrHandler:
    ' User pressed the Cancel button
    Exit Sub
End Sub
```

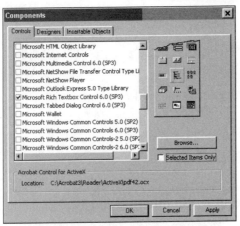

Figure 9.13 To add the RichTextBox to your Toolbox, enable it in the Components dialog.

Figure 9.14 Double-click the RichTextBox control to add it to your form.

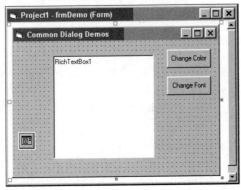

Figure 9.15 Size and position the RichTextBox control on your form.

To add the RichTextBox control to your Toolbox:

1. From the Project menu, choose Components.

   The Components dialog opens (**Figure 9.13**).

2. On the Controls tab, scroll down to the Microsoft Rich Textbox Control 6.0.

3. Check the checkbox on the left side of the dialog to enable the control.

4. Click OK, or click Apply and Close.

   The RichTextBox control is added to your Toolbox.

To add a RichTextBox control to your form:

1. With a form open, select the RichTextBox control in the Toolbox (**Figure 9.14**).

2. Double-click, or drag and drop, to add the control to the form.

3. Size and position the control on the form (**Figure 9.15**).

✔ Tip

■ In the example, the default name for an instance of the RichTextBox control, RichTextBox1, is used.

THE FONT DIALOG

To invoke the Font dialog:

1. Open the Code Editor.

2. From the Objects list, choose cmdFont.

3. From the Procedures list, choose Click. The cmdFont Click event procedure is created.

4. Add a line of code that sets CancelError to True:

   ```
   CommonDialog1.CancelError = True
   ```

5. Add a line of code that processes errors:

   ```
   On Error GoTo ErrHandler
   ```

6. Add a line of code that sets Common Dialog flags (for more information on flags, see the sidebar, "Common Dialog Flags"):

   ```
   CommonDialog1.Flags = cdlCFBoth
   ```

   This flag tells the Common Dialog control to display both printer and screen fonts.

7. Add a line of code that displays the Font dialog:

   ```
   CommonDialog1.ShowFont
   ```

8. Change the RichTextBox's Font property depending on the font selected:

   ```
   RichTextBox1.Font.Name =
   → CommonDialog1.FontName
   RichTextBox1.Font.Size =
   → CommonDialog1.FontSize
   RichTextBox1.Font.Bold =
   → CommonDialog1.FontBold
   RichTextBox1.Font.Italic =
   → CommonDialog1.FontItalic
   ```

9. Add code to handle error processing:

   ```
   Exit Sub
   ErrHandler:
       'User pressed the Cancel button
   ```

10. Run the project.

11. Type some text in the RichTextBox control (**Figure 9.16**).

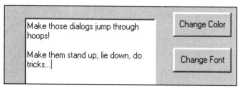

Figure 9.16 With a project running, you can enter text in a RichTextBox.

Common Dialog Flags

The Flag property of the Common Dialog control is used to set a variety of configuration options for the dialogs that will be opened. (The Common Dialog flag values are also called Common Dialog control constants. For a full list, look up this phrase in Visual Basic's online Help.)

Here are a few of the Flag values that are commonly used:

◆ `cdlOFNFileMustExist`
  User can enter only names of existing files in the File Open/Save dialogs.

◆ `cdlOFNOverwritePrompt`
  Causes the Save As dialog to request confirmation before overwriting an existing file.

◆ `cdlCCRGBInit`
  Sets the initial values for the Color dialog.

◆ `cdlCFBoth`
  Causes the Font dialog to display printer and screen fonts. (Note: A flag must be set for either printer or screen fonts—or both—or no fonts will be displayed in the dialog.)

◆ `cdlCFEffects`
  Includes strikethrough, underline, and color effects in the Font dialog.

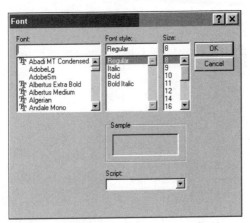

Figure 9.17 When the Font dialog opens, no font is selected.

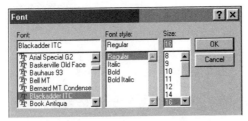

Figure 9.18 You can choose font, font style, and size.

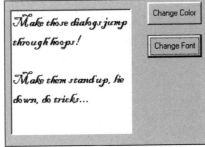

Figure 9.19 Your choice of font is applied to the text in the RichTextBox.

12. Click Change Font.

The Font dialog opens, with no font selected (**Figure 9.17**).

13. Select a font, font style, and size (**Figure 9.18**). The fonts that appear in the dialog depend on what is available on your system.

14. Click OK.

The font you selected is used to display the text in the RichTextBox (**Figure 9.19**).

Changing Selected Text

If you are truly enamored of that "ransom note" effect, you can use the Font dialog to change the font attributes for selected text in the RichTextBox (rather than the overall font).

Listing 9.3 shows the complete event procedure code for changing the font attributes of selected text only.

To change selected text:

1. With RichTextBox and Common Dialog controls already in place on a form, add a command button.

2. Use the Properties window to name the button cmdSel and caption it Change Selection.

3. Position the button on the form (**Figure 9.20**).

Figure 9.20 The Selected Text button will be used to change only selected text.

Listing 9.3 Changing Selected Text

```
Code                                                    _ □ ×
Private Sub cmdSel_Click()
    ' Set Cancel to True
    CommonDialog1.CancelError = True
    On Error GoTo ErrHandler
    ' Set the Flags property
    CommonDialog1.Flags = cdlCFEffects + cdlCFBoth
    ' Display the Font dialog box
    CommonDialog1.ShowFont
    RichTextBox1.SelFontName = CommonDialog1.FontName
    RichTextBox1.SelFontSize = CommonDialog1.FontSize
    RichTextBox1.SelBold = CommonDialog1.FontBold
    RichTextBox1.SelItalic = CommonDialog1.FontItalic
    RichTextBox1.SelUnderline = CommonDialog1.FontUnderline
    RichTextBox1.SelStrikeThru = CommonDialog1.FontStrikethru
    RichTextBox1.SelColor = CommonDialog1.Color
    Exit Sub

ErrHandler:
    ' User pressed the Cancel button
    Exit Sub
End Sub
```

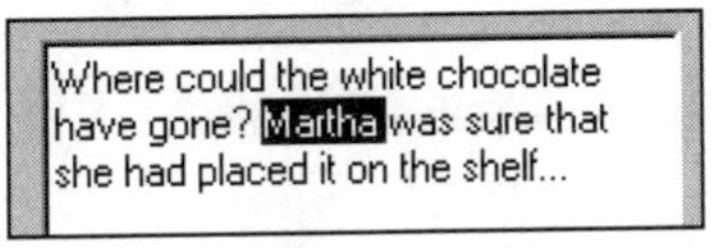

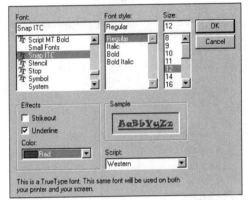

Figure 9.21 Your users can select as much or as little text as they want.

Figure 9.22 The extended Font dialog—invoked by the Flag cdlCFEffects value— includes strikethrough, underline, and color options.

Figure 9.23 You can select and apply font attributes as many times as you want.

4. Use the Code Editor to add code to cmdSel's Click event, starting with the CancelError and Flags properties:

```
CommonDialog1.CancelError = True
On Error GoTo ErrHandler
CommonDialog1.Flags = cdlCFEffects +
→ cdlCFBoth
```

5. Display the expanded Font dialog:

```
CommonDialog1.ShowFont
```

6. Apply the user's choices to the selected text in the RichTextBox:

```
RichTextBox1.SelFontName =
→ CommonDialog1.FontName
RichTextBox1.SelFontSize =
→ CommonDialog1.FontSize
RichTextBox1.SelBold =
→ CommonDialog1.FontBold
RichTextBox1.SelItalic =
→ CommonDialog1.FontItalic
RichTextBox1.SelUnderline =
→ CommonDialog1.FontUnderline
RichTextBox1.SelStrikeThru =
→ CommonDialog1.FontStrikethru
RichTextBox1.SelColor =
→ CommonDialog1.Color
```

7. Run the project.

8. Select some text (**Figure 9.21**).

9. Click Select Text.
   The Font dialog opens (**Figure 9.22**).

10. Make a font and style selection.

11. Click OK.

12. Repeat the process of selecting text and applying fonts.
   You have successfully generated ransom-note-style text in the RichTextBox (**Figure 9.23**).

The Save Dialog

The RichTextBox control includes methods that take care of the nasty details of saving and opening files. Combining these methods with the Save and Open aspects of the Common Dialog controls makes it easy to create and then open document files in your applications.

I'll show you how to save the contents of a RichTextBox as an RTF file before I show you how to open it. That way, you will have something on your file system to open.

Listing 9.4 contains the complete code for an event procedure that saves the contents of a RichTextBox.

To save the contents of a RichTextBox:

1. With RichTextBox and Common Dialog controls already in place on a form, add a command button.

2. Use the Properties window to name the button **cmdSave** and caption it **Save**.

3. Position the button on the form (**Figure 9.24**).

4. Use the Code Editor to add code to cmdSave's Click event, starting with a declaration for a string variable that will hold the file name selected by the user:

   ```
   Dim strNewFile As String
   ```

5. Add CancelError and Flags properties:

   ```
   On Error GoTo ErrHandler
   CommonDialog1.CancelError = True
   CommonDialog1.Flags =
   → cdlOFNHideReadOnly +
   → cdlOFNOverwritePrompt
   ```

6. Add a Filter property (which establishes the kinds of files that are displayed in the Save dialog):

Listing 9.4 Saving a File

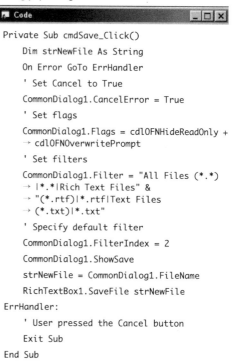

```
Private Sub cmdSave_Click()
    Dim strNewFile As String
    On Error GoTo ErrHandler
    ' Set Cancel to True
    CommonDialog1.CancelError = True
    ' Set flags
    CommonDialog1.Flags = cdlOFNHideReadOnly +
    → cdlOFNOverwritePrompt
    ' Set filters
    CommonDialog1.Filter = "All Files (*.*)
    → |*.*|Rich Text Files" &
    → "(*.rtf)|*.rtf|Text Files
    → (*.txt)|*.txt"
    ' Specify default filter
    CommonDialog1.FilterIndex = 2
    CommonDialog1.ShowSave
    strNewFile = CommonDialog1.FileName
    RichTextBox1.SaveFile strNewFile
ErrHandler:
    ' User pressed the Cancel button
    Exit Sub
End Sub
```

Figure 9.24 The Save button will be used to save the contents of the RichTextBox as a file.

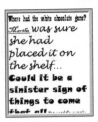

Figure 9.25 Using RTF format, you can save formatting information as well as text.

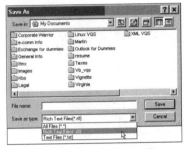

Figure 9.26 The Save As dialog allows users to choose a file location, name, and type.

Figure 9.27 The user can type a file name.

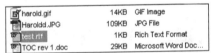

Figure 9.28 You can use Explorer to verify that the file has been added to your file system.

Figure 9.29 You can open the file in Word to make sure that the contents are intact.

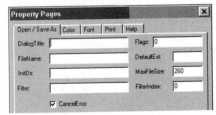

Figure 9.30 You can set Common Dialog properties using Property Pages rather than code.

```
CommonDialog1.Filter = "All Files
→ (*.*)|*.*|Rich Text Files" &
→ "(*.rtf)|*.rtf|Text Files
→ (*.txt)|*.txt"
CommonDialog1.FilterIndex = 2
```

7. Show the dialog:

   `CommonDialog1.ShowSave`

8. Assign the file name (and path) selected by the user to the variable:

   `strNewFile = CommonDialog1.FileName`

9. Use the SaveFile method of the RichTextBox to save its contents:

   `RichTextBox1.SaveFile strNewFile`

10. Run the project.

11. Enter some text in the RichTextBox.

12. Use the Font dialogs that you developed earlier in this section to format the text (**Figure 9.25**).

13. Click Save.

    The Save As dialog opens, with Rich Text Files selected (**Figure 9.26**).

14. Type a name in the File Name box—for example, "test" (**Figure 9.27**).

15. Click Save.

    The file is saved.

16. Open Windows Explorer.

    You find a listing for the file you just saved (**Figure 9.28**).

17. Open the file in Microsoft Word.

    You see that its formatting has been preserved (**Figure 9.29**).

✔ Tip

■ Remember, you can set the Common Dialog properties—such as Filter—in the control's Property Pages (**Figure 9.30**) rather than in code, if you prefer.

The Open Dialog

Now that you know how to save RTF files, let's complete the loop by learning how to load an RTF file into a RichTextBox.

The complete event code for loading a file into a RichTextBox is shown in **Listing 9.5.**

To open a file in the RichTextBox:

1. With RichTextBox and Common Dialog controls already in place on a form, add a command button.

2. Use the Properties window to name the button cmdOpen and caption it Open.

3. Position the button on the form (**Figure 9.31**).

4. Use the Code Editor to add code to cmdSave's Click event, starting with a declaration for a string variable that will hold the name of the file selected by the user:

```
Dim strOpenFile As String
```

Figure 9.31 The Open button will be used to load a file's contents into the RichTextBox control.

Listing 9.5 Opening a File

```
Code                                                    _ □ ✕
Private Sub cmdOpen_Click()
    Dim strOpenFile As String
    On Error GoTo ErrHandler
    ' Set Cancel to True
    CommonDialog1.CancelError = True
    ' Set flags
    CommonDialog1.Flags = cdlOFNFileMustExist + cdlOFNHideReadOnly
    ' Set filters
    CommonDialog1.Filter = "All Files (*.*)|*.*|Rich Text Files" &
    → "(*.rtf)|*.rtf|Text Files (*.txt)|*.txt"
    ' Specify default filter
    CommonDialog1.FilterIndex = 2
    CommonDialog1.ShowOpen
    strOpenFile = CommonDialog1.FileName
    RichTextBox1.LoadFile strOpenFile
ErrHandler:
    ' User pressed the Cancel button
    Exit Sub
End Sub
```

Figure 9.32 The Open dialog allows users to select a file.

Figure 9.33 You can type a file name.

Figure 9.34 Depending on the Flag property values you set, if you type a file name that doesn't correspond to an actual file, you get an error message.

Figure 9.35 You can add a file to the File name box by selecting it.

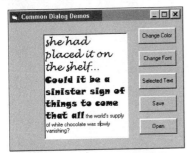

Figure 9.36 The contents of the file you selected are added to the RichTextBox control.

5. Add CancelError and Flags properties:

```
On Error GoTo ErrHandler
CommonDialog1.CancelError = True
CommonDialog1.Flags =
→ cdlOFNFileMustExist +
→ cdlOFNHideReadOnly
```

6. Add a Filter property (which establishes the kinds of files that are displayed in the Open dialog):

```
CommonDialog1.Filter = "All Files
→ (*.*)|*.*|Rich Text Files" &
→ "(*.rtf)|*.rtf|Text Files
→ (*.txt)|*.txt"
CommonDialog1.FilterIndex = 2
```

5. Show the dialog:

```
CommonDialog1.ShowOpen
```

6. Assign the file name (and path) selected by the user to the variable:

```
strOpenFile = CommonDialog1.FileName
```

7. Use the LoadFile method of the RichTextBox to save its contents:

```
RichTextBox1.LoadFile strOpenFile
```

8. Run the project.

9. Click Open.
The Open dialog opens (**Figure 9.32**).

10. Try entering a nonexistent file (**Figure 9.33**) and clicking Open.
You get an error message (**Figure 9.34**).

11. Select a file that exists (**Figure 9.35**).

12. Click Open.
The contents of the file are loaded in the RichTextBox (**Figure 9.36**).

THE OPEN DIALOG

Summary

In this chapter, you learned to:

- Add an instance of the Common Dialog control to your form.

- Add a RichTextBox control to your form.

- Use the Color dialog.

- Set fonts and attributes for text (and selected text) using the Fonts dialog.

- Save the contents of a RichTextBox control to the file system using the Save dialog.

- Load the contents of a file into a RichTextBox control using the Open dialog.

The OLE Container Control

The OLE Container control is a container for OLE objects—such as Word documents, Word paragraphs, and PowerPoint slides. Using the OLE Container control, you can link or embed these objects in your Visual Basic applications.

By the way, OLE is short for object linking and embedding. OLE objects are created with ActiveX applications or components, using Microsoft's paradigm for interapplication communication.

Linking means that the object placed in your Visual Basic application—such as a Word document saved in a file—is connected to your VB application. If the contents of the file change, so does the object in your application—and vice versa.

Embedding means that a copy of the object has been included in your VB application. Changes made to this copy do not affect the original object—nor do changes made to the original affect the copy.

For information on the advantages and disadvantages of each method, see the "Linking Versus Embedding" sidebar in this chapter.

Objects can be linked or embedded by using the OLE Container control visually at design time, as I'll show you in this chapter. Keep
in mind—although the topic is not covered in this chapter—that objects and the OLE Container control can be manipulated dynamically in code via the control's properties and methods.

Inserting Objects

The OLE Container control is automatically available in your Toolbox. In fact, it cannot be removed from the VB Toolbox.

When you add the control to a form, the Insert Object dialog automatically opens. Please be patient: there normally is a slight delay before this dialog opens, because it does have to catalog all the kinds of insertable OLE objects on your system.

When an object has been loaded in the OLE Container control, you can remove the object and insert another one in its place by using the control's special pop-up menu. (This menu is different from the pop-up menu displayed by other controls, which allow you to set properties and view code, for example.)

You'll also notice that when you insert an object—this does depend on the kind of object inserted—and select the object in the Visual Basic design-time environment, the Visual Basic menus become an odd amalgamation of VB's menus and the menus of the inserted object's application (for example, Word). The general term for this phenomenon is *menu contention*.

To create a new object:

1. With a form open, double-click the OLE Container control in the Toolbox (**Figure 10.1**).

   Wait patiently for the Insert Object dialog to open (**Figure 10.2**). Create New is preselected.

2. Scroll down the Object Type list and select the type of object you want to create.

   A Microsoft Word document is being created in **Figure 10.3**.

3. Click OK.

   The new object is indicated on your Visual Basic form with a special border (**Figure 10.4**).

Figure 10.1 Double-click the OLE Container control to add it to a form.

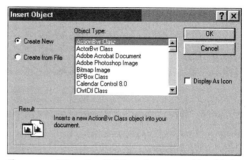

Figure 10.2 When the OLE Container control is added to a form, after a short delay, the Insert Object dialog opens automatically.

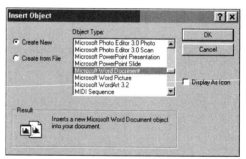

Figure 10.3 The Insert Object dialog lists all the kinds of insertable objects registered on your system.

Figure 10.4 When a new object has been added to the OLE Container control, the border around the control changes.

Figure 10.5 To open the Insert Object dialog when the OLE Container control has already been added to a form, choose Insert Object from the pop-up menu.

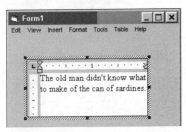

Figure 10.6 The menus of the application that the object belongs to appear on the running form.

Figure 10.7 Selecting an item from the menus opens the dialog that come from the object's application.

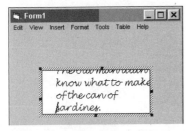

Figure 10.8 Applying the Font dialog changes the formatting of the text in the contained object.

✔ Tip

■ When the OLE Container control has been added to the form, you can open the Insert Object dialog by right-clicking the OLE Container control and choosing Insert Object from the pop-up menu (**Figure 10.5**).

To work with the new object:

1. With a new object inserted into the OLE Container control, run the project.

2. On the running form, double-click the OLE Container control.

   The new object opens on the form, with its menu appearing in the form's menu area. A Microsoft Word document is shown in **Figure 10.6**.

3. Enter text in the Word object.

4. Select the text that you entered, and format it by choosing items from the Word Format menu.

   The Font dialog is shown in **Figure 10.7**. The changes that you make by using menu items are shown in the object's text (**Figure 10.8**).

✔ Tip

■ When the OLE Container control is selected in the VB design environment, the VB menus may be an amalgam of the object's menus and the normal Visual Basic menus. To see the normal VB menus, select something else on the form.

To create an object from a file:

1. Use the Properties window to set the SizeMode property of the OLE Container control to 1 - Stretch (**Figure 10.9**).

   If this property is left at the default setting (0 - Clip), the OLE Container control displays only a small corner of the object.

2. Right-click the OLE Container control. and choose Insert Object from the pop-up menu.

   The Insert Object dialog opens.

3. Click the Create from File option button.

   The File box now displays a file system path with the current path and a Browse button (**Figure 10.10**).

4. Click the Browse button.

   The Browse dialog opens (**Figure 10.11**).

5. Select a file belonging to an application that can create OLE objects, such as Microsoft Word.

6. Click OK.

   The file name and path now appear in the File box in the Insert Object dialog.

7. Click OK to close the Insert Object dialog.

   The object—a Word document, in this example—is added to the OLE Container control (**Figure 10.12**).

Figure 10.9 Change the OLE Container control's SizeMode property to 1 - Stretch to see more than an itty, bitty bit of a Word document in the control.

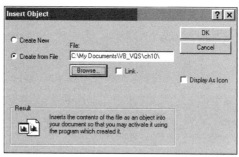

Figure 10.10 When the Create from File option button is selected, the File box and Browse buttons appear.

Figure 10.11 You can use the Browse button to find an existing file, or you can type the path and name of the file in the File box.

Figure 10.12 The object contained in the file you selected is added to the OLE Container control.

INSERTING OBJECTS

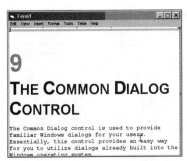

Figure 10.13 Run the project and double-click the object to activate the menus belonging to the object's application.

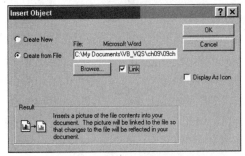

Figure 10.14 When Link is checked, an existing object in a file is linked rather than embedded.

8. Run the project.

9. Double-click the object in the OLE Container control.

   Its application's menu bar appears along the top of the form (**Figure 10.13**).

✔ Tip

- If you already have an object in the OLE Container control, you will be asked whether you want to delete it before the new object that you selected is added. Click Yes to insert the new object, or No to revert to the old object.

To create a link to an object:

1. With the Insert Object dialog open and the Create from File option selected, check the Link checkbox (**Figure 10.14**).

2. Click OK.

Linking Versus Embedding

It's up to you whether to link or to embed. (I can just see Hamlet on the ramparts of Elsinore, asking whether 'tis nobler to link, or not to link.)

A linked object remains stored in its own file with two-way links to your Visual Basic application. An embedded object is copied lock, stock, and barrel into the Visual Basic application and has no existence apart from it.

An advantage of embedding is that the object is completely under the power of your application and cannot be moved or changed by another application.

A disadvantage is that applications with embedded objects are larger than applications with links to objects.

To display an OLE object as an icon:

1. Open the Insert Object dialog.

2. With either Create New or Create from File selected, check the Display As Icon checkbox (**Figure 10.15**).

3. Click OK.

   The object appears in the OLE Container control as an icon (**Figure 10.16**).

✔ Tip

■ If you want, you can change the default icon for an embedded object by clicking the Change Icon button in the Insert Object dialog. You still activate the object in the same way: by running it and double-clicking the icon in the OLE Container control.

To delete an embedded object:

◆ Right-click the OLE Container control, and from the pop-up menu, choose Delete Embedded Object (**Figure 10.17**).

✔ Tip

■ If you have linked rather than embedded an object, to delete the link, choose Delete Link from the OLE Container control's pop-up menu.

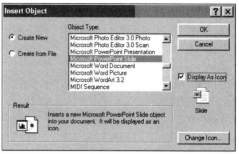

Figure 10.15 To display an icon, rather than an object, in the OLE Container control, check Display As Icon.

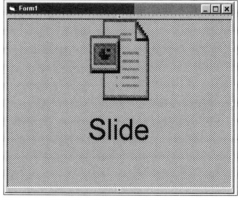

Figure 10.16 The icon for a PowerPoint slide rather than a slide itself is displayed.

Figure 10.17 Use the OLE Container control's pop-up menu to delete an embedded object.

INSERTING OBJECTS

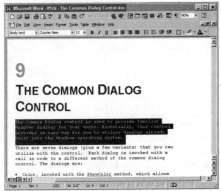

Figure 10.18 You can select a paragraph of a Word document for embedding or linking.

Figure 10.19 The Paste Special dialog is opened by choosing Paste Special from the OLE Container control's pop-up menu.

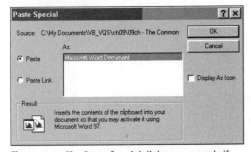

Figure 10.20 The Paste Special dialog opens only if the Windows Clipboard holds an OLE object capable of being linked or embedded.

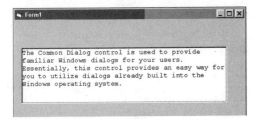

Figure 10.21 Your selection is embedded in the OLE Container control.

Using the Paste Special Dialog

The Paste Special dialog allows you to link or embed a portion of an OLE object. You can link or embed an Excel cell or a Word paragraph, for example, rather than the entire spreadsheet or document.

To paste and embed an OLE object:

1. Select the portion of the object that you want to embed in its native application.

   A Word paragraph is shown selected in Microsoft Word in **Figure 10.18**.

2. Copy the selection to the Windows Clipboard.

3. In Visual Basic, right-click the OLE Container control, and from the pop-up menu, choose Paste Special (**Figure 10.19**).

   The Paste Special dialog opens (**Figure 10.20**).

4. Click OK.

   The portion of the object that you selected is embedded in the OLE Container control (**Figure 10.21**).

To paste an OLE object link:

1. Copy a selection to the Windows Clipboard.

2. In Visual Basic, right-click the OLE Container control, and choose Paste Special from the pop-up menu.

   The Paste Special dialog opens.

3. Select the Paste Link option (**Figure 10.22**).

4. Click OK.

   Your selection is linked to the OLE Container control.

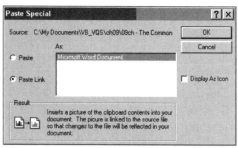

Figure 10.22 Use the Paste Link option—rather than Paste—to link instead of embed your selection.

✔ Tips

■ If you have linked a subpart of an OLE file to the OLE Container control, your users can navigate to the subpart's location in the full object by double-clicking the contained object. If the OLE Container control is linked to a paragraph in a Word document, for example, running the VB project and double-clicking the OLE Container control opens the Word document in Word with the insertion point positioned at the paragraph.

■ The Paste Special dialog opens only if the Windows Clipboard already holds an OLE object capable of being linked or embedded.

Summary

In this chapter, you learned to:

◆ Use the OLE Container control.

◆ Create a new object in the OLE Container control.

◆ Create an object from a file.

◆ Create a link to an object.

◆ Display an object as an icon.

◆ Use the Paste Special dialog.

THE TIMER CONTROL

The Timer control is used to fire an event at specified intervals. The code you want executed is placed in this event (called the Timer control's Timer event).

Once you get the idea, you'll find the Timer control extremely simple to use.

This control has no methods, only one event (the Timer event, already mentioned), and only seven properties. Only a few of these properties are actually used. In addition, the control is invisible at run time.

In this chapter, I'll show you how to use the Timer control. In addition, the examples in the chapter explain some important techniques and concepts, including:

◆ How to wire a simple animation

◆ How to use a subroutine to write the code once

◆ How to validate input and trap input errors

Understanding a Timer

Basically, once you put a Timer on a form, its Enabled property is True or False. You can set the Enabled property at design time, using the Properties Window, or at run time in code.

When Enabled is set to True, the Timer's Timer event is regularly fired at intervals. The length of the interval depends, as you might expect, on the Interval property.

The Interval property can also be set at either design or run time. The unit of measure is milliseconds, so `Timer1.Interval = 1000` means "fire this puppy once a second." (In case you are wondering, setting the Timer interval to 0 is equivalent to disabling the Timer.)

Let's have a look at this in the context of a simple example. **Listing 11.1** shows the complete code for counting how many times a Timer has been fired and displaying the current Timer count in a form's caption bar.

To count the number of Timer events:

1. Double-click the Timer in the Toolbox (**Figure 11.1**) to add it to a form (**Figure 11.2**).

2. Use the Properties Window to set the Timer's Enabled property to True.

3. Set the Timer's Interval property to 100 (**Figure 11.3**), meaning 1/10 second.

4. Open the Code Editor.

5. From the Objects list, choose Timer1. The Timer's only event, Timer, is selected in the Procedures list, and an event procedure framework is created:

```
Private Sub Timer1_Timer()

End Sub
```

Listing 11.1 Counting the number of times a Timer is fired

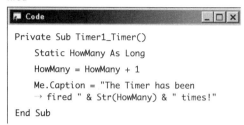

```
Private Sub Timer1_Timer()
    Static HowMany As Long
    HowMany = HowMany + 1
    Me.Caption = "The Timer has been
    → fired " & Str(HowMany) & " times!"
End Sub
```

Figure 11.1 Double-click the Timer control to add it to a form.

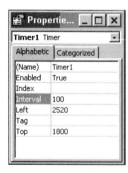

Figure 11.2 The Timer control is not visible at run time, so it does not matter where you position it on a form.

Figure 11.3 The two important Timer properties are Enabled (is the Timer on?) and Interval (how often is the Timer code triggered?).

Figure 11.4 The number of times the Timer has been fired is displayed in the form's caption.

6. At the top of the event procedure, add a static variable declaration so that the variable starts with the value it had the last time the Timer was fired:

```
Static HowMany As Long
```

7. Increment the counter variable to reflect the fact the Timer has been fired once more by virtue of this code's being invoked:

```
HowMany = HowMany + 1
```

8. Add code that displays the number of times the Timer has been fired in the form's caption:

```
Me.Caption = "The Timer has been
→ fired " & Str(HowMany) & " times!"
```

9. Run the project.

The Timer is being fired 10 times a second, and each time it is fired, the count displayed in the form caption is incremented (**Figure 11.4**).

✔ Tips

- If you have only one or two Timers on a form, there is no need to rename the control. The default names (Timer1, Timer2, and so on) work well enough. If your application requires many Timers, however, you should name them so that their functions are clear at a glance—for example, tmrAnimate and tmrRemind.

- The str() function converts numbers to strings. If you left the function off, the variable HowMany would still display correctly—but it is better coding practice to make explicit variable type conversions.

The Static and Long Keywords

A variable declared as long is a double-wide integer. If you are interested in the gory details, in Visual Basic, an integer variable has 2 bytes of storage reserved and can range from -32768 to 32767. A long variable has 4 bytes of storage space and can range from -2,147,483,648 to 2,147,483,647.

When you use the Static keyword in a variable declaration instead of the Dim keyword, you are saying that this variable retains its value as long as the project it is in is running. Without the Static keyword, a variable declared in a procedure loses its value when that procedure stops running.

Creating Simple Animation

A Timer control is often used to create a simple animation effect. The animation mechanism is often something—for example, an ImageBox control containing a graphic—steadily moved by code in the Timer's Timer event.

In this section, an ImageBox is moved around a form via the ImageBox's Move method. Each time the ImageBox hits an edge of the form, it starts over at the other side of the form.

Listing 11.2 shows the complete Timer event code that handles the animation.

To animate an ImageBox:

1. Add a Timer control to a form.

2. Use the Properties Window to set the Timer's Enabled property to True and its Interval to 100 (**Figure 11.5**).

3. Double-click the ImageBox control in the Toolbox (**Figure 11.6**) to add it to the form.

4. Using the Properties Window, set the name of the ImageBox to imgSnow (**Figure 11.7**).

   We will be animating a snowflake.

5. In the Properties Window, select imgSnow's Picture property (**Figure 11.8**).

6. Click the ellipsis on the right side of the Properties Window to open the Load Picture dialog (**Figure 11.9**).

7. Select the snow icon that ships with Visual Basic (Snow.ico) and Click OK.

   The snow icon is loaded in the ImageBox.

8. Open the Code Editor.

9. Choose Timer1 from the Objects list.

   The Timer event is selected in the Procedures list, and a Timer event procedure framework is created.

Listing 11.2 Animating an ImageBox

```
Private Sub Timer1_Timer()
    Dim MoveH As Integer, MoveV As Integer
    If imgSnow.Top > Me.ScaleHeight Then
        imgSnow.Top = 0
    Else
        MoveV = -100
    End If
    If imgSnow.Left > Me.ScaleWidth Then
        imgSnow.Left = 0
    Else
        MoveH = -100
    End If
    imgSnow.Move imgSnow.Left - MoveH,
    ↪ imgSnow.Top - MoveV
End Sub
```

Figure 11.5
A Timer Interval of 100 (1/10 second) is used to smoothly animate the snowflake.

Figure 11.6 Double-click the ImageBox control in the Toolbox to add it to your form.

Figure 11.7
The ImageBox is named imgSnow, because it will be holding a snowflake.

Figure 11.8
The ImageBox's Picture property is used to load a graphic image into the ImageBox.

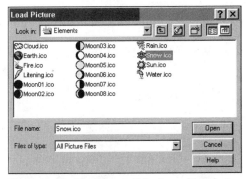

Figure 11.9 The Load Picture dialog is used to select the file that will be loaded.

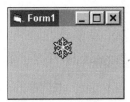

Figure 11.10 When the form is run, the snowflake is happily animated, running on the form until the project is stopped.

11. Within the event procedure, declare variables for horizontal and vertical increments of motion:

```
Dim MoveH As Integer, MoveV As Integer
```

12. Add code to reset the ImageBox position if it has hit the top of the form, and otherwise to increment the vertical movement of the ImageBox:

```
If imgSnow.Top > Me.ScaleHeight Then
    imgSnow.Top = 0
Else
    MoveV = -100
End If
```

13. Add code to reset the ImageBox's position if it has hit the right wall of the form and otherwise to increment the horizontal movement of the object:

```
If imgSnow.Left > Me.ScaleWidth Then
    imgSnow.Left = 0
Else
    MoveH = -100
End If
```

14. Add a call to imgSnow's Move method to actually move the control:

```
imgSnow.Move imgSnow.Left - MoveH,
→ imgSnow.Top - MoveV
```

15. Run the project.

The snowflake is smoothly animated on the form (**Figure 11.10**).

✔ Tip

■ The Snow.ico file is usually located in the Program Files\Microsoft Visual Studio\ Common\Graphics\Icons\Elements directory. If you didn't elect to install graphic files when you installed Visual Basic, you may have to go back and rerun the installation program.

Using a Subroutine

Do you know the saying, "It never rains, but it pours?" This probably applies to animations, in which too much is never enough.

To prove the point, we are going to add rain, cloud, and sun animations to the snowflake that is already falling forever across the form.

Each animation will be achieved by moving an ImageBox named as shown in **Table 11.1**.

The complete code for animating all four ImageBoxes is shown in **Listing 11.3**.

The real point of this is to show you how to do it without retyping the Timer code for each ImageBox. Because the code is the same for each, a *subroutine*—that is, a procedure or routine called from another procedure or routine—can be written in which the name of the control is a variable.

To animate many ImageBoxes by using a subroutine:

1. Add a Timer control to a form.

2. Use the Properties Window to enable it and to set its interval to 100 (**Figure 11.11**).

3. Add the four ImageBoxes listed in **Table 11.1**, with their Picture properties set as indicated in **Table 11.1.**

4. Open the Code Editor.

5. Type Sub MoveObject(ctrl As Control).

6. Press Enter.

   Visual Basic adds the line of code to close the procedure:

   ```
   Sub MoveObject(ctrl As Control)

   End Sub
   ```

Table 11.1

ImageBox names	
IMAGEBOX NAME	PICTURE FILE
imgCloud	Cloud.ico
imgRain	Rain.ico
imgSnow	Snow.ico
imgSun	Sun.ico

Listing 11.3 Using a Subroutine to Animate Many ImageBoxes

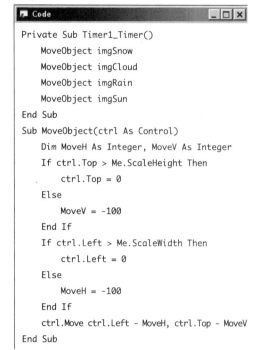

```
Private Sub Timer1_Timer()
    MoveObject imgSnow
    MoveObject imgCloud
    MoveObject imgRain
    MoveObject imgSun
End Sub
Sub MoveObject(ctrl As Control)
    Dim MoveH As Integer, MoveV As Integer
    If ctrl.Top > Me.ScaleHeight Then
        ctrl.Top = 0
    Else
        MoveV = -100
    End If
    If ctrl.Left > Me.ScaleWidth Then
        ctrl.Left = 0
    Else
        MoveH = -100
    End If
    ctrl.Move ctrl.Left - MoveH, ctrl.Top - MoveV
End Sub
```

Figure 11.11
One Timer control is used to animate all four ImageBoxes.

Figure 11.12 All four icons are smoothly moving on the form.

You just created a subroutine named MoveObject that expects to be invoked with a control as a parameter. ctrl is the variable name for that control within the subroutine.

7. Generalize the code that was used in the preceding section to move the snowflake by replacing references to imgSnow with ctrl.

   For example,

   ```
   If imgSnow.Top > Me.ScaleHeight Then
   ```
   becomes
   ```
   If ctrl.Top > Me.ScaleHeight Then
   ```

8. Place the modified code within the MoveObject subroutine.

9. Use the Objects list to open the Timer's Timer event procedure.

10. Add four calls to the MoveObject subroutine within the Timer's event procedure, one for each of the ImageBoxes:

    ```
    Private Sub Timer1_Timer()
        MoveObject imgSnow
        MoveObject imgCloud
        MoveObject imgRain
        MoveObject imgSun
    End Sub
    ```

11. Run the project.

    All four weather icons happily dance on your form (**Figure 11.12**).

USING A SUBROUTINE

Turning the Timer On

The way we've set the animation up, it goes on and on, as long as the project is running. It's often a good idea to let the user control turning an animation off and on. Toggling the Timer control's Enabled property in code achieves this purpose

The code that toggles the Timer control is shown in **Listing 11.4**.

To control the Timer dynamically:

1. Using the multiple animation project developed in the preceding section, add a command button to the form.

2. Use the Properties Window to caption the button Start Timer and name the button cmdStart.

3. Use the Properties Window to set the Timer's Enabled property to False.

4. Open the Code Window.

5. Choose cmdStart from the Objects list and Click from the Procedures list to create a Click event procedure framework.

   ```
   If Timer1.Enabled = False Then
       Timer1.Enabled = True
       cmdStart.Caption = "Stop Timer"
   ```

6. Add code that disables the Timer if it is enabled and changes the caption of the command button back to Start Timer:

   ```
   Else
       Timer1.Enabled = False
       cmdStart.Caption = "Start Timer"
   End If
   ```

7. Run the project. The animations are not moving (**Figure 11.13**).

8. Click the Start Timer button. The animations start (**Figure 11.14**).

9. When you get tired of watching them, click the Stop Timer button to stop the animations.

Listing 11.4 Enabling and Disabling the Timer

```
Private Sub cmdStart_Click()
    If Timer1.Enabled = False Then
        Timer1.Enabled = True
        cmdStart.Caption = "Stop Timer"
    Else
        Timer1.Enabled = False
        cmdStart.Caption = "Start Timer"
    End If
End Sub
```

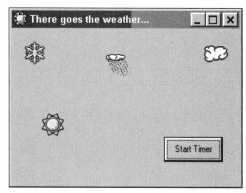

Figure 11.13 Click the Start Timer button to start the animations.

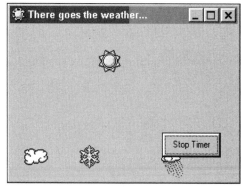

Figure 11.14 Click the Stop Timer button to stop the animations.

Listing 11.5 Setting the Timer Interval

```
Code                              _ □ ×
Private Sub cmdStart_Click()
    Dim I As Long
    On Error GoTo ErrHandle
    If Timer1.Enabled = False Then
        I = Abs(Int(txtInterval.Text))
        Debug.Print I
        Timer1.Interval = I
        Timer1.Enabled = True
        cmdStart.Caption = "Stop Timer"
    Else
        Timer1.Enabled = False
        cmdStart.Caption = "Start Timer"
    End If
    Exit Sub
ErrHandle:
    MsgBox "You must enter an integer value
    → between 1 and 65535!"
End Sub
```

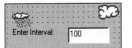

Figure 11.15 A TextBox control is used to accept the user's input for the Timer's Interval value.

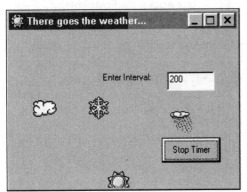

Figure 11.16 The user can speed and slow the animations.

Setting the Interval

Another embellishment you might want to make in the animation program is to allow the user to set the Timer interval. That way, the user can decide whether she likes her animations fast or verrry slow.

The complete code for allowing the user to set the interval is shown in **Listing 11.5.**

To set the Timer interval dynamically:

1. Add a Label control and a TextBox to the form (**Figure 11.15**).

2. Use the Properties Window to set the Label's caption to `Enter Interval:`.

3. Name the TextBox `txtInterval`, and set its Text property to 100.

4. Using the Code Editor, modify the code in cmdStart's Click event that turns the Timer on to use the input in txtInterval for the Timer interval:

```
If Timer1.Enabled = False Then
    Timer1.Interval = txtInterval.Text
    Timer1.Enabled = True
    cmdStart.Caption = "Stop Timer"
Else
    Timer1.Enabled = False
    cmdStart.Caption = "Start Timer"
End If
```

Provided that she enters an integer value that is acceptable to the Timer control, the user can now control the Timer interval used to determine the speed of the animations (**Figure 11.16**).

✔ Tip

- There are a couple of problems with setting the interval this way. Both problems fall within the purview of what's generally known as *validating the input*.

continues on next page

For one thing, nothing stops the user from entering a text string, such as frodo, rather than a number in txtInterval. For another, the valid values of a Timer Interval are integers between 1 and 65,535. Nothing in place prevents the user from attempting to enter a number larger or smaller than this range or one that includes decimals—for example, -234234.8989. If a user were to provide input of this sort and then click the Start Timer button, your application would come crashing down with an error message.

Using the Immediate Window

Suppose that you've added the Int and Abs functions to the procedure setting the Timer Interval. But you'd just like to be very sure of what value is being passed as the Timer interval after the user input goes through the Int and Abs functions.

You can use the Immediate Window to determine the value of any variable at any point during program execution. The Immediate Window is invoked via the Print method of the Debug object.

To use the Immediate Window:

1. In the Code Editor, add a line of code to the cmdStart Click event after the Abs and Int functions have been applied, to display the current value in the Immediate Window:

```
. . .
I = Abs(Int(txtInterval.Text))
Debug.Print I
Timer1.Interval = I
. . . .
```

2. Run the project.

3. Type a noninteger value in the Interval box—for example, -34.56 (**Figure 11.17**).

4. Click Start Timer. The Immediate Window displays the rounded-off value.

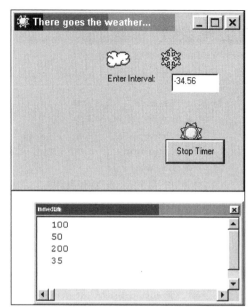

Figure 11.17 The Immediate Window displays the value of variables during your program's execution.

Int and Abs Functions

The Int() function rounds a number to the nearest integer. The Abs() function returns the absolute value of a number. Int(34.12) is 34, for example, and Abs(-23) is 23. You can use the Int and Abs function to take care of some of the problems with setting the Timer interval dynamically:

```
Dim I As Long
If Timer1.Enabled = False Then
    I = Abs(Int(txtInterval.Text))
    Timer1.Interval = I
```

For a complete list of mathematical functions available in Visual Basic, look up Math Functions in online Help.

SETTING THE INTERVAL

Trapping Errors

All our problems haven't been solved by Int() and Abs(), however. What if the user enters a text string or a number outside the allowable range?

It would be possible to test for these conditions and then either give the user another chance or automatically enter a value if something erroneous was input. But it is far easier to *trap the error*.

If the error is trapped, the Timer does not get activated—so the program isn't brought down by an error. A message box can detail the problem for the user, so that she can try again.

To trap input errors:

1. Add an On Error statement near the top of the cmdStart Click procedure.

   ```
   On Error GoTo ErrHandle
   ```

   ErrHandle is a *label* to which execution control is passed in the event of an error condition. (A label is used to mark a specific location in code to which execution can be transferred. Excessive use of labels and GoTo statements is called "spaghetti" code. It is generally a bad idea.)

2. Add an Exit Sub statement at the end of the existing Click event code before the End Sub statement.

3. Create a label for the error handler below the Exit Sub statement:

   ```
   ErrHandle:
   ```

   continues on next page

4. Add a message box that tells the user what the problem is.

The error handler now reads:

```
...
ErrHandle:
    MsgBox "You must enter an integer
    → value between 1 and 65535!"
End Sub
```

5. Run the project.

6. Enter something entirely bogus in the Interval box, such as `frodo`.

7. Click Start Timer.

Your message box is displayed (**Figure 11.18**), but you can't start the Timer (or crash your program).

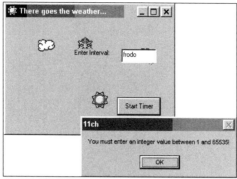

Figure 11.18 You can trap errors to protect your program from spurious input values.

Summary

In this chapter, you learned to:

- Work with the Timer control.
- Create a simple animation effect.
- Use a subroutine to write code once.
- Turn a Timer on and off dynamically.
- Set the Timer Interval property dynamically.
- Use the Int() and Abs() functions.
- Use the Immediate Window.
- Trap errors.

VISUAL BASIC ADD-INS

Visual Basic Add-Ins are programs that are extensions to the Visual Basic environment. These programs connect seamlessly with Visual Basic, so you may not know that you are using an Add-In rather than part of Visual Basic itself.

Add-Ins can be written in the Professional or Enterprise Edition of Visual Basic 6, but this is an advanced topic not covered in *Visual Basic: Visual QuickStart Guide*.

Five Add-Ins ship with the Learning Edition of Visual Basic 6:

- ◆ The Visual Data Manager, which is a tool for working with databases (explained in Chapter 15).

- ◆ The Package and Deployment Wizard, which helps you write setup programs and deploy your applications (explained in Chapter 16).

- ◆ The Application Wizard, which helps you quickly put together the visual parts of an application (see Chapter 13).

- ◆ The Resource Editor, which is used to create and edit resource files.

- ◆ The Template Manager, which provides some code, menu, and control templates.

It's possible for other Add-Ins to appear in the Add-In Manager so that they can be loaded and unloaded from your Visual Basic environment. This task is something that the Add-In itself accomplishes when it is executed, however.

Whether or not Add-Ins appear as part of your Visual Basic environment primarily depends on the settings in the Visual Basic Add-In Manager. (The Visual Data Manager is always available and cannot be unloaded via the Add-In Manager. I'll also show you ways to invoke the Package and Deployment Wizard and the Application Wizard that do not involve the Add-In Manager.)

This chapter explains how to use the Add-In Manager. I'll also provide an overview explanation of the Resource Editor and show you how to use the Template Manager to quick-start ListBox functionality.

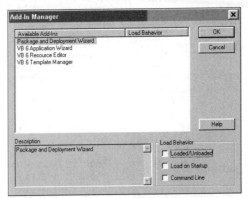

Figure 12.1 The Add-In Manager is used to load and unload Add-Ins.

Figure 12.2 Select an Add-In to alter its load behavior.

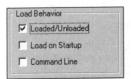

Figure 12.3 Check Loaded/Unloaded to load the Add-In if it is currently unloaded.

Figure 12.4 When the Add-In is loaded, it is listed as Loaded in the Load Behavior frame.

Using the Add-In Manager

The Add-In Manager is used to load or unload Visual Basic Add-Ins. In other words, a loaded Add-In can be started via a Visual Basic menu item. An unloaded Add-In cannot be started via the Visual Basic menus.

You can also use the Add-In Manager to configure an Add-In to load automatically when Visual Basic starts.

To open the Add-In Manager:

◆ From the Add-Ins menu, choose Add-In Manager.

The Add-In Manager opens (**Figure 12.1**).

To load an Add-In:

1. In the list of Available Add-Ins, select the Add-In that you want to load (**Figure 12.2**).

2. Check Loaded/Unloaded in the Load Behavior frame (**Figure 12.3**).

The Add-In is listed as Loaded (**Figure 12.4**).

3. Click OK.

The Add-In is now available in the Visual Basic menus.

To unload an Add-In:

1. Select a loaded Add-In (**Figure 12.5**).

2. Uncheck Loaded/Unloaded in the Load Behavior frame (**Figure 12.6**).

   The Add-In no longer appears as loaded in the Load Behavior list.

3. Click OK.

   The Add-In's menu item is removed.

To load an Add-In automatically when VB starts:

1. From the list of available Add-Ins, select a loaded or unloaded Add-In (**Figure 12.7**).

2. In the Load Behavior frame, check Load on Startup (**Figure 12.8**).

   The Add-In now includes Startup in the description of its Load Behavior (**Figure 12.9**).

3. Click OK.

   The next time VB starts, the Add-In is loaded automatically.

✔ Tip

- Unless an Add-In is set to Load on Startup, it will not be loaded with a project, even if the project was saved with it loaded.

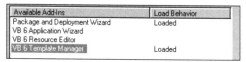

Figure 12.5 To unload a loaded Add-In, select it in the Available Add-Ins list.

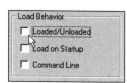

Figure 12.6 Uncheck the Loaded/Unloaded box to unload the selected Add-In.

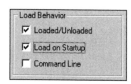

Figure 12.7 Select the Add-In you want to load automatically with VB.

Figure 12.8 Check Load on Startup to initiate automatic loading.

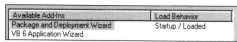

Figure 12.9 The Add-In's Load Behavior now includes the word Startup.

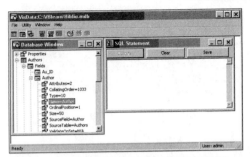

Figure 12.10 Select Visual Data Manager to start the Visual Data application.

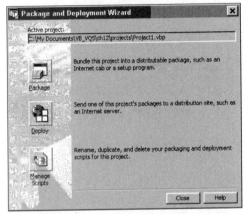

Figure 12.11 You can start the Package and Deployment Wizard from the Add-Ins menu if your project is saved.

Starting Add-Ins

Each Add-In decides for itself—meaning that its developers have decided—where it is placed in the Visual Basic menu structure.

To start the Visual Data Manager:

◆ From the Add-Ins menu, choose Visual Data Manager.

The Visual Data application opens (**Figure 12.10**).

✔ Tips

■ The Visual Data Manager is built into Visual Basic and cannot be loaded or unloaded through the Add-Ins Manager.

■ See Chapter 16 for more information on using the Visual Data Manager.

To start the Package and Deployment Wizard:

1. Make sure that the wizard is loaded in the Add-In Manager.

2. Save your current project.

3. From the Add-Ins menu, choose Package and Deployment Wizard.

The first screen of the Package and Deployment Wizard is displayed (**Figure 12.11**).

✔ Tips

■ To start the wizard, you must have saved your project. If you have not, a message box asks whether you want to save the project before starting the wizard.

■ You can also start the wizard by choosing Package and Deployment Wizard from the Windows Start menu.

■ For more information on using the wizard to create setup programs for your applications, see Chapter 16.

To start the Application Wizard:

1. Make sure that the wizard is loaded in the Add-In Manager.

2. From the Add-Ins menu select Application Wizard.

   The first panel of the Application Wizard opens (**Figure 12.12**).

✔ Tips

■ You can also start the Application wizard by choosing VB Application Wizard in the New Project dialog (**Figure 12.13**).

■ For information on using the Application Wizard to jump-start building your application, see Chapter 13.

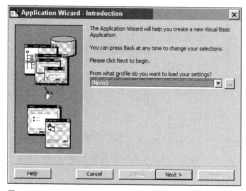

Figure 12.12 The Application Wizard presents a series of screens that help you jump-start building an application.

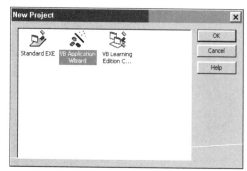

Figure 12.13 You can also start the Application Wizard from the New Project dialog.

Figure 12.14 The Resource Editor is used to store strings and graphics in .res files, which you can change without changing program code.

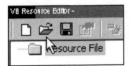

Figure 12.15 To open an existing resource file, click the Open button in the Resource Editor toolbar.

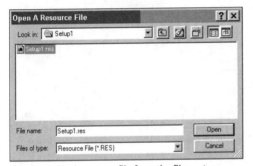

Figure 12.16 Select a .res file from the file system.

Figure 12.17 The resource file is displayed in the Resource Editor.

Using the Resource Editor

Resource files—identified with the .res file extension—are used to hold text strings and graphics that are part of an application. As an example, the text strings might be used to supply the text used for a command-button caption or a menu item.

The program that uses the resource files loads the strings and graphics in it when it runs to displays buttons and menus.

The point of this is that the text strings and graphics in the resource file can be changed without changing the program itself. Alternatively, different strings and graphics in the resource file can be loaded depending on—as a common real-life example—which language version of the program is needed.

To open the Resource Editor:

1. Make sure that the Resource Editor is loaded in the Add-In Manager.

2. From the Tools menu, choose Resource Editor.
   The Resource Editor opens (**Figure 12.14**).

To open a resource file:

1. In the Resource Editor toolbar, click the Open file button (**Figure 12.15**).
   The Open a Resource File dialog opens (**Figure 12.16**).

2. Use the Open dialog to browse the file system and select a .res file.

3. Click Open.
   The resource file is loaded in the Resource Editor (**Figure 12.17**).

To edit a resource string:

1. With a resource file open in the Resource Editor, click the plus sign to the left of the String Table folder (**Figure 12.18**) to expand it and view all the string tables present in the resource file (**Figure 12.19**).

2. Double-click the expanded string table to open it in edit mode (**Figure 12.20**).

3. Select the text string that you want to modify.

4. Type your new string (**Figure 12.21**).

5. Close the string table.

   When you close your Visual Basic project, you are asked whether you want to save or discard the changes in the resource file. To keep the changes you have made, select Save.

✔ Tips

- Be cautious about making changes in resource files—otherwise, you may start running into strange application messages!

- The Code Snippet template, which is part of the Template Manager, provides the code necessary for managing resource-file items in your programs.

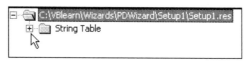

Figure 12.18 The String Table folder can contain many string tables.

Figure 12.19 The expanded String Table folder shows all the string tables in the resource file.

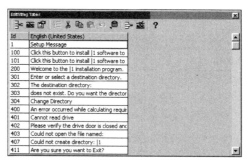

Figure 12.20 Double-click a string table to edit the strings that it contains.

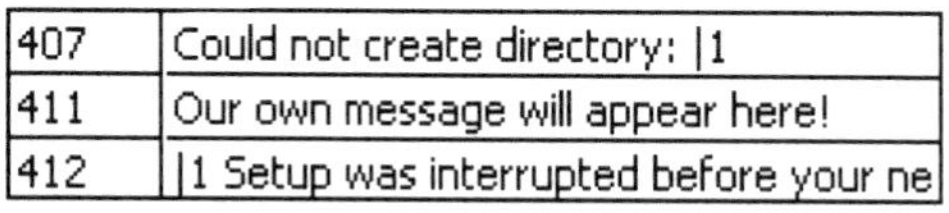

407	Could not create directory:	1
411	Our own message will appear here!
412		1 Setup was interrupted before your ne

Figure 12.21 If you select a string and start typing, the new text appears in place of the old text in the string table.

Figure 12.22
The Template Manager adds three new items to the Tools menu.

Figure 12.23 Code snippets help simplify two common programming chores.

Using the Template Manager

If the Template Manager is loaded in the Add-In Manager, you'll find three new items in the Tools menu (**Figure 12.22**):

◆ Add Code Snippet

◆ Add Menu

◆ Add Control Set

Code snippets are bits of code that handle common Visual Basic programming chores.

Menus are preconstructed menu-item combinations that conform to the menus used in most Windows applications.

Control sets are groups of controls prewired to work together—for example, a pair of list boxes with arrows that let you move items from one list box to the other and up and down within the lists.

To add a code snippet:

1. With the Template Manager loaded, select a module in your project to receive the code snippet.

2. From the Tools menu, choose Add Code Snippet.
   The Add Code Snippet dialog opens (**Figure 12.23**).

3. Select Load Resources, which adds code that manages resource-file items, or Registry Access, which adds code that manages storing and retrieving Registry information.

4. Click Open.
   The code is added to your module.

To add a menu to a form:

1. Make sure that the Template Manager is loaded in the Add-In Manager.

2. Open a form.

3. From the Tools menu, choose Add Menu. The Add Menu dialog opens (**Figure 12.24**).

4. Select a menu—for example, Edit Menu.

5. Click Open. The menu is added to the form (**Figure 12.25**).

✔ Tip

- See Chapter 15 for information about working with menus.

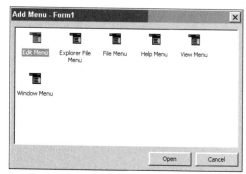

Figure 12.24 The Add Menu dialog allows you to choose among several prebuilt menus.

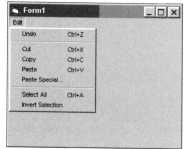

Figure 12.25 The menu you selected is displayed on the form.

USING THE TEMPLATE MANAGER

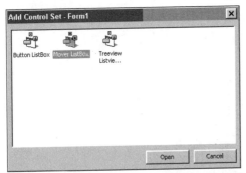

Figure 12.26 The Add Control Set dialog is used to add combinations of controls that are prewired to work together in your form.

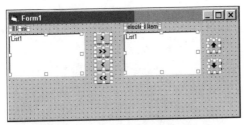

Figure 12.27 The Mover ListBox control set uses arrows to move items between the ListBoxes.

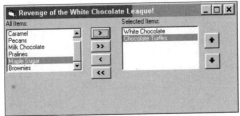

Figure 12.28 When you run the Mover ListBox control set, you'll find that it is fully functional.

To add a control set to a form:

1. Make sure that the Template Manager is loaded in the Add-In Manager.

2. Open a form.

3. From the Tools menu, choose Add Control Set.
   The Add Control Set dialog opens (**Figure 12.26**).

4. Select a control set—for example, the Mover ListBox.

5. Click Open.
   The code and controls for a pair of ListBoxes with arrows that allow items to move between them (and up and down) is added to the form (**Figure 12.27**).

6. If you run the form, you'll see that the controls all work together and are fully functional (**Figure 12.28**).

USING THE TEMPLATE MANAGER

Summary

In this chapter, you learned to:

- ◆ Work with the Add-In Manager.
- ◆ Start the Add-Ins.
- ◆ Use the Resource Editor Add-In.
- ◆ Work with the Template Manager.

THE VISUAL BASIC APPLICATION WIZARD

13

The Visual Basic Application Wizard is intended to provide you with a starting point for developing your applications. The wizard builds the common objects and forms used in many applications, such as toolbars and About boxes. It also adds some of the code required to makes these user interfaces work. (This code contains ToDo comments, indicating the additions that you will need to make for the application to fully work.)

It's up to you to customize the resulting forms, dialogs, and applications.

You can save a great deal of time by using the wizard. An additional benefit is that you can save particular styles of applications that you generate by using a wizard *profile* file. (The profile file is used to record your choices in the Application Wizard.) This means that you can use a wizard to provide a common look and feel for several applications that you write.

Running the Wizard

You can use the wizard to generate three styles of applications:

◆ Multiple Document Interface (MDI) (see Chapter 3 for an explanation of the MDI interface).

◆ Single Document Interface (SDI), which is the simplest, standard interface.

◆ Explorer-style, which creates a main form that mimics Windows Explorer.

The process for generating each of these applications is pretty much the same, except for the differences in the primary form generated.

To start the wizard:

1. In the New Project dialog, select VB Application Wizard (**Figure 13.1**).

2. Click OK.

or

1. Use the Add-In Manager to load the VB 6 Application Wizard (**Figure 13.2**).

2. From the Add-Ins menu, choose Application Wizard.

In either case, the first screen of the wizard opens (**Figure 13.3**).

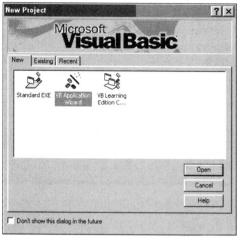

Figure 13.1 You can open the Application Wizard by selecting it in the New Project dialog.

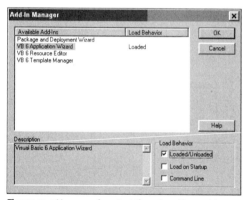

Figure 13.2 You can also start the wizard by making sure that it is loaded in the Add-In Manager and then choosing Application Wizard from the Add-Ins menu.

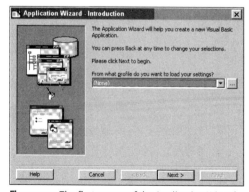

Figure 13.3 The first screen of the Application Wizard allows you to select a saved profile.

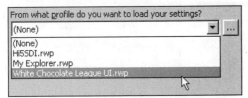

Figure 13.4 You can select the saved profile from the drop-down menu if it was saved in the default location.

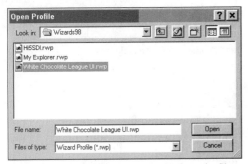

Figure 13.5 You can also select a profile from the file system.

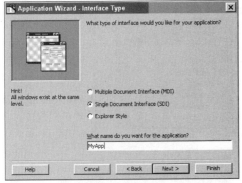

Figure 13.6 The Interface Type screen is used to choose an MDI, SDI, or Explorer-style interface.

To select a profile:

◆ If you have previously saved a profile, open that profile by choosing it from the drop-down menu in the Application Wizard - Introduction screen (**Figure 13.4**).

This has the effect of starting the wizard with the selections made in the profile as the default.

or

1. If you have not saved a profile, choose (None).

2. Click Next to continue with the wizard.

✔ Tip

■ If you saved a wizard profile in a location other than the wizard's home directory, you can open it from the Open Profile dialog (**Figure 13.5**), which you access by clicking the ellipsis in the Introduction screen.

To select an interface:

1. With the Interface Type screen open, choose the MDI, SDI, or Explorer interface (**Figure 13.6**) for your application's main form.

2. Provide a name for your application.

3. Click Next to continue.

To add menus to the main form:

1. With the Menus screen open (**Figure 13.7**), check the items in the Menus list that you want to include as upper-level menus (**Figure 13.8**).

2. With an upper-level menu selected, use the Sub Menus list to include, exclude, and order menu items (**Figure 13.9**).

3. Click Next to continue.

✔ Tip

■ To add a new menu or submenu, click the plus icon. The Add New Menu dialog opens (**Figure 13.10**). You can use this dialog to add a new menu caption and name to the lists. Adding menus is explained in Chapter 15.

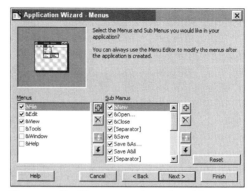

Figure 13.7 The Menus screen is used to add menus and menu items to the main form.

Figure 13.8 Selected items in the Menus list appear as menus on the form.

Figure 13.9 Selected items in the Sub Menus list appear as menu items on the form.

Figure 13.10 You can add new menus and menu items by using the Add New Menu dialog.

RUNNING THE WIZARD

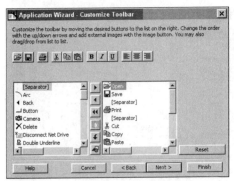

Figure 13.11 The Customize Toolbar screen is used to configure the toolbar that will appear along the top of the main form.

Figure 13.12 You can drag and drop or use the button control to add buttons to the Toolbar list box.

Figure 13.13 The current toolbar configuration is displayed across the top of the form.

Figure 13.14 The wizard can set up your application to load text strings from a Resource file.

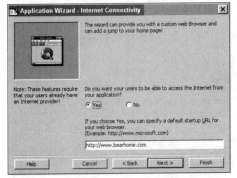

Figure 13.15 The wizard can add a Web browser to your application.

To customize the toolbar:

1. With the Customize Toolbar screen open (**Figure 13.11**), add buttons to the right list box to add them to the toolbar (**Figure 13.12**), and remove them from the right list box to remove them from the toolbar.

   The toolbar is displayed toward the top of the form (**Figure 13.13**).

2. Click Next to continue.

To complete the wizard:

1. Use the Resources screen to determine whether the text strings in your application will be read from a resource file (**Figure 13.14**).

   See Chapter 12 for an explanation of Resource files.

2. Click Next to continue.

3. Use the Internet Connectivity screen to specify whether you want the wizard to add a Web browser to your application (**Figure 13.15**).

4. Click Next to continue.

continues on next page

RUNNING THE WIZARD

5. Use the Standard Forms screen to select forms for inclusion in your application (**Figure 13.16**).

You can choose to add a splash screen, a login dialog, an Options dialog, and an About Box.

6. Click Form Templates to make additional form choices (**Figure 13.17**).

7. Select any template-based form that you'd like to add to your application.

8. Click Next.

The Data Access Forms screen (**Figure 13.18**) requires the Professional or Enterprise Edition of VB6. If you have the Learning Edition and attempt to use this screen by clicking Create New Form, you get an error message (**Figure 13.19**).

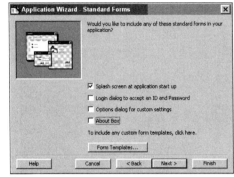

Figure 13.16 You can add a splash screen, a login dialog, an Options dialog, or an About box to your application.

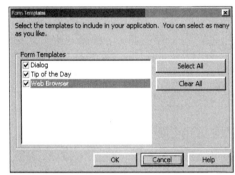

Figure 13.17 You can also add template-based forms to your application.

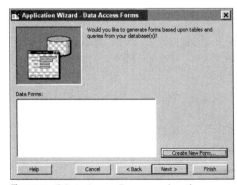

Figure 13.18 Data Access Forms requires the Professional or Enterprise Edition.

Figure 13.19 If you click Create New Form in the Learning Edition, you get an error.

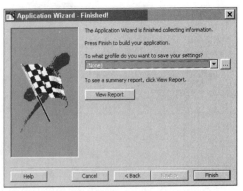

Figure 13.20 The Finished! screen is used to save your current wizard settings.

Figure 13.21 You can give your settings any profile name.

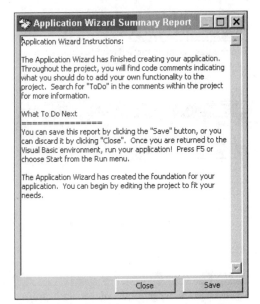

Figure 13.22 You can view a report on the wizard's activities—but you will not learn a great deal from it.

9. Click Next.

10. The Finished! screen of the wizard (**Figure 13.20**) lets you save your configuration choices as a profile by choosing a profile name from the drop-down list.

    To give the profile a new name, click the ellipsis to open the Save Profile dialog (**Figure 13.21**).

11. Click View Report to view a report on the wizard's activities (**Figure 13.22**).

12. Click Finish to finish the wizard process.

    Your application is generated, and a dialog states that the wizard is complete (**Figure 13.23**).

Figure 13.23 After you click Finish, the application is generated.

Running the Application

The project that the wizard has created is a normal Visual Basic application. You can run it as you would any other VB app: by choosing Start from the Run menu or by pressing the F5 key.

Your application will vary, depending on whether you selected a Multiple Document Interface (**Figure 13.24**), Single Document Interface (**Figure 13.25**), or Explorer-style application (**Figure 13.26**).

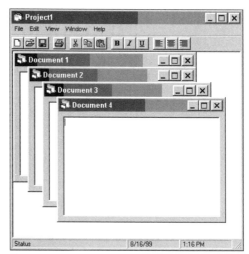

Figure 13.24 The MDI application created by the wizard includes MDI children that use the RichTextBox control.

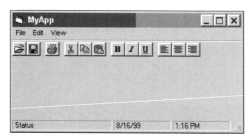

Figure 13.25 The main form of the SDI application created by the wizard is a normal form with a toolbar.

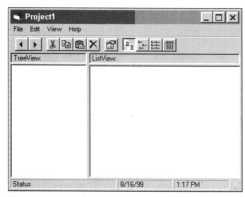

Figure 13.26 The Explorer-style interface includes controls that replicate the functionality of Windows Explorer.

Figure 13.27 The splash screen needs to have the blanks filled in.

Figure 13.28 The menus and toolbar that you specified are on the main form.

Figure 13.29 If you choose to add a Web browser, it is fully capable of browsing the Web.

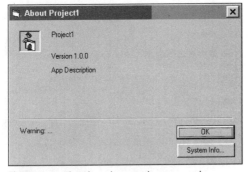

Figure 13.30 The About box needs some work.

To view the forms in the application created in the wizard:

1. Run the project.

   The splash screen is displayed (**Figure 13.27**) while the main form is loading (**Figure 13.28**).

2. From the View menu, choose Web Browser.

   The Web browser opens (**Figure 13.29**).

3. Close the Web browser.

4. From the Help menu, choose About.

   The About box opens (**Figure 13.30**).

5. Click System Info to open the Microsoft System Information utility (**Figure 13.31**).

✔ Tip

■ If a menu item (for example, Options in the View menu) doesn't do anything, a message box appears, telling you to add code for this item (**Figure 13.32**). This kind of placeholder, or reminder, is sometimes called a *stub*.

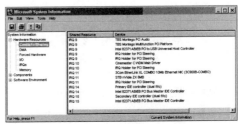

Figure 13.31 The Microsoft System Information utility is invoked from the About box.

Figure 13.32 Placeholder code is used for menu items that have no functionality yet.

Modifying the Application

The Application Wizard has created a Visual Basic application with quite a few forms and a code module. The project is shown in Project Explorer in **Figure 13.33**.

To customize the application:

1. In turn, open each of the forms shown in Project Explorer.

2. Using the Properties Window, modify control values until the text displayed and other properties are the way you want them.

3. Open each of the forms and modules in the Code Editor.

4. Every time you see a ToDo comment,

   `'TODO:`

   add the code suggested by the comment.

5. Save and run the project.

6. Make further modifications as you desire.

✔ Tip

■ The splash screen and the About box read some of the values that they display from properties of the project:

```
Private Sub Form_Load()
    lblVersion.Caption = "Version " &
    → App.Major & "." & App.Minor &
    → "." & App.Revision
    lblTitle.Caption = App.Title
End Sub
```

You can set these properties on the Make tab of the Project Properties dialog (**Figure 13.34**).

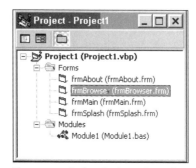

Figure 13.33 Project Explorer shows the forms and code module created by the Application Wizard.

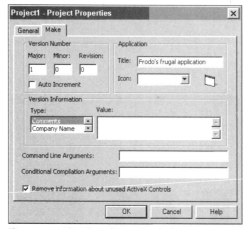

Figure 13.34 The About box and splash screen use values supplied on the Make tab of the Project Properties dialog.

Summary

In this chapter, you learned to:

◆ Run the VB Application Wizard.

◆ Run an application created by the wizard.

◆ Modify an application created by the wizard.

14

MENUS

An application without menus is like an opera singer without a voice. Fortunately, Visual Basic makes it easy to add menus to your applications.

In theory, every aspect of the user interface in a Windows application should be accessible in three ways: by clicking controls, by clicking menu items, and by using the keyboard. You've already seen how to make parts of an application available to users via control events. The good news is that you can add keyboard access at the same time that you add menus, with little extra work.

As you probably know, menus usually are arranged in hierarchies. A top-level menu, referred to simply as a *menu*, is used to display a list of menu items. (This list is sometimes called a *submenu*.) A menu item can itself be a menu when it is used to display submenu items. (As an example, consider the New submenu in the File menu of Windows Explorer.)

To confuse this terminology a bit more, *menu* is sometimes used to mean both menus and menu items.

As a general rule, no application should have submenus nested more than two levels below the primary application menus.

The Visual Basic Menu Editor makes it easy to understand and manage menu hierarchies because these relationships are shown visually with indentation.

In this chapter, I'll show you how to work with the Menu Editor to create menus and menu items. You'll learn how to add keyboard access at the same time.

For many of the examples in this chapter, I'll use the Common Dialog project from Chapter 9 as the starting place. Many of the menu items invoke the procedures that were developed in Chapter 9. As you'll see, this doesn't take much code—just a one-line call to the Click event of the command button. In this way, your code can do double duty.

After you learn how to add menus to your applications, you'll move on to learn how to dynamically enable, disable, and check your menu items in response to user actions.

Finally, I'll show you how to create pop-up menus, which are menus that appear when the right mouse button is clicked.

So let's get on with it! Your poor, menuless applications are whining and wailing. It's time to give them back their voices so that they can be the Pavarottis they were meant to be!

MENUS

Naming Menus and Menu Items

The name of a menu or menu item is not the menu's caption, which appears on the form—for example, File or Edit. The menu's name is, instead, a programmatic label for the menu object that users never see.

It's conventional to use the prefix mnu for menus and menu items. The suffix for a menu should be the menu's caption—for example, mnuFile and mnuEdit.

Menu items should start with the menu that they are part of and append their caption. The New menu item in the File menu should be named mnuFileNew, for example, and the Open menu item in the File menu should be named mnuFileOpen.

Because the Objects list in the Code Editor is alphabetical, this practice serves the purpose of grouping all the menu items on a menu.

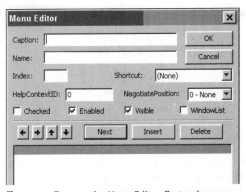

Figure 14.1 To open the Menu Editor, first make sure that you have a form selected.

Adding Menus

Menus are the top level of a window's menu hierarchy, running along a window from left to right. In most cases, selecting a menu opens a submenu of menu items.

In this section, I'll assume that you are creating the entire top level of menus before creating menu items. In the real world, a mix-and-match technique is more likely to apply; menus and menu items are created as part of the same process.

To open the Menu Editor:

1. Make sure that a form is open and selected.

2. From the Tools menu, choose Menu Editor. The Menu Editor opens (**Figure 14.1**).

Access Keys

Access keys are used to navigate a menu hierarchy in conjunction with the Alt key. If the access key for the File menu is F and the access key for the New item in the File menu is N, pressing Alt+F followed by Alt+N has the same effect as clicking the New menu item —that is, it invokes the code in the New menu item's Click event.

It's a principle of interface usability that every menu item can be reached via a combination of access keys.

To create an access key, use the Menu Editor to place an ampersand (&) in the caption of the menu or menu item before the letter that will be used for access.

It's important that access keys be unique at each menu level. (If you don't follow this technique, the results are unpredictable.) The upper-level menu access keys must not be duplicated, for example, and all access keys for menu items in the File menu must be unique. The Save menu item in the File menu and the Select All menu item in the Edit menu, however, could both use S as their access key. Although access keys are often the first letter of the caption, to avoid duplication, you can use a subsequent letter instead— for example, E&xit, making Alt+X the access key for the Exit menu item.

To add menus:

1. With the Menu Editor open, type a caption for the first menu in the Caption box—for example, &File.

   The caption is the text that appears along the window's menu bar. The ampersand (&) means that the letter next to it (F) is an *access* key: the Alt key plus the access key have the same functionality as clicking the menu.

2. Type a name for the menu in the Name box— for example, mnuFile.

   The menu caption now appears in the menu list (**Figure 14.2**).

3. Click Next to move to the next menu.

4. Repeat the process to add a mnuEdit, mnuColor, mnuHoudini, and mnuHelp (**Figure 14.3**).

5. Click OK.

   The menus have been added to the window's title bar (**Figure 14.4**).

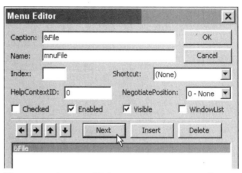

Figure 14.2 As you add them, menus appear in the Menu Editor's list.

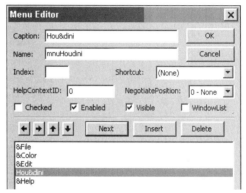

Figure 14.3 Menus are entered top to bottom.

Figure 14.4 Menus are displayed across a window from left to right.

ADDING MENUS

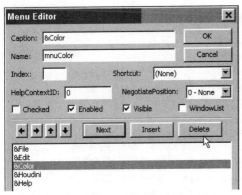

Figure 14.5 Select a menu so that you can delete it.

Figure 14.6 After you delete the menu, it is not displayed in the window's menu bar.

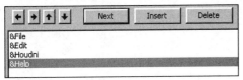

Figure 14.7 To insert a new menu, first select the menu below the new menu's proposed location.

Figure 14.8 Click the Insert button to add a new menu.

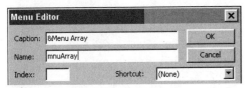

Figure 14.9 Type a name and caption for the new menu in the Menu Editor.

Figure 14.10 Menus appear from left to right on the window's menu bar.

To delete a menu:

1. In the Menu Editor's menu list, select the menu that you want to delete (**Figure 14.5**).

2. Click Delete.

3. Click OK.
   The menu no longer appears in the window (**Figure 14.6**).

✔ Tip

- To edit a menu's name or caption, select the menu and type the new information.

To insert a new menu:

1. In the Menu Editor, select the menu below your proposed new menu (**Figure 14.7**).

2. Click Insert (**Figure 14.8**).
   A space is added for the new menu (**Figure 14.9**).

3. Type a caption for the menu in the Caption box.

4. Type a name for the menu in the Name box.

5. Click OK.
   The new menu appears in the window's menu bar (**Figure 14.10**).

ADDING MENUS

To move a menu up:

1. In the Menu Editor's menu list, select the menu that you want to move up (**Figure 14.11**).

2. Click the up-arrow button to move the menu up one position.

   The menu moves left (by one menu) in the window's menu bar (**Figure 14.12**).

To move a menu down:

1. In the Menu Editor's menu list, select the menu that you want to move down (**Figure 14.13**).

2. Click the down-arrow button to move the menu down one position.

   The menu moves right in the window's menu bar.

Figure 14.11 Select a menu to change its position.

Figure 14.12 A menu that has been moved up moves left in the window's menu bar.

Figure 14.13 The up- and down-arrow buttons are used to position menus and menu items.

Shortcut Keys

Shortcut keys differ from access keys in that they provide immediate invocation of the functionality of a menu item. To reach a menu item using access keys, you must navigate the menu hierarchy.

Shortcut keys are assigned to menu items (not menus) via a drop-down menu in the Menu Editor.

Shortcut keys—actually, keyboard combinations, such as Ctrl+O—must be unique across an entire application.

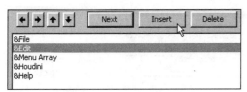

Figure 14.14 Select the menu below the menu to which you want to add menu items.

Figure 14.15 Click the right-arrow button to indent the menu item, placing it below the menu above it in the hierarchy.

Figure 14.16 The indentation, and order in the hierarchy, are indicated by an ellipsis.

Figure 14.17 You can assign a shortcut key to a menu item by using the drop-down menu.

Menu Items

Menu items appear when you select a menu. You then choose a menu item to get the application to perform a task.

It is also true that menu items can themselves be menus. In this case, when you choose the menu item, a submenu appears.

You create and position menu items in the Menu Editor by using the same methods that you use for menus (see the preceding section). There are only a few differences between menu items and menus in the Menu Editor.

The most important distinction is that a menu item is indented to the right below a menu. Indeed, the series of menu items indented below a menu becomes that menu's submenu (sometimes called a *flyout menu*). The little right arrow, which performs the indentation in the Menu Editor, precipitates this consequence.

Another difference between menu items and menus is that you can assign a shortcut key to the former in the Menu Editor.

To insert menu items:

1. In the Menu Editor's menu list, select the menu to which you want to add menu items (**Figure 14.14**).

2. Click the Insert button to add a space below the menu.

3. Click the right-arrow button to indent the menu one level in the hierarchy (**Figure 14.15**).

   An ellipsis appears, representing the indentation (**Figure 14.16**).

4. Type a caption for the menu item in the Caption box (**Figure 14.17**).

continues on next page

5. Type a name for the menu item in the Name box (**Figure 14.17**).

Be sure to include the menu name as a prefix of the menu item's name.

6. Use the drop-down menu to assign a shortcut key to the menu item (**Figure 14.17**).

7. Click OK.

You now see the menu item with its shortcut key indicated as part of the window's menu system (**Figure 14.18**).

8. Repeat the process to add more menu items (**Figures 14.19** and **14.20**).

9. Click OK.

The menu items appear as part of the window's menu system (**Figure 14.21**).

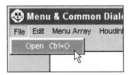

Figure 14.18 When you choose the menu, the menu item appears.

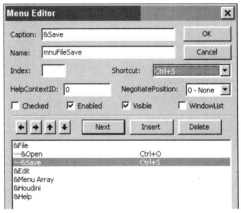

Figure 14.19 Menu items that are indented at the same level below a menu form a submenu.

Figure 14.20 Shortcut keys that have been assigned to menu items appear to the right of the menu item.

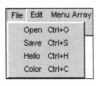

Figure 14.21 When you choose the menu, the entire submenu appears.

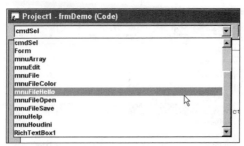

Figure 14.22 It's a great convenience to name menu items so that they appear with the other menu items in their submenu in the Objects list of the Code Editor.

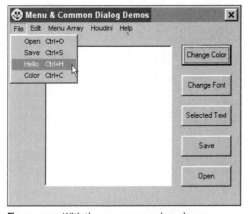

Figure 14.23 With the program running, choose a menu item to execute the code in the menu item's Click event.

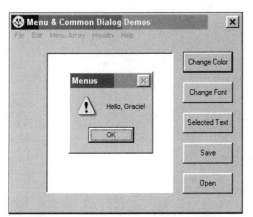

Figure 14.24 The message box invoked in the menu item's Click event is displayed.

Menu Click Events

Each menu item has an associated Click event. This event is fired when the user chooses the menu item.

For the user's menu-item choice to have any consequences, code must be placed in the menu item's Click event.

When you use the Code Editor to add code to a menu Click event, you first must use the Objects list to locate the menu item. This task makes it important that you name menu items by following the suggestions in the "Naming Menus and Menu Items" sidebar earlier in this chapter.

To add code to a menu item's Click event:

1. Open the Code Editor.

2. From the Objects list, choose select mnuFileHello (which is a menu item in the File menu with the caption Hello) (**Figure 14.22**).

   An event code framework is created for you.

3. Add code to display a message box:

```
Private Sub mnuFileHello_Click()
    MsgBox "Hello, Gracie!",
      → vbExclamation, "Menus"
End Sub
```

4. Run the project.

5. Choose the Hello menu item (**Figure 14.23**).

   The message box appears (**Figure 14.24**).

✔ Tip

■ You should also verify that the access key and the shortcut key assigned to the menu item also invoke the message box.

Separators

Separators appear in a submenu as lines that separate menu items. They are used to categorize menu items.

To add menu-item separators:

1. In the Menu Editor's menu list, click Insert to add a space for the separator.

2. Click the right-arrow button to indent the separator into its appropriate submenu.

3. In the Caption box, type a hyphen (-).

4. In the Name box, enter any unique name.

   It's a good idea to name your separators something like mnuSep0 and mnuSep1, so that you know what they are, even though separators do not generate Click event code and are not used programmatically.

5. Repeat the process.

   Each separator appears in the menu list as a dash (**Figure 14.25**).

6. Click OK.

   The separators now appear on the menu (**Figure 14.26**).

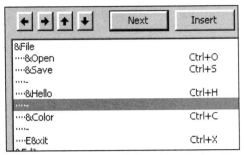

Figure 14.25 A separator is indicated by a dash in the Menu Editor.

Figure 14.26 Separators are used in submenus to group menu items by subject matter.

Listing 14.1 Wiring Menu Items by Using Existing Event Procedures

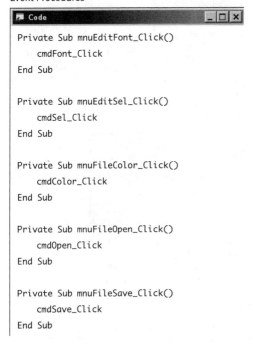

```
Private Sub mnuEditFont_Click()
    cmdFont_Click
End Sub


Private Sub mnuEditSel_Click()
    cmdSel_Click
End Sub


Private Sub mnuFileColor_Click()
    cmdColor_Click
End Sub


Private Sub mnuFileOpen_Click()
    cmdOpen_Click
End Sub


Private Sub mnuFileSave_Click()
    cmdSave_Click
End Sub
```

Figure 14.27 The ampersand—indicating the access key for a menu or menu item—can be placed in front of any letter in the menu text string.

| Change Font |
| Change Selected Text |

Figure 14.28
The Edit menu now has a submenu.

Replacing Buttons with Menus

To have a menu system with menu items that access the functionality of the application developed in Chapter 9, it's necessary to add a few more menu items (**Figures 14.27** and **14.28**). These features were originally accessed via command buttons.

The plan is to wire the menu items that use the existing event procedures, so that no new code has to be written. **Listing 14.1** contains the complete code for connecting menu items to the command-button functionality of the application.

To wire the menu items with existing code:

1. For each menu item that you want to connect to an existing event procedure, use the Objects list in the Code Editor to open a Click event procedure.

   For example:

   ```
   Private Sub mnuFileOpen_Click()

   End Sub
   ```

2. Within the menu event framework, place a call to the related command-button event procedure:

   ```
   cmdOpen_Click
   ```

3. Run the project to verify that choosing the menu item achieves the same functionality as clicking the button.

✔ Tip

- If you look at an event procedure itself, you'll see that its declaration uses parentheses—for example, cmdOpen_Click(). To call the event procedure, leave the parentheses off.

To add code to unload a form:

◆ The following code works well as an exit Click event:

```
Private Sub mnuFileExit_Click()
    Unload Me
End Sub
```

To add submenus:

1. In the Menu Editor, click the right-arrow button to make indented menu items below a menu.

2. Add names and captions for the menu items (**Figure 14.29**).

3. Click the right-arrow button to indent again below one of the menu items you just created (**Figure 14.29**).

4. Add several menu items at the new level of indentation, providing names and captions for the menu items (**Figure 14.29**).

5. Click OK.

   When you run the project, if you select the initial menu, you'll see the submenus that you created (**Figure 14.30**).

Figure 14.29 Menu items in a submenu can themselves be menus and have their own submenus.

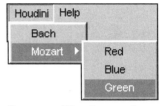

Figure 14.30 When the user chooses a menu item that has menu items below it, a flyout menu appears.

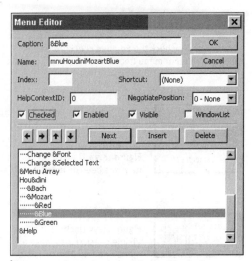

Figure 14.31 Put a check mark in the Checked checkbox to check a menu item.

Figure 14.32 A check mark appears next to the menu item.

Dynamic Menu Items

Dynamic means to change something at run time in response to a user action. In the case of menu items, three properties are often manipulated dynamically:

◆ *Checked,* meaning that a check mark is placed next to the menu item.

◆ *Enabled,* meaning that the menu or menu item responds to the mouse (and keyboard). A disabled menu or menu item appears grayed out. You will not be able to access menu items below a disabled menu.

◆ *Visible,* meaning that the menu item appears on the screen in the menu hierarchy. If a menu is not visible, menu items below it are automatically not visible. Also, a menu or menu item that is not visible is not enabled.

These properties can all be set at design time in the Menu Editor. Before learning how to change these properties dynamically in code, let's run through setting them in the Menu Editor.

To check a menu item:

1. With the Menu Editor open, select the menu item that you want to check (**Figure 14.31**).

2. Check the Checked checkbox.

3. Click OK.

   The menu item appears with a check next to it (**Figure 14.32**).

✔ Tip

■ Top-level menus—as opposed to menu items—cannot be checked.

To disable a menu or menu item:

1. With the Menu Editor open, select the menu or menu item that you want to disable.

2. Uncheck the Enabled checkbox (**Figure 14.33**).

3. Click OK.

   The menu or menu item is grayed out (**Figure 14.34**).

To render a menu or menu item invisible:

1. With the Menu Editor open, select the menu or menu item that you want to make invisible.

2. Uncheck the Visible checkbox (**Figure 14.35**).

3. Click OK.

   The menu or menu item is no longer visible (**Figure 14.36**).

Figure 14.33 Uncheck the Enabled checkbox to disable a menu or menu item.

Figure 14.34 The Red menu item has been disabled.

Figure 14.35 Uncheck the Visible check box to make a menu or menu item invisible.

Figure 14.36 The Red menu item is no longer visible.

Listing 14.2 Toggling Menu Check Marks

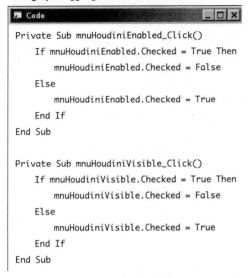

```
Private Sub mnuHoudiniEnabled_Click()
    If mnuHoudiniEnabled.Checked = True Then
        mnuHoudiniEnabled.Checked = False
    Else
        mnuHoudiniEnabled.Checked = True
    End If
End Sub


Private Sub mnuHoudiniVisible_Click()
    If mnuHoudiniVisible.Checked = True Then
        mnuHoudiniVisible.Checked = False
    Else
        mnuHoudiniVisible.Checked = True
    End If
End Sub
```

Figure 14.37 Add two new menu items, one to toggle the Red menu item's Enabled property and the other to toggle the Mozart menu's Visible property.

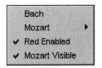

Figure 14.38 The menu items are initially checked.

Dynamic Menu Manipulation

It's time to move on to manipulating the Checked, Enabled, and Visible properties dynamically. To demonstrate this, we'll add Red Enabled and Mozart Visible menu items to the Houdini menu in the sample project. Each of these menu items presents a checked or unchecked state, which can be toggled by the user. When Red Enabled is checked, the Red menu is enabled; when it is unchecked, the Red menu is disabled. When Mozart Visible is checked, the Mozart menu and its submenu are visible; if it is unchecked, the Mozart menu and submenu are not visible.

To toggle check marks:

1. In the Menu Editor, add the Red Enabled and Mozart Visible menu items (**Figure 14.37**).

   Make sure that you check the Checked checkbox for both menu items.

2. Click OK.

   The menu items are added to the Houdini menu (**Figure 14.38**).

3. Use the Code Editor to add to each of the two menu items' Click events code that determines whether the menu item is checked (see **Listing 14.2**).

   If it is, the code unchecks the menu item. If the menu is not checked, the code checks it.

4. Run the project.

   You'll find that the check marks next to these two menu items toggle when you click the menu items.

The next step is adding code that actually enables the menu or menu item (or makes the menu or menu item visible) inside the check mark toggle.

DYNAMIC MENU ITEMS

To enable and disable a menu or menu item in code:

1. Use the Code Editor to add two lines of code to the mnuHoudiniEnabled_Click procedure to toggle the Enabled state of mnuHoudiniMozartRed (see **Listing 14.3**).

2. Run the project.

3. Choose the Houdini menu.

   The Red Enabled item is checked, and the Red menu item is enabled (**Figure 14.39**).

4. Choose the Red Enabled item.

   It is unchecked, and the Red menu item is now grayed out (**Figure 14.40**).

Listing 14.3 Enabling and Disabling a Menu Item

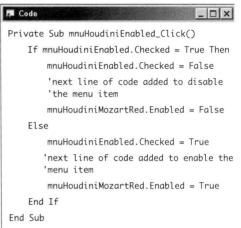

```
Private Sub mnuHoudiniEnabled_Click()
    If mnuHoudiniEnabled.Checked = True Then
        mnuHoudiniEnabled.Checked = False
        'next line of code added to disable
        'the menu item
        mnuHoudiniMozartRed.Enabled = False
    Else
        mnuHoudiniEnabled.Checked = True
        'next line of code added to enable the
        'menu item
        mnuHoudiniMozartRed.Enabled = True
    End If
End Sub
```

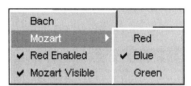

Figure 14.39 The Red menu item is enabled.

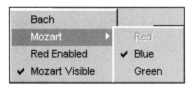

Figure 14.40 When you click the Red Enabled menu item, its check mark toggles, and the Red menu is disabled.

Listing 14.4 Making a Menu Visible or Invisible

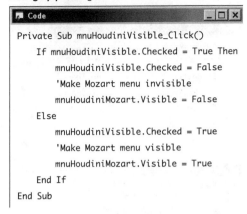

```
Private Sub mnuHoudiniVisible_Click()
    If mnuHoudiniVisible.Checked = True Then
        mnuHoudiniVisible.Checked = False
        'Make Mozart menu invisible
        mnuHoudiniMozart.Visible = False
    Else
        mnuHoudiniVisible.Checked = True
        'Make Mozart menu visible
        mnuHoudiniMozart.Visible = True
    End If
End Sub
```

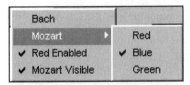

Figure 14.41 The Mozart Visible item is checked, and the Mozart menu item and submenu are visible.

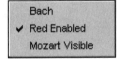

Figure 14.42 The Mozart Visible item is unchecked, and the Mozart menu item and submenu are nowhere to be seen.

To make a menu or menu item visible or invisible:

1. Add two lines of code to the mnuHoudiniVisible_Click event to toggle the visible state of mnuHoudiniMozart (see **Listing 14.4**).

2. Run the project.

3. Choose the Houdini menu.

    The Mozart Visible item is checked, and the Mozart item and submenu are visible (**Figure 14.41**).

4. Choose Mozart Visible.

    The Mozart Visible item is unchecked, and the Mozart item and submenu has disappeared (**Figure 14.42**).

5. To restore the Mozart item and submenu, choose Mozart Visible again.

DYNAMIC MENU ITEMS

Pop-Up Menus

You create a pop-up menu by setting the Visible property of a menu to False. For a menu to pop up, the menu must contain a submenu. The PopupMenu method of a form is used to display the submenu when the user right-clicks the form. Actually, you can use the PopupMenu method to pop the menu when either mouse button is clicked, but it's more typical to use it with the right mouse button only.

The complete event code for generating a right-mouse-button pop-up menu is shown in **Listing 14.5.**

To create a right-mouse-button pop-up menu:

1. With the Menu Editor open, create a menu item named PopUp in the Houdini menu to host the pop-up submenu (**Figure 14.43**).

2. Make sure that the Visible box is unchecked.

3. Use the Menu Editor to add submenu items below PopUp (**Figure 14.44**).

4. Click OK.

   Notice that PopUp and its submenu do not appear in the form's menu display (**Figure 14.45**).

5. Use the Code Editor to open the framework for the form's MouseDown event.

6. Add code to the event framework that tests for the right mouse button's having been clicked:

   ```
   If Button = vbRightButton Then

   End If
   ```

Listing 14.5 Popping a Menu When the Right Mouse Button Is Clicked

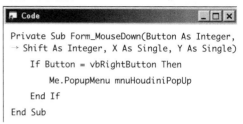

```
Private Sub Form_MouseDown(Button As Integer,
   Shift As Integer, X As Single, Y As Single)
      If Button = vbRightButton Then
         Me.PopupMenu mnuHoudiniPopUp
      End If
End Sub
```

Figure 14.43 To create a pop-up menu, first add a menu item that is not visible.

Figure 14.44 Menu items placed below the invisible menu become the pop-up menu submenu.

Figure 14.45 When you run the form, the pop-up menu is not visible.

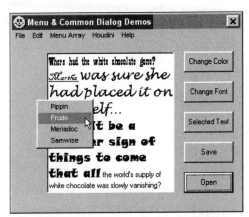

Figure 14.46 When the form is running, right-clicking opens the pop-up menu.

7. Add code to the If statement that invokes the form's PopupMenu method:

```
Me.PopupMenu mnuHoudiniPopUp
```

8. Run the project.

9. Right-click anywhere on the form. The pop-up menu is displayed (**Figure 14.46**).

✔ Tips

■ To open the pop-up menu no matter which mouse button was clicked, add the PopupMenu method to the form's Click event instead:

```
Private Sub Form_Click()
    Me.PopupMenu mnuHoudiniPopUp
End Sub
```

■ You can add code to the Click events of the pop-up menu items the way that you would for normal menu items.

Summary

In this chapter, you learned to:

◆ Use the Menu Editor to add menus.

◆ Work with menus and menu items.

◆ Add access keys and shortcut keys.

◆ Invoke a control's event code from a menu's Click event.

◆ Add submenus.

◆ Create menus that respond dynamically to user actions.

◆ Create pop-up menus.

15

DATABASES

Ultimately, all programs of any sophistication require access to stored data. This access can be accomplished in ways ranging from reading and saving information to files to interacting with sophisticated database programs.

Without the ability to work with stored values, your program has no memory from one time it is run to the next. Programs that handle tasks such as managing inventory or handling accounting chores must be able to save their work—and pick up where they left off.

Using the resources in the Learning Edition, this chapter explains how to create programs that work with stored data. You'll be glad to know that you can create database applications in Visual Basic with little programming knowledge. You also do not need a sophisticated understanding of databases. All you really need to know about databases is that they are internally organized in tables. Each table contains rows and columns, called *fields*, of information. A row across the table is called a *record*.

You may have heard the term *relational* database. Essentially, this term means that the data resides in tables of the sort I just described that are largely independent of one another. SQL (Structured Query Language) is the common language used to manipulate and obtain information from relational databases.

This chapter explains how to use the Data control to bind intrinsic controls, such as text boxes and list boxes, to a database. You learn how to populate the fields in a grid without using any code.

Next, I'll show you how to work with the Visual Data Manager, a tool that lets you view the structure of databases. You can also use the Visual Data Manager to run SQL queries against databases and create new databases.

The Data Manager can greatly speed development; it will automatically build a data-aware form for you.

Using the Data Control

The Data control is an intrinsic control used to *bind*—that is, create a connection—between a database and controls such as text boxes. A database is assigned to the Data control via its properties. Then individual controls are bound to the Data control.

To add a Data control to a form:

1. With a form open, double-click the Data control in the Toolbox (**Figure 15.1**).

   The Data control is placed on the form (**Figure 15.2**).

2. Using the Properties Window, change the caption of the Data control to something descriptive, such as Click here to control data display (**Figure 15.3**).

✔ Tip

- Figure 15.2 shows the navigation buttons that are built into the Data control.

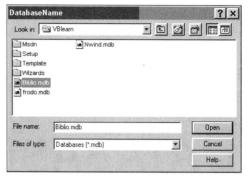

Figure 15.1 Double-click the Data control to add it to a form.

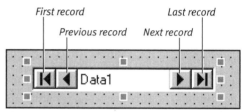

Figure 15.2 The Data control allows users to navigate forward and backward in a data set.

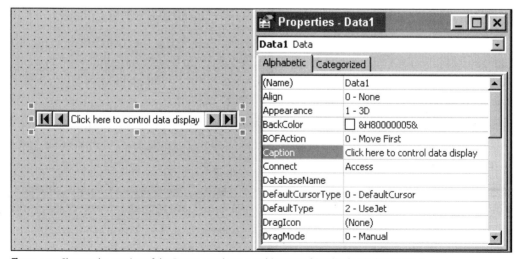

Figure 15.3 Change the caption of the Data control to something user-friendly that indicates its purpose.

USING THE DATA CONTROL

Figure 15.4 The DatabaseName property is used to connect a database to the Data control.

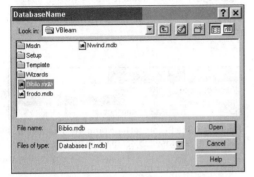

Figure 15.5 You can browse the file system to find a database file.

Figure 15.6 The database file that you select is assigned to the DatabaseName property.

To connect the Data control to a database:

1. With the Data control open in the Properties Window, select the DatabaseName property in the left column (**Figure 15.4**).

2. Click the ellipsis in the right column.

   The DatabaseName dialog opens (**Figure 15.5**).

3. From your file system, select a database.

4. Click Open.

The database file now appears in the right column of the Properties Window (**Figure 15.6**). The sample Biblio.mdb database is shown in the figure.

✔ Tips

- Visual Basic is often used with Microsoft Access databases. Access database files have the .mdb suffix.

- Visual Basic ships with two sample Access databases—Biblio.mdb and Nwind.mdb—for you to experiment with. You can find these databases in your Visual Basic home directory.

- Data control property assignments can also be made in code.

   Biblio consists of publisher, author, and book tables. Nwind is the inventory database of a fictional food-trading company.

USING THE DATA CONTROL

The RecordSource Property

To bind other controls to the Data control, you must specify a table within the database that will be used to supply data. To do so, you use the Data control's RecordSource property.

To specify the RecordSource:

1. With the Data control selected in the Properties Window, select the RecordSource property in the left column.

   Provided that a valid DatabaseName property has been set, a drop-down menu of tables appears in the right column.

2. Select the table that you want to be the data source for bound controls (Publishers is shown in **Figure 15.7**).

You can use the Data control's RecordSetType property to determine the type of recordset object that is used to manipulate data (**Figure 15.8**). You have three choices:

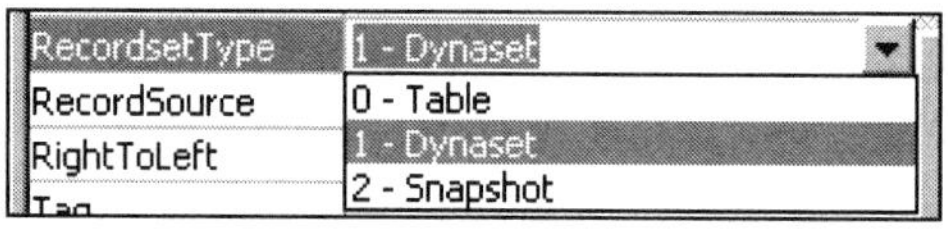

◆ **Table-type recordset.** This is a normal table view that can be used to add or edit records.

◆ **Dynaset-type recordset.** This is the default setting. A *dynaset* contains fields from one or more tables—possibly resulting from a query. It is editable and updatable.

◆ **Snapshot-type recordset.** This is a read-only set of static records that can be examined but not edited.

Figure 15.7 The RecordSource property determines the table that will be used to provide data to bound controls.

Figure 15.8 The RecordsetType property determines the kind of recordset object that will be accessed.

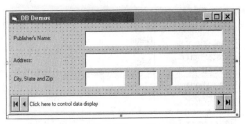

Figure 15.9 You can bind different text boxes to different fields in a table.

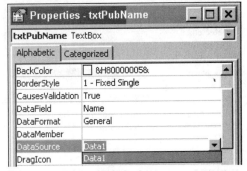

Figure 15.10 Each TextBox's DataSource property must be set to the data control (Data1).

Figure 15.11 The DataField property of the txtPubName control is set to the Name field.

Figure 15.12 The DataField property of the txtAddress control is set to the Address field.

Binding Controls

The next step is to bind controls to the Data control that you created in the preceding section. We'll start by displaying the name, address, city, state, and ZIP codes of the publishers in the Biblio database. You'll be pleased to learn that this process requires no use of code.

To bind text boxes to the Data control:

1. Add text boxes to the form containing the Data control to represent the required fields (**Figure 15.9**).

2. Name the text boxes txtPubName, txtAddress, txtCity, txtState, and txtZip.

3. Using the Properties Window, set the Text property of each TextBox so that it is empty.

4. With txtPubName active in the Properties Window, select its DataSource property.

5. Use the drop-down menu in the right column to set the DataSource to Data1, the default name for a Data control (**Figure 15.10**).

6. Select txtPubName's DataField property.

7. Use the drop-down menu in the right column to set the DataField property to Name (**Figure 15.11**).

8. Select txtAddress in the Properties Window.

9. Set its DataSource property to Data1.

10. Use the drop-down menu in the right column to set the DataField property to Address (**Figure 15.12**).

11. Select txtCity in the Properties Window.

12. Set its DataSource property to Data1.

continues on next page

13. Use the drop-down menu in the right column to set the DataField property to City (**Figure 15.13**).

14. Select txtState in the Properties Window.

15. Set its DataSource property to Data1.

16. Use the drop-down menu in the right column to set the DataField property to State (**Figure 15.14**).

17. Select txtZip in the Properties Window.

18. Set its DataSource property to Data1.

19. Use the drop-down menu in the right column to set the DataField property to Zip (**Figure 15.15**).

20. Run the project.

Data from the first record in the table appears in the text boxes. You can click the navigation arrows on the Data control to move through the records in the table (**Figure 15.16**).

✔ Tip

■ The DataSource and DataField properties can also be set dynamically in code.

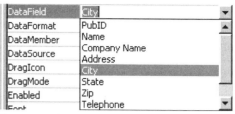

Figure 15.13 The DataField property of the txtCity control is set to the City field.

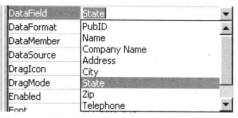

Figure 15.14 The DataField property of the txtState control is set to the State field.

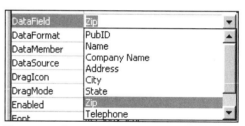

Figure 15.15 The DataField property of the txtZip control is set to the ZIP Code field.

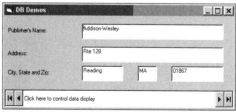

Figure 15.16 As you use the Data control to navigate the table, different records are displayed in the text boxes.

BINDING CONTROLS

Figure 15.17 You must first add a Data control to a form.

Figure 15.18 Click the ellipsis in the right column to open the DatabaseName dialog.

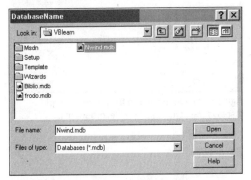

Figure 15.19 Nwind.mdb is a sample database built around a fictitious food-trading company.

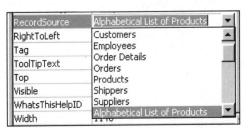

Figure 15.20 Choose a RecordSource from the drop-down menu.

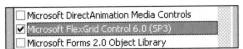

Figure 15.21 If the FlexGrid is not already in your Toolbox, you must first enable it by using the Components dialog.

Figure 15.22 Double-click the FlexGrid in your Toolbox to add it to your form.

To bind a grid to the data control:

1. Start a new project.

2. Add a Data control to the project's default form (**Figure 15.17**).

3. In the Properties Window, select the DatabaseName property (**Figure 15.18**).

4. Click the ellipsis in the right column to open the DatabaseName dialog (**Figure 15.19**).

5. Select the Nwind.mdb database.

6. Click Open to assign Nwind.mdb to the DatabaseName property.

7. In the Properties Window, select the RecordSource property.

8. Use the drop-down menu in the right column to select Alphabetical List of Products as the RecordSource (**Figure 15.20**).

9. Use the Properties Window to set the Visible property to False (because the user will not be using the Data control to navigate records).

10. If the MSFlexGrid is not already in your Toolbox, use the Components dialog to enable Microsoft FlexGrid Control 6.0 (**Figure 15.21**).

11. Double-click the MSFlexGrid control in the Toolbox (**Figure 15.22**).
A FlexGrid is added to your form.

12. Position the FlexGrid in the top-left corner of the form.

13. Use the Properties Window to set the FlexGrid's DataSource to Data1.

continues on next page

BINDING CONTROLS

14. Set the AllowUserResizing property to 3 - flexResizeBoth (**Figure 15.23**).

This allows users to resize column and cell sizes.

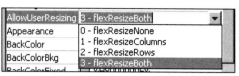

Figure 15.23 You can set the grid to allow users to resize columns and cells.

15. Set the FixCols property to 0 and the FixedRow property to 1.

This generates a header row across the top of the grid but not one down its left side.

16. Using the Code Editor, add to the form's Resize event code that keeps the grid the same size as the form:

```
Private Sub Form_Resize()
    MSFlexGrid1.Width =
    ➞ Me.ScaleWidth
    MSFlexGrid1.Height =
    ➞ Me.ScaleHeight
End Sub
```

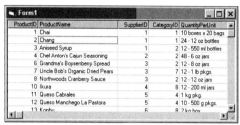

Figure 15.24 When you run the project, the grid displays the contents of the RecordSource.

17. Run the project.

The data is neatly displayed in the grid (**Figure 15.24**).

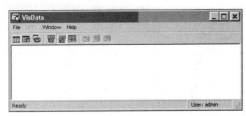

Figure 15.25 To open the Visual Data Manager, choose it from the Add-Ins menu.

Figure 15.26 Select a database from the file system to use with the Visual Data Manager.

Figure 15.27 The tables, dynasets, and snapshots in a database are displayed.

Figure 15.28 You can drill down to determine the fields in a table.

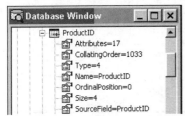

Figure 15.29 You can drill down further to determine the properties and attributes of individual fields.

Using the Visual Data Manager

The Visual Data Manager is a Visual Basic Add-In that provides a great many tools for working with databases.

To open the Visual Data Manager:

◆ From the Add-Ins menu, choose Visual Data Manager.

The Visual Data Manager opens (**Figure 15.25**).

✔ Tip

■ The Visual Data Manager is always loaded, so you do not have to load it through the Add-In Manager.

To examine the structure of a database:

1. With the Visual Data Manager open, from the File menu, choose Open Database.

   The Database Type flyout menu appears.

2. Choose Microsoft Access.

   The Open Microsoft Access Database dialog opens (**Figure 15.26**).

3. Choose Nwind.mdb.

4. Click OK.

   The database's tables are displayed in the Visual Data Manager's Database Window (**Figure 15.27**).

5. Click the plus sign next to a table such as Products to expand it, so that you can view the fields it contains (**Figure 15.28**).

6. Click the plus sign next to a field such as ProductID to view that field's properties (**Figure 15.29**).

✔ Tip

■ You can use the Visual Data Manager with many kinds of databases, including any database with an ODBC (Open Database Connectivity) interface.

To run a SQL query:

1. Use the Database Window to make note of the table and fields that you want to query (**Figure 15.30**).

2. In the SQL Statement window, type a SQL query (**Figure 15.31**).

   For example:

   SELECT CompanyName, ContactName,
   Phone FROM Suppliers ORDER BY
   CompanyName;

3. Click Execute.

4. Click No when you are asked whether this is a SQLPassThrough query (**Figure 15.32**).

   The results of the SQL query are displayed by the Visual Data Manager one record at a time (**Figure 15.33**).

Figure 15.30 Use the Database Window to determine the table and fields that you want to query.

Figure 15.31 Your query is entered in the SQL Statement window.

Figure 15.32 Click No when asked whether it is an SQLPassThrough query.

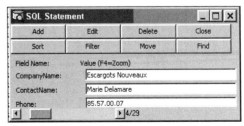

Figure 15.33 The results of your query are displayed one record at a time.

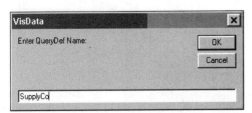

Figure 15.34 Provide a name to identify your query in the Database Window's table list.

Figure 15.35 You see the query at the bottom of the list in the Database Window.

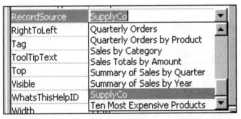

Figure 15.36 The query, identified by name, appears in the RecordSource drop-down menu in the Properties Window.

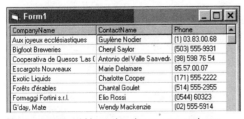

Figure 15.37 A grid bound to the query saved as a RecordSource shows the information specified in the SQL query.

To save a query:

1. With a valid SQL query in the SQL Statement window, click Save.

2. Provide a name for the query when you are prompted (**Figure 15.34**).

3. Click OK.

The query appears at the bottom of the table list in the Database Window (**Figure 15.35**). It also appears in the RecordSource drop-down menu for a Data control set to the database (**Figure 15.36**). A grid bound to the Data control displays the information specified in your SQL query (**Figure 15.37**).

To create a database:

1. From the Visual Data Manager's File menu choose New.

2. From the flyout menu, choose Access (**Figure 15.38**).

3. From the flyout menu, choose Version 7.0 MDB (**Figure 15.39**).

4. Provide a name and location in the file system for the database (**Figure 15.40**).

5. Click Save.

   The new database is created.

To create a table:

1. With a database open in the Database Window, right-click.

2. From the pop-up menu, choose New Table (**Figure 15.41**).

   The Table Structure Dialog opens (**Figure 15.42**).

3. Provide a name for your table.

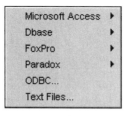

Figure 15.38 You can create databases of several kinds, including Access databases.

Figure 15.39 Select the most current version of Access available.

Figure 15.40 Provide a name and location for the database.

Figure 15.41 To create a table, choose New Table from the pop-up menu in the Database Window.

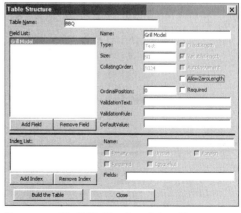

Figure 15.42 The Table Structure dialog allows you to add fields and indexes.

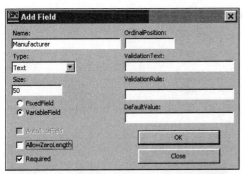

Figure 15.43 Use the Add Field dialog to specify fields.

Figure 15.44 The table and fields you created are displayed in the Database Window.

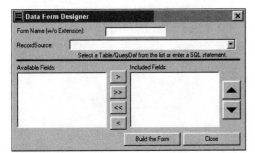

Figure 15.45 The Data Form Designer allows you to specify the RecordSource and fields that will be included in the generated form.

Figure 15.46 The RecordSource you select could be an SQL query that you created and saved earlier.

4. Click Add Field.

The Add Field dialog opens (**Figure 15.43**).

5. Create some fields.

6. Click OK.

You return to the New Table dialog, which displays the fields that you added.

7. Click Build the Table.

The table is created, with its structure displayed in the Database Window (**Figure 15.44**).

To create a data-aware form:

1. With a Visual Basic project open and a database open in the Visual Data Manager, from the Utility menu, choose Data Form Designer.

The data Form Designer opens (**Figure 15.45**).

2. Supply a form name.

The Data Form Designer supplies both the frm prefix and the .frm extension automatically when it creates the form, so you don't need to include them.

3. From the drop-down menu, choose a RecordSource (**Figure 15.46**).

This can be a query that you created earlier. The fields from the record source appear in the Available Fields list (**Figure 15.47**).

continues on next page

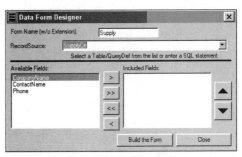

Figure 15.47 When a RecordSource has been selected, the Available Fields list is populated.

4. Use the arrow controls to move the fields that you want to included in the form into the Included Fields list (**Figure 15.48**).

5. Click Build the Form.

A data-aware form is generated and added to your Visual Basic project (**Figure 15.49**).

6. To display the form, use the Project Properties dialog to set the StartUp Object to the newly created form (**Figure 15.50**).

7. Run the project.

A data-aware form has been created that provides access to the recordset and fields that you specified (**Figure 15.51**). The arrows on the data control are used to "cycle through" the data.

✔ Tip

■ Although the generated form is functional, you may want to view it as being a starting place for your own forms. You can use the Code Editor to modify the code that was generated for the form and add new controls to it.

Figure 15.48 Use the arrow keys to select — and order — fields that will be included in the generated form.

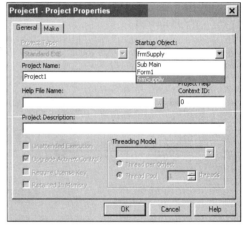

Figure 15.49 The Data Form Designer adds a data-aware form to your Visual Basic project.

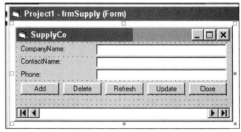

Figure 15.50 To run the new form, you can set the project to start with it.

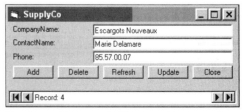

Figure 15.51 The generated form provides access to the records in the fields that were included.

Summary

In this chapter, you learned to:

- Connect the Data control to a database.

- Configure the Data control's RecordSource property.

- Bind text boxes to the Data control.

- Bind a grid to the Data control.

- Use the Visual Data Manager to examine the structure of a database.

- Use the Visual Data Manager to execute a SQL query.

- Use the Visual Data Manager to save a SQL query as part of a database.

- Create a database.

- Create a table.

- Use the Visual Database Manager to generate a data-aware form.

COMPILING AND DISTRIBUTING

16

A Visual Basic project does not do the world—or you—much good unless the world has access to it. By and large, the world does not have Visual Basic running on its computers, so your Visual Basic project must be uncoupled from the Visual Basic environment.

The first step in converting a Visual Basic project for general use is compiling the project. *Compiling* means translating the language and objects (such as forms) that Visual Basic understands—and that run in the Visual Basic design- *and* run-time environments— to more general code. The goal is to produce a stand-alone program that will run in the Windows environment.

Compiling a program is only the first step. Next, the program needs to be distributed to users. This is accomplished with a setup program: an executable file that, when run, installs an application.

Setup programs can be created with VB's Package and Deployment Wizard (which was called the Setup Wizard in earlier versions of Visual Basic). The programs that this wizard creates are themselves based on Visual Basic projects.

If you stop to think about it, a setup program needs to take care of a great many tasks. It needs to make sure that all the components required for an application to run are present on the target machine. It needs to create program groups, items, and a program icon on the target machine. It needs to handle various possible installation errors gracefully. It needs to provide a way to uninstall the software. Isn't it nice that we have a wizard to handle these details for us?

The process of compiling and distributing your programs can be broken into three steps:

1. Compiling an executable

2. Packaging the executable

3. Deploying the package on distribution media

This chapter explains each of the three steps.

Compilation

In the Learning Edition of Visual Basic 6, you can make only one kind of compiled file: an executable file. This is a file with a name that ends with the extension .exe. When you double-click it in Windows Explorer, the program the file contains is executed. (In the Professional and Enterprise Editions, you can make other kinds of compiled files. These include libraries, with a .dll extension, and ActiveX controls, with an .ocx extension.)

Pseudo-Code Compilation vs. Full Compilation

In the Professional and Enterprise Editions of Visual Basic 6, you have the choice of two compilation modes: pseudo-code (also called P-code) compilation and full (or native-code) compilation. Learning Edition users do not have to worry about the difference; they can compile only to P-code.

In P-code compilation an intermediate kind of code, also called pseudo code, is created. A translation library, called the Visual Basic run-time library, is required to execute the pseudo code. (This pseudo-code situation is a little like running a Java program, which requires a Java Virtual Machine [VM] to execute. The VB run-time library can be considered to be a VB virtual machine.)

In full compilation, the VB project is completely compiled to machine code.

When you select full compilation, you can choose from many compiler optimization options. None of these is available with P-code compilation. It is likely that a well-tweaked native-code program will be faster than a P-code program made from the same project.

As a general matter, native-code programs made from a project are a bit bigger than P-code programs made from the same program. P-code programs, however, rely on the presence of the VB run-time library (itself a large file).

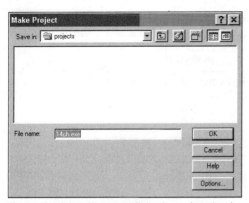

Figure 16.1 The Make Project dialog is used to give the executable file a name and location.

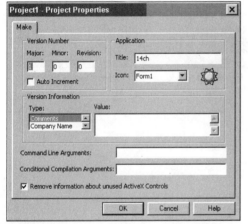

Figure 16.2 When you click Options, the Make tab of the Project Properties dialog opens.

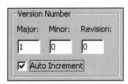

Figure 16.3 You can enter version numbers for your compilations.

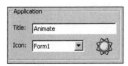

Figure 16.4 Icons are selected from a list of the icons that have previously been assigned to forms in the project.

To make a compiled program:

1. With a project open in VB, from the File menu, choose Make.

   The Make Project dialog opens (**Figure 16.1**).

   Notice that the default name for the executable file is the file name under which the project was saved, followed by the .exe extension. If myproj.vbp is the project file, for example, the File Name box in the Make Project dialog suggests myproj.exe as the name of the executable.

2. Click Options.

   The Make tab of the Project Properties dialog opens (**Figure 16.2**).

3. The default version number for a project is 1.0.0; change this setting, if you want, in the Version Number frame (**Figure 16.3**).

4. Check Auto Increment to have Visual Basic keep track of the version numbers for successive recompilations (**Figure 16.3**).

5. If you want, provide an application title (**Figure 16.4**).

   This corresponds to the Product Name on the Version tab of the executable file's Properties Page.

6. Select an icon for the application by choosing an icon (you can only select an icon that has previously been assigned to a form in the project) (**Figure 16.4**).

   This icon is used to identify the program in Windows Explorer and in the Windows Taskbar.

   continues on next page

COMPILATION

7. Type the Version Information that you want to embed in the executable (**Figures 16.5** and **16.6**).

At minimum, you probably should include a Description and a Legal Copyright notice. This information appears on the Version tab of the executable file's Properties Page.

8. Click OK.

You return to the Make Project dialog.

9. Specify the name and location that you want to use for your compiled program (**Figure 16.7**).

10. Click OK.

A compiled, executable program is created in an .exe file.

✔ Tip

■ You can also open the Make tab of the Project Properties dialog by first choosing Properties from the Project menu and then choosing the Make tab.

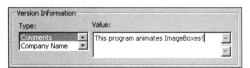

Figure 16.5 The Version Information that you type is embedded in the executable file.

Figure 16.6 It's a good idea to include a Legal Copyright notice in the Version Information.

Figure 16.7 Provide a name for your executable file.

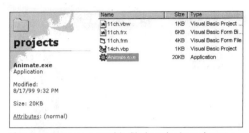

Figure 16.8 Your executable file has the icon that you assigned to it.

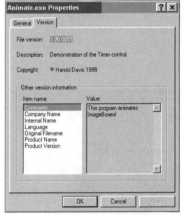

Figure 16.9 The Version Information that you typed in the Make tab can be viewed in the Version tab of the program's Properties Page.

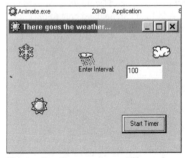

Figure 16.10 Your program will run when it is launched from Windows Explorer.

To view the program's version information:

1. Locate the executable file, using Windows Explorer (**Figure 16.8**).

You'll notice that it is represented by the icon you selected.

2. Right-click the file in Windows Explorer, and from the pop-up menu, choose Properties.

The executable file's Properties Page opens.

3. Click the Version tab.

The version information that you entered in the Make tab is displayed (**Figure 16.9**).

To run the program:

◆ Double-click the program's icon in Windows Explorer.

The program starts (**Figure 16.10**).

Packaging

Packaging is the term that Microsoft uses for creating a setup program and placing it, along with your compiled application and all the files it needs to run, in one directory folder. The Package and Deployment Wizard that ships with Visual Basic 6 automates this job for you. (You may be interested to know that industrial-strength third-party products are available that also handle the creation of setup programs and deployment.)

Before you can run the Package and Deployment Wizard, you should save your project. The wizard creates a package around a specific Visual Basic project, and it requires a compiled executable to create the package. If no compiled executable is associated with the project, or if the files in the project have been changed after it was compiled, the wizard will give you an opportunity to compile the project.

To start the wizard with a project active in VB:

1. With the project that you want to package open in Visual Basic, use the Add-In Manager to make sure that the Package and Deployment Wizard is loaded (**Figure 16.11**).

   For more information on the Add-In Manager, see Chapter 12.

2. From the Add-Ins menu, choose Package and Deployment Wizard.

   The Package and Deployment Wizard opens, with the active project targeted (**Figure 16.12**).

✔ Tip

- If you start the wizard as an Add-In, only the current, active project can be targeted for packaging.

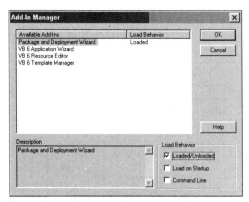

Figure 16.11 Before the Package and Deployment Wizard can be loaded as an Add-In, it must be activated in the Add-In Manager.

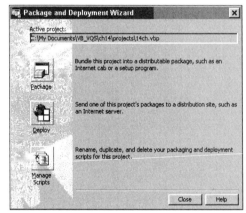

Figure 16.12 If the Package and Deployment Wizard is activated as an Add-In, it can be used only to package the current project.

Figure 16.13 You can start the Package and Deployment Wizard from the Windows Start menu.

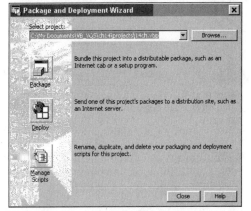

Figure 16.14 When started from Windows, the Package and Deployment Wizard has a Browse button that allows you to select a project.

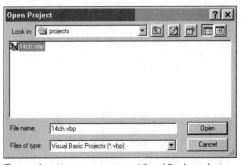

Figure 16.15 You can target any Visual Basic project when the wizard is started from Windows.

Figure 16.16 If you have changed anything in your project, the wizard gives you a chance to recompile it.

To start the wizard from the Windows Start menu:

1. From the Windows Start menu, choose Package and Deployment Wizard from the Microsoft Visual Basic 6.0 Tools flyout menu. This flyout menu is accessed from the Visual Basic 6.0 flyout in the Programs menu (**Figure 16.13**).

   The wizard opens (**Figure 16.14**).

2. Click Browse.

   The Open Project dialog opens (**Figure 16.15**).

3. Select the Visual Basic file that you want to package.

4. Click Open.

To package a project:

1. With the Package and Deployment Wizard open, and a project targeted for Packaging, click Package.

2. If you have changed any source files since the project was compiled, you should recompile when prompted by clicking Yes (**Figure 16.16**).

continues on next page

3. In the first wizard screen, select Standard Package Setup for Package type (**Figure 16.17**).

4. Click Next.

5. Select the directory where your package will be assembled (**Figure 16.18**).

The package is assembled in a directory named Package, placed in the location that you select. If the Package directory doesn't exist, the wizard creates it.

6. Click Next.

The Included Files screen shows the files that are included in your package (**Figure 16.19**).

7. Remove files from the package, if you want, by unchecking them.

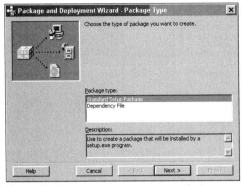

Figure 16.17 To create a setup program, select Standard Package Type.

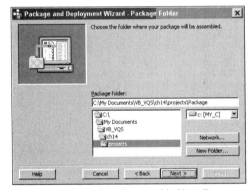

Figure 16.18 The package is assembled in a directory named Package in the location that you specify.

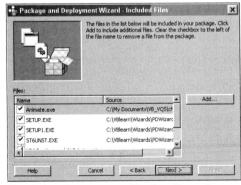

Figure 16.19 You can remove files from the package.

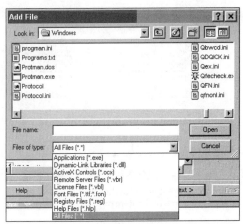

Figure 16.20 You can add files not selected by the wizard.

Figure 16.21 If a single cab file is too large for your distribution medium, you need to split the package into multiple cab files.

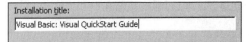

Figure 16.22 The text that you type is displayed when the setup program runs.

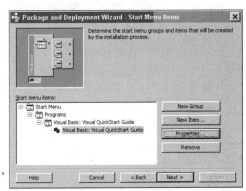

Figure 16.23 You can specify the Windows Start menu groups and items that the setup program will create.

8. Click the Add button to add a file to the package.

The drop-down Files of Type menu shows the file types that you would most likely want to add to a package (**Figure 16.20**).

9. Click Cancel or Open to return to the Included Files screen.

10. Click Next.

11. Select a single archive (cab) file if the estimated file size is such that it will fit on your distribution medium, such as disks; select multiple cab files if you need to place your package on several disks (**Figure 16.21**).

Notice that even the smallest Visual Basic program is likely to require two 1.44MB floppy disks by the time you include the VB run-time library and other support files.

12. Click Next.

13. Provide text that will be displayed when the setup program is run (**Figure 16.22**).

14. Click Next.

15. Use the Start Menu Items screen to determine the Windows Start menu groups and items that will be created by the installation program (**Figure 16.23**).

continues on next page

If you want to change a group or item name, you can do that by clicking Properties and changing the name in the Start Menu Item Properties dialog (**Figures 16.24** and **16.25**).

16. Click Next in the Start menu items screen.

17. Use the Install Locations screen (**Figure 16.26**) to change the installed location of the files created by your project.

    You can't change the location arbitrarily. You can only choose it from a drop-down menu of symbolic macros.

18. Click Next.

19. Unless your program will be used by other programs, leave it unselected in the Shared Files screen (**Figure 16.27**).

20. Click Next.

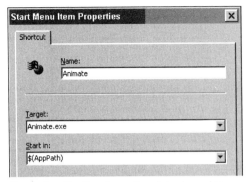

Figure 16.24 The Item Properties dialog is used to change the name of the item or group.

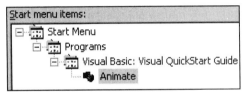

Figure 16.25 Changes in items or groups are reflected in the Start menu items screen.

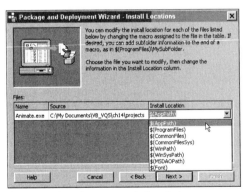

Figure 16.26 You have some choice of where your application is installed.

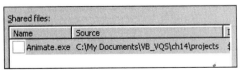

Figure 16.27 Do not select file sharing unless your program will be used by more than one other program.

PACKAGING

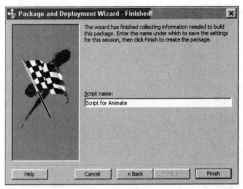

Figure 16.28 Your wizard selections use a script name so that you can easily rerun the wizard to re-create the package or reference the package in the Package and Deployment Wizard.

Figure 16.29 The wizard has created package files in the Package directory.

Figure 16.30 If you run the setup program, you'll see that it has been customized for your application.

21. Provide a script name for the package options that you selected (**Figure 16.28**), so that you can re-create the package without having to make all the choices at a future time.

This name is also used in the Deployment Wizard to refer to a package.

22. Click Finish.

A Package directory is created in the location that you specified (**Figure 16.29**)

23. If you double-click setup.exe in the Package directory to run the installation program, it displays the text that you specified (**Figure 16.30**).

✔ Tip

■ You can find the source code for the Visual Basic project that is compiled to setup.exe in the Visual Basic\Wizards\ PDWizard\Setup1 directory. Provided that you make a backup copy of this project first, you can modify it, recompile it, and use the customized version in place of the standard setup.exe.

Deployment

Deployment is the process of placing the package files on distribution media, on network servers, or on a Web server. After you copy the package files to floppy disks, if you slap labels on the floppies and shrink-wrap the ensemble—well, gosh durn golly if it isn't shrink-wrapped software.

To deploy a package:

1. Open the Package and Deployment Wizard.

2. Select a VB project.

3. Click Deploy.

4. Select the Package to deploy that you created in the preceding section by selecting its script from the drop-down menu (**Figure 16.31**).

5. Click Next.

6. Choose Floppy Disks as the deployment method (**Figure 16.32**).

7. Click Next.

8. Choose a drive for the deployment (**Figure 16.33**).

9. Click Next.

10. Provide a name for the deployment script (**Figure 16.34**).

11. Click Finish.

12. When you are prompted to insert a disk, place the first floppy disk in the drive, and click OK.

    A Visual Basic installation that includes the VB run-time library requires at least two 1.44MB disks.

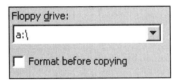

Figure 16.31 Select the script that you created with the Package and Deployment Wizard.

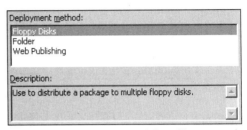

Figure 16.32 You can deploy to disks, a file or network folder, or a Web server.

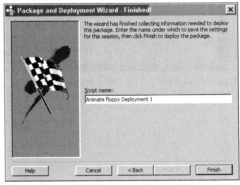

Figure 16.33 A deployment drive— used to create the installation master floppy disks—is specified.

Figure 16.34 Each deployment script can be named.

DEPLOYMENT

Figure 16.35 Even minimal VB6 programs require several floppies. You will be prompted for each floppy disk.

13. When you are prompted for a second disk (**Figure 16.35**), place the second disk in the drive, and click OK.

14. When the Deployment Wizard finishes, remove the disk from the drive.

✔ Tips

■ The deployment process overwrites any files on the floppy disks.

■ You should delete all files from the distribution floppies before starting the deployment process. Alternatively, the Deployment Wizard will reformat the floppies for you before writing to them.

■ The file setup.lst, which is copied to the first distribution disk, contains configuration information for the install. It is an ASCII text file, and you can view it in any text editor. If you are feeling adventurous, you can edit this file to change many setup parameters.

The only real way to see the package and deployment operations were successful is to use the distribution to install the application.

To install the application:

1. Place the first installation disk in the target computer's disk drive—for example, the A drive.

2. From the Windows Start menu, choose Run.

   The Run dialog box opens (**Figure 16.36**).

3. Type a:setup.

4. Click OK.

   The installation program starts and prompts you for the second disk (**Figure 16.37**).

5. Insert the second disk, and click OK.

   The main setup screen appears (**Figure 16.38**).

6. Click OK.

7. Accept the default target directory, or click Change Directory to change it (**Figure 16.39**).

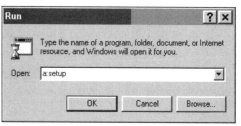

Figure 16.36 You can use the Windows Run dialog box to run the setup program on the distribution disks.

Figure 16.37 You will be prompted for multiple disks as you need them.

Figure 16.38 The setup program's welcome screen contains the text that you specified in the Package and Deployment Wizard.

Figure 16.39 You can change the directory where the program will be installed.

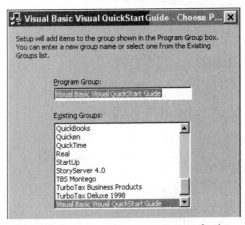

Figure 16.40 You can select a program group for the application.

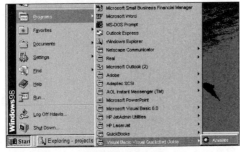

Figure 16.41 You should see a message telling that you the installation was successful.

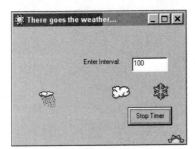

Figure 16.42 Your program item and group should be added to the Windows Start menu.

8. When you are satisfied with the target destination, click the installation button (**Figure 16.39**).

9. Choose the Program Group for the application (**Figure 16.40**).

10. Click OK.

You see a message stating that the program was successfully installed (**Figure 16.41**). An item for it has been added to the Windows Start menu (**Figure 16.42**).

When you double-click the program icon, your application starts (**Figure 16.43**). An uninstall program has been added to the Add/Remove Programs applet in the Windows Control Panel (**Figure 16.44**).

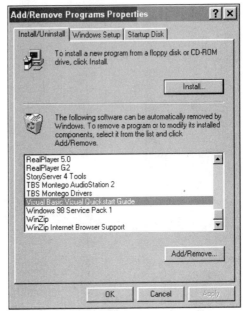

Figure 16.44 The installation program automatically adds an item to the drop-down menu in the Add/Remove Programs applet.

Figure 16.43 Double-clicking the item should start the program.

DEPLOYMENT

Summary

In this chapter, you learned to:

◆ Make a compiled program from a Visual Basic project.

◆ Use the Package and Deployment Wizard to package a project for distribution.

◆ Use the Package and Deployment Wizard to deploy a project.

◆ Create a master set of disks for distributing your program.

SUMMARY

GETTING HELP

This appendix explains where to look for more information about specific Visual Basic 6 features and functions and where to turn for help if you are stuck. The first line of defense is online Help. The online Help that is included with VB6 is an extensive library on a CD-ROM. This library is called MSDN—short for Microsoft Developers Network.

Using MSDN

MSDN online Help could be termed "the good, the big, and the ugly." This is a vast treasure trove of information. The biggest problem is finding what you need quickly—a problem compounded by the fact that the MSDN CD-ROM provides information not only for Visual Basic but also for all the applications included in Microsoft Visual Studio.

The quickest way to find information about a Visual Basic dialog is to use the Help hot key.

To use the Help hot key:

1. Make sure that the MSDN CD-ROM is in the CD-ROM drive.

2. Open the dialog containing the feature that you need help with.

   The Editor tab of the Options dialog is shown in **Figure A.1**.

3. Press F1 on your keyboard.

   After a slight delay, MSDN online Help opens to the Editor Tab topic (**Figure A.2**).

Sometimes, you may have a question that is not directly related to a Visual Basic dialog. In this case, you have to search the MSDN CD-ROM for the answers that you need.

To open the MSDN library:

1. With Visual Basic open, choose Contents, Index, or Search from the Help menu.

   The MSDN library opens to the Visual Studio start page (**Figure A.3**).

2. Use the left (navigation) pane to search the contents and the right pane to drill down on topics via links.

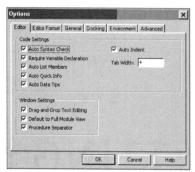

Figure A.1 Make sure the dialog you need help with is open.

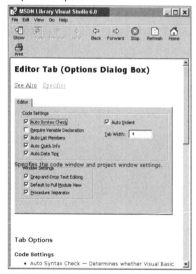

Figure A.2 Press F1 to open the relevant topic.

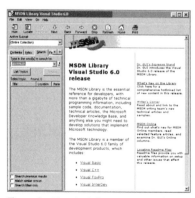

Figure A.3 Use the left pane to search MSDN and the right pane to find subjects via hyperlinks.

USING MSDN

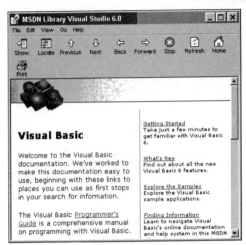

Figure A.4 The Visual Basic welcome page provides access to Visual Basic information.

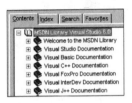

Figure A.5 You'll need to expand the contents list to find Visual Basic Documentation.

Figure A.6 Visual Basic Documentation topics are contained in a volume structure.

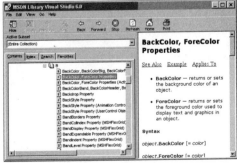

Figure A.7 When you find the topic that you are interested in, click it to display it in the right pane.

To drill down by using links:

◆ With the Visual Studio start page open, click the Visual Basic link.

The Visual Basic welcome page opens (**Figure A.4**).

To use the Contents tab:

1. With MSDN open, click the Contents tab in the navigation pane.

2. Expand the list in the Contents tab until Visual Basic Documentation is visible (**Figure A.5**).

3. Expand the Visual Basic Documentation topic until the Visual Basic volumes are visible (**Figure A.6**).

4. Keep on expanding volumes until topics are displayed.

5. Select the topic that you are interested in. The information is displayed in the right pane (**Figure A.7**).

✔ Tips

■ The Index and Search tabs allow you to locate or search for specific information without being concerned about the organization of the Visual Basic volumes.

■ It's easier to use the Contents, Index, and Search tabs if you limit the scope of MSDN to Visual Basic documentation by choosing *Visual Basic Documentation from the Active Subset drop-down menu (**Figure A.8**).

Figure A.8 If you limit the subset to Visual Basic documentation, finding Visual Basic topics will be easier.

USING MSDN

Using Web Resources

The companion Web site for this book is: http:// www.peachpit.com/vqs/visualbasic.

This site contains the source code for the projects in the book, organized by chapter in archives.

Microsoft's Web sites contain valuable information about Visual Basic. Some Microsoft sites that you will find useful are:

◆ **Microsoft Visual Studio home page**
 http://msdn.microsoft.com/vstudio/

◆ **Microsoft Visual Basic home page**
 http://msdn.microsoft.com/vbasic/

◆ **MSDN online Help**
 http://msdn.microsoft.com/

◆ **MSDN Web Workshop**
 http://msdn.microsoft.com/workshop/

Many good sites are devoted to Visual Basic. A good one is Visual Basic Programmer's Journal, at http://www.vbpj.com/. The hardcopy version of the *Visual Basic Programmer's Journal* is also a good reference.

Visual Basic Variable Types

A *variable* is a placeholder used to store a value. Every variable used in Visual Basic has a *type*, which indicates the kinds of values it can be used to store. The frequently used types are shown in **Table B.1.**

You tell Visual Basic the type of a variable by using the Dim statement. **Table B.1** lists examples of using the Dim statement for the different variable types.

Table B.1

Common Variable Types

TYPE	VALUES	SAMPLE DECLARATION	IMPLICIT CHARACTER
Boolean	True or False	`Dim flgChoice As Boolean`	N/A
Integer	-32,768 to 32,767	`Dim I as Integer`	%
Long (long integer)	-2,147,483,648 to 2,147,483,647	`Dim Counter As Long`	&
Single	Single-precision real number	`Dim HowHigh As Single`	!
Double	Double-precision real number	`Dim ThisHigh As Double`	#
Currency	Monetary value, including four decimal places	`Dim natBudget As Currency`	@
Date	January 1, 100 to December 31, 9999	`Dim Today As Date`	N/A
Object	An object reference	`Dim objCont As Object`	N/A
String	A variable-length string of text	`Dim strHeader as String`	$
String	A fixed-length string of text	`Dim strFixed As String * 12`	$
Variant	Numbers, strings, objects, and so on	`Dim Frodo As Variant`	N/A

Variant Variables

If you don't declare the type of a variable, it is assumed to be a *variant*. It is good practice, however, to explicitly declare all variables, including variants.

A variant variable can store any kind of data that is acceptable to Visual Basic. There are only two caveats:

◆ If you use the variant in an arithmetical calculation, it must contain a number.

◆ If you concatenate string values contained in variant variables, you should use the & operator (not +).

Although using variants may seem to be an easy thing to do—you don't have to worry about the type of your data—you should avoid the practice except in special circumstances.

Explicit Typing

You can enforce explicit typing of variables in your programs by adding the keywords Option Explicit in the Code Editor before any other code. Visual Basic automatically adds the Option Explicit keywords to your programs if you enable Require Variable Declaration in the Editor tab of the Options dialog.

Implicit Declaration and Typing

An *implicitly typed* variable is simply one that is used in a statement with no previous variable declaration. An identifying character is used to type the variable. If no identifying character is present, the implicitly typed variable is a variant.

For example, if there has been no declaration for lname:

```
lname = "Smith"
'the value "Smith" is stored in the
'variant variable lname

lname$ = "Smith"
'the value "Smith" is stored in the
'string variable lname
'$ is the identifying character for a
'string variable
```

It's better practice to avoid using implicit declarations of your variables. But you should at least know about the identifying characters, because it is not uncommon to see them in code that you may come across (not, of course, in this book!).

Operators, Keywords, and Commands

Keywords and commands are the meat and potatoes of Visual Basic code. They are used—in conjunction with object references, variables, and operators—to make your program actually do something. (An example of an object reference is using a control method or setting a form property.)

This appendix provides a reference for some of the operators, commands, and keywords that you will use frequently.

Operators

An *operator* is used to do, compare, or assign one thing to something else. The most common example of an operator is a mathematical operator, such as +.

Visual Basic has four kinds of operators (see **Table C.1**) and several operators that don't fit into a standard category—for example, the dot operator and the assignment operator.

The *arithmetic operators* include +, -, *, /. It's worth noting that / stands for real number division, and \ is used to stand for integer division (the round-offs are discarded).

String concatenation is represented by & and +, both of which are string-concatenation operators, with minor functional differences. String concatenation joins two strings.

Comparison operators include = (confusingly, = is also used in Visual Basic as the assignment operator), <, >, and Is, which compares the equivalence of two object references. When = is used as the comparison operator, it tests to see whether two values are equal.

Logical operators are used to perform logical manipulations of variables and values, often as part of a comparison.

The dot operator, denoted by a period (.), is used to connect objects with a child object and properties and methods with objects.

For example:

```
frmMain.cmdClick.Caption
```

identifies the Caption property of cmdClick seated on frmMain.

The *assignment operator* is denoted by an equal sign (=). It is used to transfer a value from the right side of an equal sign to the identifier on the left side. For example:

```
strFish = "Shark"
```

Table C.1

Types of Operators	
OPERATOR TYPE	**PURPOSE**
Arithmetic	Perform operations on numbers
String Concatenation	Combines strings
Comparison	Compares
Logical	Performs Boolean operations

Keywords and Commands

Keywords are words reserved by Visual Basic for special purposes. You cannot use a keyword as a variable name.

All commands are keywords, but some keywords are not commands. *Commands* are keywords that cause something in the code to perform some action.

Visual Basic has many kinds of keywords. For a complete categorization, see the online MSDN topic "Keywords by Task." The links in this topic show you all the keywords and commands available in a given area.

Table C.2 lists some of the keywords and commands that you are likely to use as you get started with Visual Basic. For the complete syntax of each keyword, see online Help.

Table C.2

Common Keywords and Statements	
KEYWORD	MEANING
Abs	Returns the absolute value of a number.
Beep	Makes a beep sound.
ChDir	Changes to a directory.
Close	Closes a file.
Const	Declares a constant to be used in place of a literal value.
Dim	Declares variables, and allocates storage space for them.
Do...Loop	Repeats a block of statements until a condition becomes True, or while a condition is True.
End	Ends code execution immediately.
Exit	Exits a block or procedure.
FileCopy	Copies a file.
FileLen	Returns the length of a file.
For...Next	Repeats a block of statements the specified number of times.
Format	Converts a number to a string and, provides formatted output.
FV	Calculates future value.
GoTo	Goes to a line in a procedure.
If...Then...Else...End If	Conditionally executes a block of statements.
Int	Returns the integer portion of a number.
InStr	Finds the position of one string within another string.
Len	Finds the length of a string.
LCase	Converts a string to all lower case.
Me	Refers to the current object.
MkDir	Makes Creates a directory.
Now	Returns the current date and time.
On Error	Enables an error- trapping routine within a procedure.
Open	Accesses or creates a file.
Option Explicit	Requires explicit variable declarations.
Randomize, Rnd	Generates random numbers.
Rate	Calculates an interest rate.
Resume	Resumes execution following an error-handling routine.
RGB	Returns a number representing an RGB color value.
Select Case...End Select	Conditionally executes one of a group of statements.
SendKeys	Sends keystrokes to an application.
Static	Used to declare variables at the procedure level that keep their value as long as code is running.
Str	Converts a number to a string.
UCase	Converts a string to all upper case.

KEYWORDS AND COMMANDS

INDEX

A

About box 220
Abs() function 196
accepting user input with controls 115–140
access keys 223, 229
accessing array elements 124
ActiveX control. *See* controls
Add Form dialog, adding forms to projects 10
Add Module dialog 86
Add-In Manager 201–209
Align property 145
animating ImageBoxes 190–193
Application Wizard 204, 211–220
applications. *See* programs
architecture, user interface 115
arguments. *See* parameters
arithmetic operators 280
arrays, option button 124–129
assignment operators 280
associating icons with forms 15
attributes. *See* properties

B

BackColor property
    obtaining color values for 166–167
    setting 11–12, 53–58
base-16 numbers. *See* hexadecimal numbers
binding controls 245–248
birth events 76
BorderStyle property 59–60
button frames 33
Button parameter 26–28
button responses 129

buttons. *See also* controls
    adding
        code to 156
        to invoke dialogs 166, 168
        to projects 19–21
        to toolbars 155
    closing forms when clicked 91
    copying and pasting 38
    determining selections of by users 42–43
    displaying 27–30
    evaluating responses 47–48
    replacing with menus 231–232

C

calling event procedures 231
"Cancel" buttons 30
CancelError 165
captions
    menus, changing 225
    setting 13–14
categorizing properties 16
centering forms 10–11, 95–96
changing. *See also* setting
    BackColor properties 55–56
    default tab names 158–159
    fonts while programs run 62
    menu names and captions 225
    programs 220
    resource strings 206
    selected text 172–173
    sizes of images 154
check marks, toggling 135
checkboxes 116–119
Checked property 233, 235
choosing. *See* selecting

V

validating input 195–196
Value property 116
values 26
variables. *See also* specific variables
  declaring in forms 78–79
  requiring declarations 6
  storing color values in 56–57
  types of 277–278
variant variables 278
vbOKOnly message box 29
versions of programs, displaying 261
viewing. *See* displaying
visible menus and menu items 237
Visible property 233, 235
Visual Basic Add-Ins 199–209
Visual Basic Programmer's Journal 276
Visual Data Manager 203, 249–254

W

Web sites with information about Visual Basic 276
width properties, setting for forms 63
windows. *See* forms, specific windows
Windows Start menu, starting Package and Deployment Wizard from 263
wiring
  forms 42–46
  menu items with existing code 231
  toolbars 156
wizards. *See* specific wizards

Y

"Yes" button 30, 89–90